A Leader's Guide to Storytelling

Part manual, part memoir and part call to action, this book demonstrates why the core skill needed by leaders in the next decade and into the future will be authentic and effective communication.

Communications based on character, integrity and values will be critical in helping leaders navigate the two mega trends of accelerated technological change and increasing demands for social change. This book is the first to marry practical advice on deepening communication skills with insight from a coaching and cognitive point of view into what techniques work and why, and to pull together the wider societal issues and the operating context for leaders.

Counter-intuitive and written to provoke thought and awareness, the author looks at the psychological and emotional effects of our communications and what leaders can do to inspire and engage, guiding them through three sections:

- A framework for effective communications
- A toolkit, detailing what good looks like in practical situations
- The authentic leader, an exploration of the changing communications landscape and why a different kind of leadership is needed

C-suite executives, leaders about to take that last step into the C-suite or millennial leaders about to enter the boardroom will value this book as an advisory guide, as a handbook to be used in internal coaching and training sessions and as a manual and aide memoir for themselves.

Mark Dailey is a director at the Madano Partnership and advises leaders on strategy, positioning and storytelling. He has worked in television, and has been a speechwriter, a head of communications, a PR consultant and a business coach. He is married and lives in north London.

To effectively motivate their teams, leaders must engender trust and respect via their actions. Mark Dailey has spent his career coaching these principles and working across the globe with multi-national organisations. His wide-ranging experiences provide him with the insights to deal with most modern leadership challenges. I would not be the manager I am today without Mark's coaching.

Max Sinclair, Head of UK Division, Wells Fargo Commercial Real Estate

As the CEO of Swinton Group between 2014 and 2018, Mark's helping hand for engaging with my colleagues in town halls or with the directors in Board meetings has been decisive for driving a complete overhaul at a fast pace of a 60-year-old regulated business. This book is an invaluable *vade mecum* for the bumpy coming years, as many managers will have to lead their teams through accelerated transformation and uncertainty. Indeed, the way most CEOs have shouldered their way to the top in steady situations is not fit anymore for these daunting times which require genuine authenticity to talk about the meaning of change and that will lead many to reinvent not only their jobs but also their lives as a whole.

Gilles Normand, former Swinton Group CEO

This is a remarkable book: some of it is wholly unexpected, other parts we know – but resist...But Mark makes the case so persuasively, and his practical tips are so abundant, that I am a complete convert! A must-have for all our bookshelves.

Anne Scoular, Co-Founder Meyler Campbell

You can have no better guide than Mark to help you navigate communications as a leader in the post-pandemic world. Mark has become a trusted advisor to many leaders for his innate ability to understand that authenticity and meaning have always mattered. Now, his advice has never been more important as the "right thing to do" for companies shifts from legal obligations to a complex mix of moral, ethical and social challenges. In this book, Mark both pinpoints the under currents of today's communications landscape with wisdom and insight and offers practical ways for leaders to put change into practice.

Andrea Carpenter, Co-Founder of Women Talk Real Estate

A superlative guide for current and future leaders who, by embracing authentic and effective communications, will accelerate the success of their organisations, while enriching their careers and their personal lives. This practical and insightful book is based on strong theoretical frameworks, the author's broad career experience, numerous personal insights and the science of how one processes information. A must-have communications book for any leader.

Stephen Swatridge, CEO, Not-for-Profit Organizations

I've worked with Mark for years to help my team gain consciousness and capability in clear, concise and compassionate communication. The chance to read the early drafts and this final product has proven incredibly helpful during COVID. I can hear Mark's true, warm voice in the stories he tells to breathe life into his advice. This book has a menu of hard-earned and well-honed wisdom, packaged in meaningful morsels. Enjoy!

Jonathan Sullivan, Managing Director of Seabury Consulting in Europe, Middle East, Africa from 2012 to 2017, now a Managing Director at Accenture

Mark Dailey has been advising me on internal and external communications for over 5 years. I am certain that the success of my firm is correlated to this relationship. Mark has allowed me to progress towards the best version of myself as a leader, never by changing my intention or message, but by articulating, laser focusing and growing the most valuable attributes within my leadership skillset – both hard and soft. The best leaders, he understands, are those true to themselves.

Ghada Sousou, CEO and Co-Founder, Sousou Partners

Mark Dailey draws upon years of experience working at the highest level in Europe, Asia and North America to identify the most urgent issues facing communicators in today's rapidly changing world. Clearly and concisely he sets out the challenges, and shows that authentic and compelling communication is a skill the lies within us all.

Martin Evans, European Communications Manager,
from 1988–2021 Hong Kong Trade Development Council

Drawing on experience of working with leaders in various sectors and countries, Mark Dailey argues for the importance of renewed authenticity with warmth, clarity and insight, and sets this against the transforming events that have marked the beginning of this decade. In doing so, he promotes a focus on audience and client that benefits from his considerable expertise in communications and experience as a business coach. Anyone concerned with the need for agile leadership, the emergence of multi-generational semi-remote workforces, sustainability and ESG, and individual and collective purpose will welcome this engaging and accessible book.

Jon Hayes, Partner, DLA-Piper

As technological change accelerates and the business world becomes ever more complex, leaders face an extraordinary challenge in how they communicate about what's important. Mark has reminded us that authenticity, character and storytelling will lie at the heart of navigating the changes that lie ahead.

Maggie Buggie, Chief Business Officer, SAP Services

This book is so much more than a guide to storytelling, it truly captures the essence of leadership. Mark is a great teacher in storytelling, and with this book he places it in context of the problems we all face in today's challenging times.

Lonneke Löwik, Chief Executive Officer, INREV

Mark Dailey is a master storyteller. A consummate communications professional, a strategic thinker and a trained coach, he has the perfect combination of skills to guide you through the 'cauldron of disruption.' *A Leader's Guide to Storytelling* is full of wise advice and astute observations. It is elegantly written as well as relevant, informative and practical. Mark makes an impassioned case for effective communication and why it is at an even greater premium in the current context; then he shows his readers how to communicate authentically and meaningfully. If your job involves leading or engaging people, this book tells a story you need to read.

Dr. Liz Gooster, Professional Coach and Meyler Campbell Faculty Member

A Leader's Guide to Storytelling

Restoring Authentic Communication
in a World of Change

Mark Dailey

Routledge
Taylor & Francis Group

NEW YORK AND LONDON

First published 2022
by Routledge
605 Third Avenue, New York, NY 10158

and by Routledge
2 Park Square, Milton Park, Abingdon, Oxon, OX14 4RN

Routledge is an imprint of the Taylor & Francis Group, an informa business

Library of Congress Cataloging-in-Publication Data
Names: Dailey, Mark, author.
Title: A leader's guide to storytelling : restoring authentic communication
in a world of change / Mark Dailey.
Description: New York, NY : Routledge, 2022. | Includes bibliographical
references and index.
Identifiers: LCCN 2021020173 (print) | LCCN 2021020174 (ebook) |
ISBN 9781032057453 (hardback) | ISBN 9781032057446 (paperback) |
ISBN 9781003198994 (ebook)
Subjects: LCSH: Communication in management. | Communication in
organizations. | Leadership. | Storytelling. | Organizational change.
Classification: LCC HD30.3 .D327 2022 (print) | LCC HD30.3 (ebook) |
DDC 658.4/5—dc23
LC record available at https://lccn.loc.gov/2021020173
LC ebook record available at https://lccn.loc.gov/2021020174

ISBN: 978-1-032-05745-3 (hbk)
ISBN: 978-1-032-05744-6 (pbk)
ISBN: 978-1-003-19899-4 (ebk)

DOI: 10.4324/9781003198994

Typeset in Sabon
by codeMantra

For Mimi, Lara and Liam
And for my Mother: the best storyteller of them all

Contents

Figures

Tables

Boxes

Part I

Setting the Scene

Introduction

It is the thesis of this book that authentic and effective communication – from everyone, but leaders particularly – will be needed more than ever in the years to come, not only to deal with the immediate, lingering and longer-term effects of COVID-19 but also to help us find our way between two conflicting mega trends – *accelerated disruption driven by digitisation and technological change* and *the rise of social values* and the significantly increasing pressure on leaders to take a stand on the great societal issues of the day.

We are entering an age which will be typified by these two mega trends, and this will require a substantial upgrade in how leaders communicate. In the shorter term, it will be imperative for leaders to be able to show empathy and to articulate in an authentic and effective way what is happening to individuals and organisations, as the wave of business restructuring and redundancies signals the start of the great realignment that will happen when the implications of COVID start to become more apparent.

Then, as the two mega trends accelerate, leaders will need to redouble their efforts to explain change, build resilience and inspire others to be confident.

The first trend will be seen in the wave of disruption that will gather pace as automation, artificial intelligence and algorithms begin to profoundly reshape business. The digital divide will describe the gap between those who are able to find employment directing this effort and adding value through advisory, creative and insight services and those who will be increasingly marginalised.

The second trend – *the rise of the importance of social values* and the demand for action on issues such as fairness, racism, climate change and sustainability – will be accompanied by roiling emotion and rising expectations.

The quantum of expected disruption and change over the next ten years will be of such a magnitude that the core business skill needed will be effective communication. To find a workable balance between the detached, inexorable logic of automated change on the one hand, and the visceral emotion of those yearning for social change but experiencing so much economic and structural disruption on the other hand.

A 'third way' of communicating will be needed between the 'cool' imperative of technological progress and the 'hot' emotions brought to the fore by surging concern for social justice. Leaders will need to be authentic and effective to intermediate between these two 'zeitgeist-driven' modes of communicating.

A perfect example of the gulf between these two ways of communicating was seen in the summer of 2020 with the great exam fiasco in the UK.

On the one hand, there were the apostles of automation with their outsized faith in an algorithm's ability to make the correct determination of A level and GCSE grades in the absence of exams. Their position was marked by bloodless and technocratic explanations for why this was the best available and fairest methodology process-wise.

DOI: 10.4324/9781003198994-2

On the other hand was the hugely negative reaction from parents, teachers and students to the perceived unfairness of the process. Their unified and visceral response went viral in intensity and caused an embarrassing U-turn in Scotland and in England a couple of weeks later.

This kind of emotional and communications face-off between these two trends will only intensify and multiply as both accelerate.

It is the increasing dissonance wrought by these two conflicting trends that will make the ability to communicate what is really happening and what is really of value so important. Questions like what is fair, where do our best interests lie, what is important and worth preserving and what must we let go of, and how can we navigate our way forward and embrace change without marginalising whole segments of society will cry out for authentic and effective articulation unsullied by either technocratic impulses or feral emotion.

And so what does authentic and effective communication look like? I think the core of the answer lies with our strange relationship to storytelling.

People are innately articulate and eloquent provided the forum is relaxed, informal and the subjects are themselves or something they hold dear. In conversations, facilitation or training exercises and certainly in one-on-one coaching sessions – where there is no requirement other than to talk – *when people are telling their story*, they show all the hallmarks of effective communications: authenticity, engagement, brevity and above all a willingness and facility to say what it means.

This is easily disrupted by the weight of expectations, formality, the feeling that storytelling is inadequate in a business setting and above all performance, time and peer pressure. This easy-going eloquence dissipates as people react to what they feel they should do in a business setting. But in its purest, storytelling form – the story of me – people are eager to share and innately know how to do well.

We all know what good looks like. When directly asked, people always respond the same way:

- A topic that is relevant to me
- Delivery that is engaging, confident and authentic
- Content that is concise, meaningful and has clear takeaways

We are also able to translate this recognition and knowledge of what good looks like into extremely accurate and useful feedback. And what is astonishing is that the feedback always comes in the same order. People always give feedback starting with how it made them feel (audience), how well it engaged them (engagement) and then what they remember (content/structure). And they are robust, cogent and articulate in offering insight.

So the question is if we intuitively know what good looks, why *do we find it so difficult to do for ourselves*?

We have an innate ability to recognise what is good, identify the ingredients that made it good and articulate precisely when, how and why we perceive the communication this way.

Why having started with such a built-in competitive advantage in our ability to communicate informally about ourselves and easily recognise what good looks like in others do we squander that advantage? Why do we communicate well about other people's communications but forget all this great feedback when it comes to ourselves?

This is the first great conundrum in communications – *we intuitively recognise, understand and can articulate what good looks like in others – but we find it very difficult to do for our own communications.*

What is responsible for holding us back?

I think the answer revolves around how we perceive ourselves and how we wish to be perceived by others. We tend to have deeply rooted beliefs and strong feelings about how we come across publically, what we feel our strengths are, what 'being professional' means, the reputations we want to build and strengthen, what we were taught at school, university and on the job, our innate personalities and confidence levels and our ability to trust ourselves and others.

And this complex ecosystem translates primarily into a yearning to be safe that manifests itself in the *need to say more rather than less*. Less leaves us open to being perceived as lightweight, perhaps deficient in expertise and knowledge. More is safer. And so, although we exhort other people to be concise, we exempt ourselves from this advice.

If you asked me to sum up the one thing most responsible for holding us back from being good communicators it would be that *we vastly prefer to seek solace and safety in rationally delivering detail rather than emotionally engaging with others about meaning*. For many of us, detail represents not only a safe haven but the chance to showcase expertise, buttress our point of view and garner external validation.

Detail means content and for many people content is synonymous with presentation. When you ask people preparing a presentation to estimate how much time they put into the three key buckets they have identified as constituting good communications – audience, structure/content and engagement – they usually score it this way:

- Thinking about what the audience needs – 5%
- Structure and content – 90%
- Engagement – 5%

Many presenters don't think much about the audience – what they need, what will be important and what will resonate best with them. And yet, surely this is the primary requirement of communication – that we attempt to understand our audience and make it easy and worthwhile for them to hear our message.

Likewise, it is the same with engagement. If we think at all about engagement, it is usually as an offshoot of content – what audiovisual support do I need other than slides? What 'icebreaker' can I use to get things moving (talk about a Freudian slip and the clue being in the name)?

The fact is we actively do not want to think about our audience and we are wary of engagement. In a business context, the fear is that too much dwelling on the audience will keep us from focusing on what we have to do. And show too much concern for engagement and we open the doors to emotion and meaning.

Most people avoid emotion like the plague: too nebulous, too dangerous and too personal. We are exceedingly wary of talking about meaning: too presumptuous, too patronising and too pompous. Meaning demands commitment, prioritising and editing. It requires us to take a view. No one gets penalised too harshly for putting too much detail out there. But put too much meaning out there and you'll awaken the trolls. Instead, emotion and meaning are deemed to better belong to our personal lives, not our professional ones.

This is entirely normal and almost completely wrong. Our presentations and communications come alive at exactly those moments when we go off-piste and say what we really think. Talk directly to the audience. Show little bits of emotion and take a stab at articulating meaning. Yes, of course, we need to include facts, detail and process. But what everyone remembers is 'the other bits'.

The world is awash in information and attention spans are shortening precipitously. What we crave is meaning that is delivered in an authentic and concise manner.

And we need that now more than ever. And all of what we've just talked about applies to leaders, perhaps more than anyone else.

And so this book is a call to arms – offering guidance about what effective and authentic communications looks like and why these skills will be so needed, so soon.

The book is a distillation of what I have learned and observed about what works and what doesn't in communications – and why. It's also a warning that *in the coming years, we are going to need to be infinitely better communicators than we have been in the past.* The issues that will need explaining, the change pathways laid out and demystified, the consensus and bridge-building that will be critical to close the digital gap and the gap between cool, automated change and hot, societal change will all require significant communication skill and commitment.

The book is set out in four sections:

1 The current operating landscape and what authentic leadership looks like
2 A framework for understanding effective storytelling and authentic communications
3 A toolkit detailing what this looks like in specific types of leadership communications
4 How a coaching approach can best mobilise authentic leadership

This book begins by looking at the 'cauldron of disruption' and what will be expected of leaders in navigating a course through the current disruptive operating landscape. We'll look at some of the technological, social and generational trends that are influencing the leadership imperative and creating the need for the rise of the authentic leader.

The second part of the book posits a way of looking at storytelling and effective communications through a framework of audience, structure/content and engagement. We'll look at some important and counter-intuitive ideas like:

• The five-step cognitive map that should guide your efforts to connect with your audience
• How to combat 'second presenter syndrome'
• How the trajectory of a typical presentation generates telling insight into what are the most important parts of storytelling
• How to communicate in exactly the order in which people expect to receive information
• How to use a communications 'GPS system' to understand why and when 'you've arrived at your destination'
• Why storytelling is a leader's more efficient and powerful way of communicating

The toolkit will focus on the challenges of specific forms of communication and how leaders can optimise presenting, perform in the spotlight, handle group dynamics, manage a crisis, navigate change and deal with the media.

This book ends with a look at how authentic leadership can best be mobilised. A coaching approach to leadership typifies many of the attributes of authentic leadership and offers a guide for how to put these ideas into practice.

Coaching shares the same kind of platform of character and trust that underpins authentic leadership. The currency of authenticity has been cheapened recently by overuse and misunderstanding, and returning to the foundations of what actually generates authenticity will be at the heart of the new character-driven, values-oriented leadership that is emerging. Coaching provides leaders with insight into how to do this.

Restoring Our Sense of Story and Meaning

Some of what this book talks about will require 'unlearning' much of what we have been taught about what constitutes 'good communications'.

On an individual level, this may be somewhat akin to restoring factory-fresh settings, to returning you to your default configuration that was in place before the corporate gobbledegook, legalese and political bafflegab took its toll, to regaining some of that ease of authenticity, eloquence and storytelling that was in play when we were just talking about ourselves.

Much the same kind of process is increasingly at work on the organisational level. We are seeing far more companies talk about values and purpose and put far more emphasis on understanding and articulating the corporate narrative than ever before – what is the story of our firm, where are we on our journey and what do we stand for.

What is required in the final analysis is a reset on our ability to tell stories – the story of me and the story of what we are doing as an organisation is hugely important and fundamentally positive.

We are all innate storytellers. Stories are the most powerful form of communicating, bar none. They are in our DNA. We are hard-wired to like stories. They are the most efficient way of transmitting both information and meaning, because they are intimate, memorable, audience-friendly and engaging.

We are in for much disruption and change over the next ten years. Our ability to tell our stories clearly, honestly and with power and conviction will never be more important. We are battered and bruised and tired right now – that much is evident. But the real challenges lie ahead.

And when all the artifice is cast away and we are getting to the nub of the matter and communicating simply and honestly, we will feel a sense of liberation that is palpable. And that will be very powerful, authentic and effective.

This is what will guide, sustain and nourish us through the disruption and changes in the months and years to come.

Chapter 1

The Cauldron of Disruption

The Perfect Storm

Year 2021 may be looked back on as an historic inflection point, a kind of portal to the future, in which a series of fundamental issues came together and coalesced into a hurricane of change – a 'perfect storm' of issues.

Many of the clients I have worked with remarked on the accelerating pace of change, and one suggested that in the spring of 2020, his firm had 'moved the work force on 10 years in the last three months'. He was referring specifically to the almost wholesale adoption of remote work during the COVID-19 lockdown, but he could have been referring to a host of other issues.

The pandemic appears to have brought renewed vigour and focus to social issues such as racial equality, fairness, diversity and inclusion and inequality of opportunity. The idea of a broad societal need to 'level-up' and reduce these fundamental gaps and inequities has gathered visceral force with the protests following the killing of George Floyd in the US, the Black Lives Matter movement and the rebellion against the perceived racist nature of historical statues. And the debate has not been all one-way traffic, as we've seen in the significant backlash against the rise of the so-called 'cancel culture'.

This swelling of emotion accompanying social issues has been coming for a while now. Extinction Rebellion, the climate action protest group, the Occupy movement for social justice and against globalisation, the Umbrella revolution in Hong Kong calling for the preservation of democracy in the special administrative region of China are all examples of emotion and the thirst for social action and change, increasingly moving to centre stage.

On a more micro level, it is seen in the sharpening sensitivity to microaggression, transgender rights, 'gas-lighting' and cultural misappropriation. Everywhere, the talk is of inalienable rights and rights infringed that shouldn't have to be conferred or earned, but rather need to be recognised as inalienable and fundamental building blocks of a just world.

Plenty may say that we have seen all this before at both macro and micro level. In the 1960s, with the civil rights movement, the Vietnam War, the advent of the pill and sharply changed social mores. In the late 1980s, with demonstrations against Communism, the fall of apartheid and the 'greed is good' embrace of materialism, every decade throws up its major issues and changes.

But this social emotion does appear to be gathering pace. It almost seems as if the pandemic has served as some kind of 'Great Awakening', with many people yearning to deliberately not go back to the 'old normal' but to use this portal moment to reset basic modalities.

The pandemic has also accelerated business change: from hollowing out whole industries like hospitality and aviation to changing the central nervous system of cities

DOI: 10.4324/9781003198994-3

with vastly reduced need for central office space, the undermining of business travel and 'zombification' of the transport and services backbone of central business districts.

Much of this change may prove ephemeral and the smart betting is we are in for five years of sifting and settling as the more permanent aspects of change take time to bed-in and reveal the distinction between the temporal and the lasting. It is in the area of digital and technology that the greatest acceleration and change will be seen.

The pandemic has accelerated the digital divide we talked about in the introduction. The idea is that we are at a fundamental rupture point in history, a second Renaissance and Reformation rolled into one, where the new holy trinity of artificial intelligence, automation and algorithms ushers in a completely different business ethos and world.

For example, in even the least glamorous area of business – audit – a senior partner in one of the 'big four' accountancy firms estimates that artificial intelligence can compute audit sums 1,800 times faster than the brightest person.

Machine learning, coupled with machine automation, and fuelled by machine-generated algorithms mean that the business world will increasingly be run in a very different way than in the past – with radically different roles for people. A fundamental change is happening in how business takes place.

The thesis is that we stand on the cusp of an entirely new epoch where the power, inexorability and sheer acceleration of this new technical and digitised business world may quickly become further and further removed from what has been recognisably driving business for the past 250 years.

It is the swirling vortex created by these two megatrends coalescing – social equality and the digital divide – that is creating the sense that this is an historical 'perfect storm'. It is the disparate nature of individual issues such as equality, diversity, digitisation, robotics, security of supply chains and climate change that makes their increasing connectivity so startling.

These issues are being brought closer together as they come to the fore and this gives the appearance of a wave of change, making it seem even more disruptive and momentous. A small example of this interconnectivity between the pace of digital and technological change and the power of social values can be seen by looking at what's happening in the relatively mundane and contained world of warehousing.

BOX 1.1 SMART WAREHOUSING AND SUSTAINABILITY

One of the clients we have worked with is one of the world's largest transport, logistics and supply chain firms and the changes being implemented right now are huge.

The firm has made a significant investment in artificial intelligence and automation to drive smart warehousing. It is a little like a fridge that is preprogrammed to replenish supplies when levels get depleted – smart warehouses speed up the filling and tracking of orders because everything is automated and prewired not to wait for human instigation. Human direction, supervision and strategic thinking drive the set-up, but increasingly the engine of the basic value proposition is automated.

The smart warehouse is only one element of this new 'contract' with the client. The other is a significantly ramped up commitment to sustainability and the green agenda. Electric vehicles and lower carbon emission, plus environmentally sound standards for the fully managed microclimate inside the warehouse, are key parts of what is on offer.

Increasingly, our two megatrends are joining forces. This represents a strategic opportunity and a fundamental challenge for businesses.

The Need for a Business Reset

The opportunity is to anticipate, articulate and lead change. This will require a fundamental recalibration of the two most important stakeholder relationships for business: employees and customers. At the heart of this change will be the idea of building trusted and valued partnerships with both. And that will be hugely difficult over the next few years as employees suffer uncertainty and pain as the business landscape is dominated by restructuring and redundancies and customers feel bewilderment as significant change in demand, supply and distribution alters business models irrevocably.

Implicit in capitalising on this opportunity will be the need to better understand the changing operating landscape and to build `in far more agility and flexibility, which will require a pivot to an innovative, fast reactive stance rather than the proactive or planned stance that has been standard operating procedure since Henry Ford and the first days of standardised production.

What we are really talking about is the need for a business reset in three fundamental areas:

1   A management reset on planning and control.
2   An employee reset on values and trust.
3   A customer reset on collaboration and connectivity.

All three will demand that leaders have the ability to identify what is at stake and the key components of what needs to change versus what must be preserved. Understanding the changing dynamics of business and the interplay between how the twin drivers of technological and social change are affecting business will be incredibly complicated and challenging.

But this effort to identify, understand and articulate what is at stake, where we are going, how and why must not be outsourced either technically or morally.

In order to create the conditions where employees and customers trust the road ahead and are reassured that their interests are being considered and articulated, leaders will need to both slow down and speed up. Slow down to allow for reflection, understanding and genuine dialogue, and speed up in their ability to move proactively and with agility and flexibility.

And in addition to the individual skills needed to handle communications through change, leaders will need to better understand how to identify and manage crises and the processes through which change is implemented.

Giving Up Control – The First Legacy of the Perfect Storm

The acceleration in the pace of digitisation and technological change effectively means the end of certainty. The speed of change allied to the interconnectivity and complexity of everything is a key challenge for businesses trying to plan rationally for the future. As everything changes and becomes more complex, it's impossible to be certain.

This means a weakening of the rationalist model that has driven business planning and control for perhaps the last 100 years – and this is an absolutely fundamental change in the overall psychological underpinning of the business landscape.

The natural instinct, especially given the huge increase in AI, and the technological capability for predictive analysis is to redouble efforts to analyse, rationalise and understand. Almost a 'let the robots loose to work the problem if the complexity gets too great' kind of stance.

But Daniel Kahneman's devastating critique of rational or 'system 2 thinking'[1] posits the sobering assessment that experts do no better than informed amateurs at prognosticating accurate scenarios.

Nassim Taleb, in his seminal book *The Black Swan*,[2] suggests stability was never really there anyway and that what we think is stability is anything but. That our predisposition to seeing patterns and designating rationality to what are really random events blinds us to the irrationality of much of what passes for planning. Taleb sees uncertainty as being the norm and randomness its handmaiden.

Increasingly, businesses are acknowledging this – that the paramount need is for nimbleness, agility and alertness and that abductive logic (what could be) and obliquity (pursuing goals indirectly) may actually be a better bet in a complex world than oversized faith in deductive or inductive logic.

This has not kept systems planners from trying to build in this kind of oblique thinking and intuitive, deductive and accretive machine learning to algorithms and artificial intelligence. But safe to say that there is general recognition that the days of proscriptive, carefully crafted five-year business plans are waning – the old days of command and control are on their last legs.

It is interesting that in conversations with CEOs, they sound less certain about the future, even though they are better equipped to deal with uncertainty than ever before. They recognise the difficulty in planning more than three years ahead in constantly reviewing and fine-tuning their competitive positioning, and they worry about whether the talent they have will support the shape of the business in three years' time.

They also worry that experience is at risk of being devalued. In a world of constant change, speed and above all uncertainty, experience can be framed as irrelevant. And they struggle with the challenge of leading and appearing decisive when acceptance of and comfort with ambiguity will increasingly be one of the key benchmarks of business success.

BOX 1.2 IMPLICATIONS FOR LEADERS

Leading during a time of uncertainty is hugely challenging. Leaders face tremendous pressure to try and make sense of changing trends and chart a course through uncertainty. Nimble, fast reactive and agile are all good attributes to inculcate in a firm, but the real challenge for leaders is twofold:

1   How do you separate what is a fundamental change from something that appears important or alluring but is subsequently proven to be a mere bagatelle?
2   How do you forge a united front bringing employees and customers with you when you don't know where you are going?

There is an implicit balancing act that will lie at the heart of good leadership over the next decade – the ability to engender trust and confidence in others when you don't feel that way yourself and the ability to involve others without undermining your own responsibility to lead.

In their book *Management Reset: Organising for Sustainable Effectiveness*[3], Ed Lawler, Chris Worley and David Creelman touch on many of the key themes of this fundamental management reset: the need for sustainability, the difficulty in predicting and mapping the future, coping with increased complexity and embracing uncertainty and aligning with the increasing values-driven expectations of younger employees.

And, as if *how* businesses will cope with trying to understand this increasingly complex operating environment wasn't enough – irrespective of whether human and machine learning can dovetail to produce an efficient but nuanced and humanised way of understanding complexity – *businesses are being hit at the same time by a seminal change in the values landscape.*

Embracing Values and Building Trust – The Employee/Social Imperative

We talked earlier about the huge increase in social consciousness that is one of the two drivers of the perfect storm. How firms make sense of and respond to these social issues is the second key challenge for organisations these days.

Along with navigating the pace of change, understanding how growth will happen and coping with the regulatory burden, building an attractive 'employer brand' to recruit, retain and reward 21st-century talent is fundamental. And that means engaging on values and building trust with employees.

For younger employees, working for an organisation that does well by doing good, which is cognizant of the zeitgeist and aligned to progressive values, is both a deal-breaker and a game changer. They won't work for firms that don't get it and 'live' their values – and that really means the employee's values.

If these values, increasingly centred on diversity, inclusion and fairness, are in place, the effect on commitment, engagement, productivity and morale is significant.

This argues for a reset in the way employee engagement is done – from the old top-down, directive approach to a much more grassroots, democratic, genuine and authentic stance. This fundamental reduction in hierarchies and encouragement of a more caring, engaged approach, explicitly aligned to 'refreshed' values, will be a core part of reacting positively to the perfect storm.

But here is where it gets difficult on the values front. For many people, the pivot to more inclusive and 'human' value is long overdue. One hundred years of institutional spin has resulted in two predominant emotions felt by many people, not just millennials or employees. The first is passive – a lethargic soup of widespread resignation, disgust and disengagement with authority. The other is active – a seething, roiling brew of anger where people seem to have said to themselves we 'won't get fooled again'.

This mix of frustration, alienation, marginalisation and expectation is surfacing more frequently these days and producing a perfect 'storm-within- a-storm' for leaders trying to help employees, customers and stakeholders navigate a world of change. One of the most important job leaders will have over the coming decade is to articulate the dangers of:

- Too much emotion
- The eclipsing of the rational by the irrational
- The growing addiction to randomness as a response to complexity
- The self-infantalising that occurs when people withdraw from responsibility

Leaders will need to help us navigate our responses to complexity and uncertainty, and to bolster our collective belief that we can handle what comes our way. That being involved is better than sitting on the sidelines. Calm and courageous leadership based on character, values and real authenticity will be needed to do this.

As if that wasn't challenging enough for leaders, accompanying this emotional response is *a new orthodoxy rising up that is narrowing the range of what is acceptable* to many individuals and this increasingly could be a issues minefield for many firms. Let me explain by going back 20 years to the turn of the century.

The same technology and social media platforms that facilitated the phenomenal rise in information sharing and collaboration also directly led to the values revolution.

Over the last 20 years, there has been a massive explosion in shared information, the Information Age that pundits are so fond of writing about. But the Information Age is a lazy construct and idea. The term misses the vital point – it is not the information but the *startling paucity of meaning* that has accompanied this burgeoning information that is important.

People do not crave information, they crave meaning. It is not fanciful to suggest that the ratio of meaning to information is lower and the relationship between the two more tenuous than at any time over the past 1,000 years. We are awash in information but at the same time left yearning for meaning.

They say nature abhors a vacuum, but so do people. This 'meaning gap' has been increasingly filled by the rise in concern for important global and societal issues and the development of a shared consciousness about their importance.

This was encapsulated beautifully by a throwaway comment my daughter passed on the other day. She said a friend of hers was so upset by society's lack of action on the black lives matter issue that she had said: 'with so much information available nowadays – ignorance is an active political choice not an excuse'.

This is an exceptional articulation of exactly the rise of consciousness and social values I'm talking about. There is a powerful and growing consensus, particularly among the young but noticeable across all generations, that 'something needs to change', that the old shibboleths and shuffling off of responsibility have been found wanting and that there is a new urgency to effect social and societal change.

But increasingly, there is also the idea that there is a 'right way' to do this. That the change playbook is black and white and if you articulate grey, you simply haven't evolved enough. There is a new orthodoxy afoot in the change game that is unsettling.

With this consciousness-raising about the need for change has come a significant narrowing of opinion into what constitutes the correct way forward. Proper, open and democratic dialogue is under pressure from both the right and the left. From the right, by an increasingly virulent populism driven by those who feel left behind and marginalised in the slipstream of globalisation. And from the left, by an increasingly strident and woke coalition, for whom there is only one way to view a whole range of issues from climate change and microaggression to transgender rights and police brutality.

At both extremes, there is unwillingness to compromise. On the right, it is the 'fake news' dismissal of any inconvenient point of view, the baiting of deep-seated prejudice and the succour given to feral displays of public emotion. Take this to its logical conclusion and the result is public emotional chaos.

On the left, this orthodoxy is seen in the no-platforming, cancel culture, cultural misappropriation movements that insist that some views are so heinous they simply cannot be debated. Take this to its logical conclusion and you get intellectual chaos, as any view that has not been sanctioned by each potentially affected individual is rendered invalid.

The increasing embrace of emotion is a positive development, provided it doesn't mutate into something extreme. If it moves too far into a celebration of the feral and febrile and a renunciation of rational thought or debate, then we are in real trouble.

It must be said that the virtues of this new rise in consciousness and social values far outweigh the difficulties seen in the more extreme manifestations from both ends of the political spectrum. There is a growing consensus on many issues that easily outweighs these more radical notions.

But as social values gather steam, the reputational aspects of managing these issues will also become far more complicated, as organisations work out how to balance fervently held values with business practicalities and the concerns of their employees with those of their customers.

They may not always align.

BOX 1.3 IMPLICATIONS FOR LEADERS

The implication here is one of character. Leaders will know to expect negative reactions to change, complexity and uncertainty. They will need to understand the importance of leveraging character, values and their own sense of what it means to lead.

Most of the big decisions of the next decade will not be made principally from a platform of knowledge, analysis or experience. In a throwback to earlier decades, they will be made more from a platform of character, morality and values. Evaluating information, making the decision, mobilising support and articulating the way forward will all be predicated on not only on what is understood, but also what it believed and felt.

Leveraging Customer Connectivity – The Third Challenge

The third challenge is tightly tied to both mega trends. Everyone can see the huge impact digitisation and technology change has had on customers. In retail, the advent of online distribution has seriously undermined high street shopping and led to a fundamental recalibration of the mix between bricks and clicks. Savvy retailers talk about omni-channel strategies, and there has been a fundamental shift from the selling of products and services in shopping centres to the experiential sale driven by food and beverage, entertainment and virtual reality.

Banking is another sector whose fundamental value chain is being completely reimagined. Broadly speaking, banking is being split in two between commoditised, low-end transactional banking that has migrated almost completely online and high-end, high-value, high-touch service for high-net-worth individuals and corporates who need capital raising, financial structuring and mergers and acquisitions (M&A) advisory support.

In the 2020s, it seems that a rift has opened between businesses that 'get' the changing role of the customer and those who do not. Two of the more eminent business theorists of the past 50 years, Peter Drucker and Tom Peters, have built their careers around warning of the primacy of the customer. As Drucker says, 'the purpose of business is to create and keep a customer. No matter how de-layered, outsourced, virtualised or re-imagined businesses become, the company of the future will still need to remain focused on this simple fact'.[4]

For Tom Peters, many companies have passed that point of no return. He has suggested that most big businesses are actually dying but they just don't know it. Yet.

The idea that customers *are* the business is a bit like saying the audience is the communication – it turns received wisdom on its head. Everything should be about the receiver of the communication – the audience. What they need to hear and why, how we can make it cognitively easy for them to understand by making communication concise, differentiated and memorable.

There are three big challenges for business in dealing with customers.

How to Inform a Richer Customer 'conversation'

Eric Qualman writes in his book *Socialnomics*,[5] 'it is the conversation with the customer that is the key issue – that drives the perception of service and value'. The best companies are recognising the huge opportunity of putting the customers at the centre of the conversation and making them the business.

Having a point of view on shared values first and then products and services and getting this to the customer in a user-friendly manner lie at the heart of capitalising on the customer conversation.

A key payoff of the technological change we have talked about is that there is an extraordinary amount of information being gathered on customers via loyalty programmes, scraping and analysing digital interaction and footfall patterns and information gleaned from smartphone signals and facial recognition software at the core of smart in-store shopping.

Using this information to inform a richer, more valuable experience and relationship with the customer, not just to sell to them but to anticipate need and build 'communities of shared interest', is the primary challenge for businesses.

This immediately presents leaders with a communications opportunity and challenge.

Collaboration and connectivity has created communities of shared values and interests and *turbocharged the propensity and expectation to share*. Customer expectations about the democratisation of information have skyrocketed, putting more pressure on leaders to be honest and forthcoming with information. *In the past, this expectation-to-share dynamic simply didn't exist.*

For most leaders, wading in to the customer conversation sounds time-consuming and potentially full of pitfalls.

BOX 1.4 IMPLICATIONS FOR LEADERS

Collaboration and connectivity has produced a far more challenging ecosystem for leaders: far more pressure to 'share,' be involved and have a point of view. More pressure to make decisions in real time, under more scrutiny and in full public view. For leaders, this means far more time spent explaining, defending and communicating decisions.

One of the most important implications of this explosion of sharing is that there is now a much wider range of stakeholders and commentators. But the depth and quality of discourse has narrowed, influenced by the 280 characters per message of Twitter and the visual preoccupation of Instagram.

For leaders, the right to privacy in decision-making and time to reflect under pressure is now virtually non-existent.

Going Mobile to Capitalise on the Untethered Customer

The second customer challenge for businesses is how to ensure that all products and services can be delivered to the smartphone, which has by far eclipsed laptops and ipads as the preferred and dominant purchasing device.

As many commentators have observed, it is not the sale or transaction that is key today, but rather the opportunity via that sale to access that one customer's extended network bringing their contacts into the conversation.

Joining one person's customised, very individual universe symbolised by their smartphone with thousands of other like-minded individual universes is the big opportunity made possible by ensuring that all products and services can go mobile. It is the voluntary tethering together of the initial customer's own contacts – the creation of selling, social networks that is the real opportunity for business.

How to Understand and Align with Customer Values

Trust is a key issue in connecting with customers. The best companies are not only changing the way they converse with their customers – trusting them by putting them at the centre of the conversation and making them the business – they are also spending far more time understanding their values.

Given the emotive and changeable emotional and values landscape we have just discussed, the third huge challenge for businesses is how to react to their customers' views on the social issues in play. The need to explain the company or organisation's views and values, to both lead and listen in that conversation, will for many organisations be very new and challenging.

Actively managing reputation and making sure customers understand and support your 'licence to operate' will be business critical and will fall disproportionately on CEOs and other leaders to make happen.

These three fundamental reset challenges – management, employees and customers – will of course sit alongside the more specific changes and fallout brought about directly by the COVID pandemic.

Looking though a COVID Lens

The most immediate issue confronting the post-COVID world will be the massive restructuring and reimagining of business models that will occupy much of the 2020s. How to restructure and reimagine while not disrupting current business and making sure the bets you are making are the right ones will be the key business issue of the early 2020s.

This restructuring and reimagining will happen as a three-stage process.

Stage 1 Restructuring and redundancies: Initially, the issue will have a heavily financial flavour as government furlough schemes and income protection programmes end and the true cost of COVID-19 become more apparent. Companies will move at speed to reassess their financial viability. Restructuring will focus initially on redundancies and cost control. There is likely to be a wave of business failures and bankruptcies and a wave of M&A transactions driven by distressed opportunities and bargain hunting, but also the desire to extend competitive advantage.

Stage 2 Reimagining business models: Reassessment will quickly move on from restructuring and redundancies to reimagining business models. Firms will take a close, hard look at all aspects of their business model and the entire gamut of key business indicators such as marketing strategy, product and service mix, distribution and supply chain. Many firms will want to build more security of supply into their business model, explore new strategic partnerships, outsource production (or bring it back onshore), re-shape their labour pools, divest physical office space and accelerate even further the implementation of digital strategies and new technology. Restructuring and reimagining is probably the number one business issue trending for the next 5–10 years.

Stage 3 Alignment with social values: In reimagining business models, some firms will overtly attempt to align their new ways of working with the powerful emergent social forces we described earlier. For some, this thirst for racial and gender equality, concern for the environment and sustainability, diversity and inclusion, fairness and the yearning for authenticity may appear amorphous and anathema. But others will see real opportunity to differentiate and drive first-mover advantage in this newly emerging business landscape. These firms will move to broaden efforts to reimagine, to include aligning with, leveraging and capitalising on societal trends which have the potential to materially impact the firm.

BOX 1.5 THE COVID FALLOUT – THE 10 MOST LIKELY DEVELOP-MENTS THAT WILL AFFECT BUSINESS

Likely changes

1   Societal and individual disruption caused by massive restructuring and unemployment
    - Permanent structural unemployment, lowered living standards for some, emergence of new industries and redeployment of those with transferable skills – a decade of reconstruction
2   Structural hollowing out of weaker sectors and individual firms
    - Wholesale restructuring and reshaping of aviation, public transport, hospitality, performance arts – how much of their pre-COVID infrastructure will survive in recognisable shape and at what cost?
3   Boom for remote working
    - COVID-19 to fragment the office experience that has been in place for most white-collar staff since World War II
    - Pressure on centrally located office sites to repurpose as shared living/ workplaces or creative hubs
    - Implications for employee morale, corporate culture, shared goals and corporate narrative
4   Investment in digital
    - Accelerated investment in digitisation
    - Many businesses expect to make major investments in digital capabilities as a strategic move to mitigate risk from a future pandemic, save on travel costs and change their business model
5   Wider health fallout
    - Huge backlogs created by a unilateral focus on treating COVID-19
    - Some fallout will not be so apparent: deteriorating mental health

6 Reprioritising of national health systems
- More focus on implementing permanent 'track and trace' systems
- Restructuring so health experts are moved closer to the political decision-making
- More emphasis put on early warning systems, preventative measures and scanning for new viruses

7 Rise of e-learning
- Universities already moving into distanced and e-learning
- Fully digitising the learning experience may finally complete the business case for remote learning

Possible political changes

1 Increased tolerance for surveillance and state intervention
- Third and fourth 'waves' may require turning on/off social controls – and we'll need to be vigilant that we don't inadvertently give away freedoms
- The establishment of National Health Service in the UK in 1948 ushered in a 40-year period of state intervention. We may be at the end of another 40-year period, where we see a rollback of the focus on the individual – which has held sway since Thatcher came to power in 1979

2 Pressure for business payback from governments
- In the wake of unprecedented government support, there will be pressure on business for payback and to redefine a new model of resilient, social and stakeholder capitalism

3 Increased pressure to 'level-up'
- COVID-19 will accelerate efforts to create a fairer society, but the big question will be who will shoulder the increased tax burden?

Possible societal and behavioural changes

1 Accelerated action on climate change
- COVID-19 will be good for climate change. The aftermath will not be completely dominated by the economic agenda and social values will make themselves felt

2 Changing of the guard – millennials come of age
- From clapping for carers to adapting to Zoom and Teams – the sharing economy and collaboration has moved centre stage. Millennials will quickly begin exerting more influence in boardrooms and politics

3 Collective responsibility trumps populism
- The betting is on collective responsibility, but it will be complicated because we're likely to trade some freedom for increased surveillance and protection

The Way Forward

The 2020s will be a turbulent decade, as the immediate changes caused by COVID and the major restructuring that will inevitably follow the easing of the pandemic take centre stage. The immediate COVID reparations challenge and the ongoing need for businesses to effect a management, employee and customer reset will increasingly be affected by the impact and implications of our two mega trends.

Dealing with the underlying technological change and social disruption plus the three specific challenges of resetting management, strengthening employee trust and optimising customer connectivity will last the entire decade and beyond. It's hard to imagine a more complex operating environment in which to try to grow a business, engage with employees and customers and navigate with a sense of assuredness. This environment will require a real commitment on the part of all leaders to up their communications' game.

We see two implicit communication challenges here for leaders.

The first challenge will be how to effectively balance, broker and articulate the competing requirements and imperatives of the two trends.

The first 'technological' trend will be accompanied by a rational mindset, concerned with optimisation, utility and cost savings derived by applying logic, machine learning and modelling. *This will be the discourse of efficiency and it is likely to appear ruthless and relentless.* Certainly, in the restructuring that will mark the immediate post-COVID phase, there will be an inexorable logic to communications about resizing, recalibrating and readjusting.

This coolly rational discourse will increasingly come into conflict with the more emotionally based values of trust, authenticity, honesty and transparency driving the values reset – and the thirst for fairness, justice and equality driving the wider societal change for which many are agitating.

Navigating when two very different value sets may well be in diametric opposition to each other will be very challenging.

Putting it on a more personal basis, imagine you are a leader of a firm that has made the pivot to a management and values reset and understands the need to deal with uncertainty and be agile. You genuinely embrace the need for trust and communicating honestly with your employees and customers, but also know you need to articulate the change journey ahead – embracing AI, automation and all the accompanying side effects. This balancing act will require a real step change in leaders' ability to deliver effective, empathetic, emotionally aware communications.

Being able to communicate in an authentic manner that engenders trust and clearly lays out the path of change will be the key communications challenge of the next decade. Articulating how to handle the imperatives of digitisation and technical change while explaining what the company values and beliefs in the face of social change will be exceptionally challenging.

The Second Communications Challenge

The second challenge may prove even more difficult to navigate.

We mentioned that accompanying the great awakening on social values, we are seeing a trend towards a growing orthodoxy of accepted opinion: on the great social issues of the day, there is increasingly one way of viewing what needs to happen and that any opinion that sits outside this rapidly narrowing band of what is acceptable is dismissed, marginalised and in some cases demonised.

In issue after issue, from cultural misappropriation to pulling statues down, from the cancel culture to no-platforming, from gas-lighting to referring to 'people who menstruate' (so as not to offend transgender women), there has been a radical narrowing of the range of acceptable comment.

This is the dark side of the values reset – the abrogation of multiple truths in favour of one political correctness. Increasingly, the millennial support for going against the grain, which had included a healthy swipe at political correctness in the name of being contrarian, now is marked by this new political orthodoxy.

This is the second great challenge that leaders will face this decade: how to navigate a route through what may be increasingly roiling emotions and controversial positions on social issues in a way that commands the attention and respect of what may be increasingly radicalised employees and customers.

Encouraging the older values of authenticity, trust, honesty and transparency while insisting on tolerant and inclusive debate in the face of strongly held views will require all the effective communications ability a leader can muster.

Summary

The next decade will be about change: navigating and articulating the constant interplay between 'cool' technological change and 'hot' social change. Bridging the divide between technological winners and losers and social change 'haves' and 'have-nots' will be at the heart of how businesses deal with change. It will increasingly affect every effort to engage employees, return value to shareholders and compel customers.

How can leaders articulate what is of value – the competing needs of different stakeholders and how to balance accepting and embracing technological change with caring for the human condition.

It will require nothing less than the rise of the authentic leader who can – from a base built on character and values – engender trust, reassurance, confidence and motivation to help us navigate the changes that lie ahead.

Notes

1 Kahneman, Daniel, (2012), *Thinking Fast and Slow*, London, Penguin Group.
2 Taleb, Nassim, (2008), *The Black Swan: The Impact of the Highly Probable*, London, Penguin Books.
3 Lawler, Edward, Worley, Chris and Creelman, David, (2011), *Management Reset: Organising for Sustainable Effectiveness*, London, John Wiley & Sons.
4 Drucker, Peter, (1993) *Management Tasks, Responsibilities, Practices*, New York, Harper Business.
5 Qualcom, Eric, (2010), *Socialnomics: How Social Media Transforms the Way We Live And Do Business*, New York, John Wiley & Sons.

Chapter 2

The Rise of the Authentic Leader

The Evolving Nature of Leadership

It is the dual requirement to successfully navigate and articulate an accelerated change journey and do so in a value-driven, authentic manner that will be the biggest challenge for leaders in the coming years.

This will require an appreciably different skill set from what has been the norm for leaders most of the past 25 years. Those older skills were mainly rooted in financial knowledge, strategy and market expertise. They were the concrete and tangible skills of a competitive-driven, growth-oriented marketplace where the focus was on revenue and growth.

The key leadership imperative in this landscape was to maximise the firm's competitiveness and profitability and the strategic question was 'how to grow'.

In this landscape, the type of leader you had was relatively unimportant. Leadership skills were tangible and transferable because they were typecast for this focus on growth. Where that is still the default setting for most businesses, the command and control model of leadership has been slow to give way to the kind of management reset we discussed in the last chapter.

But since the global financial crisis, this model has changed irrevocably. *The growth environment has been eclipsed by a change environment.* With the pace of change accelerating rapidly and adding far more uncertainty and complexity to the operating landscape, a collaborative-driven, change-oriented marketplace has superseded the growth model.

Here the key skills of leadership are cognitive and behavioural. The focus is on understanding the changing nature of the marketplace and aligning organisational behaviours in order to adapt quickly to change. Leaders focus on generating the analytic information needed to innovate, understand customer need and how stakeholders will react to change. And they exhort their organisations to become more lean and agile.

The change model is accretive, in that all the other leadership skills from the growth paradigm are still needed. It's just that these are not the most important skills needed to navigate change.

The lexicon in use now among the c-suite shows this transformation. The talk is all about being agile and pivoting seamlessly towards opportunity: working smarter not longer, focusing on strengths, leveraging and liberating talent and turning the once dry legalistic concerns around diversity and governance into creators of value.

The key leadership imperative in this change landscape is to maximise the firm's ability to be smart, flexible and resilient. And the key strategic question for leaders is 'how to adapt' not 'how to grow'.

DOI: 10.4324/9781003198994-4

In this landscape, the type of leader you are matters greatly. A collaborative leader who can articulate why change is happening, encourage and align required behaviours and mobilise his or her employees to guide customers and stakeholders in adapting to change is a very valuable asset to the organisation.

But this leadership model – as good as it sounds – will alone not be enough to cope with the change and challenges that lie ahead. Change-oriented leadership with a premium on understanding the marketplace and committing to agility, resilience and adaptability will by itself not be fit for purpose in the years to come.

An additional set of leadership skills will need to be added to this ability to understand and navigate change, if leaders are to effectively move through the next decade.

The Emerging Character-Driven Landscape

A third business landscape is emerging that will fundamentally alter the newly emergent change style of leadership.

The first model we looked at was the competitive-driven, growth-oriented marketplace. This has now been overtaken almost completely since the global financial crisis by the collaborative-driven, change-oriented marketplace. *Now, a new paradigm is emerging: the character-driven, values-oriented marketplace.*

As the pace of change grows exponentially, it will not be enough to try and understand or adapt to change. Employees, customers and stakeholders will increasingly want to know *what leaders feel about the changes they are facing and what is their vision; in other words, where should all this change be leading us to?* The questions will be pointed and personal: what do you value and perceive is worth holding on to? Why are you moving in this direction and what moral position lies behind the products and services you are offering and the public positions you are asking us to take?

The competitive landscape of the next ten years is likely to be dominated by questions that increasingly have a higher moral aspect to them than the more familiar concerns of revenue growth or adapting to change. Increasingly, the ability to analyse and understand change *without having a view on what constitutes desirable change and what is morally repugnant will be seen as outsourcing corporate responsibility.*

This is the legacy of the great groundswell in concern for values driven by millennials, which we saw earlier. This desire to have business decisions grounded in values will be infinitely strengthened by the mega trend of rising concern for justice and fairness, and the moral complexity of the plethora of issues that will be marked by the complex overlapping of technological and emotional imperatives.

For example, what is the moral position of your firm on job losses driven by automation and artificial intelligence? What does a legal firm feel about facial recognition software that helps robot judges determine if the accused is lying? Do we really trust algorithms to allocate exam results never mind vaccine lottery places and where does the responsibility lie to check the assumptions being made in programming these algorithms.

You can clearly see this tussle between automation and analytics on the one hand and the demand for emotional honesty and transparency on the other, in the great debate over scientists' modelling of COVID hospitalisation and death rates that propelled European lockdowns in 2020. 'Following the science' is a clarion call that has been increasingly tarnished by a lack of honesty about what the numbers really mean.

In this character-driven, values-oriented marketplace, leadership skills are focused more on identifying purpose, mobilising values and engendering trust.

Taking the time to explain your position, to show some humility, perhaps even some vulnerability, and to try and bridge the divide to other points of view will be a hallmark of emotionally mature leadership.

Given the quantum of change, leaders will increasingly need to articulate what their organisation believes in, why it exists, what it stands for and how it will interact with employees, customers and stakeholders as change unfolds.

Articulating, persuading and explaining what the organisation feels about change and why will increasingly take up the majority of leaders' time and be the core skills needed. And this will be the prime topic and reason for communicating to employees, customers and stakeholders.

Setting out a credo and charting a basis of doing business based on values, beliefs and purpose will be the biggest differentiator and creator of value in the coming business landscape.

In this marketplace, the key leadership imperative is to maximise the firm's ability to mobilise its values and beliefs. And the top strategic question for leaders is, 'how can I engender trust', not the older questions of 'how to grow' or 'how to adapt'.

This will require a very different set of leadership skills than was needed in either the growth or change marketplace. *The next decade will see the full emergence of the authentic leader.*

The Authentic Leader

Over the past few years, authenticity has become – well – inauthentic. It has been used too often in a bovine and glib manner to describe everything from leaders who blog and enjoy rap music to those in touch with their own feelings, able to show emotion and talk without using management-speak.

It is an overused and misunderstood term, and *the currency of authenticity has been cheapened* because of this. We need to restore the older meaning of authenticity by returning the notion to its original foundations – character and trust.

Authenticity is not something that is conferred from the outside, by say taking the measure of a leader's interests and activities and pronouncing him or her to be authentic. Rather, *it is a reaction or feeling on the part of the beholder or audience to a power and presence which emanates from within the leader.* Authenticity is the word we use to describe the effect produced by foundational qualities that when fully alive and activated are easy for us to see, feel and be moved by.

Authenticity develops on a dual track proceeding from character and trust. It starts by being grounded in the personal integrity and value system of the individual in question. Core values of fairness, kindness, patience, tolerance and honesty then join with a person's basic world view of others and of the human condition to produce a general outward disposition or operating stance that is readily seen by others.

The basic world view of an authentic leader is likely to be intrinsically positive and optimistic, forward-looking and fundamentally nurturing of people on an individual basis. This doesn't preclude being tough and temperamental on occasion, but there is a solidity and predictability to their emotional intelligence and awareness that engenders assurance and confidence.

We trust these leaders because we feel we know them. They are not changeable, vacillating, weak characters angling and calculating for temporal advantage. They are dependable and worthy of us investing our trust in them because we feel strongly they will not let us down. *But even more, because we feel they will not let themselves down.*

This feeling of innate trust lies at the heart of why we confer the marker of authenticity. But this trust is predicated on a deeper reading of the core character we see every day in how leaders approach the world. Although individual character traits will vary enormously from leader to leader, I think there is a commonality to authentic leadership that is easily identified.

Authentic leaders are intrinsically hard-working and egalitarian, they give off the feeling that they will gladly join you in the trenches and have done so many times before, and they know what you are going through. They are slow to judge, swift to praise and eager to see individual success, knowing that everything an organisation has and does happens only because of individuals.

Humility is an essential ingredient of authentic leadership. These leaders are humble enough to admit they don't know everything and comfortable enough in their own skin to show vulnerability. The leader as servant model acts as a powerful north star guiding their actions, and in return, we see someone to whom we can relate and is worthy of our respect and support.

Finally, *there is an essential kindness that lies at the core of their character.* They understand foibles, failure and the need for forgiveness that, along with a yearning for liberation and the need to love and be loved, are probably the three most fundamental of human desires. Authentic leaders appeal to our need to move on, to shed baggage, to receive absolution and to be rededicated to what lies ahead.

But as momentous as this sounds, *there is also a profound gentleness and generosity of spirit at work within authentic leaders* that is hugely attractive to us. That comforts and compels us in equal measure. This gentleness and generosity flows directly from this predisposition towards kindness.

And it is kindness that makes possible a leader's ability to put themselves in our shoes, to feel what we feel. Leaders who are not kind simply cannot be bothered to do this – and yet *this is the essential act of authentic leadership.* To hold yourself open to what others feel, to look kindly on their travails because you have been there as well – and to mobilise and lead – from this base of shared understanding.

So what does this authentic leader look like? A few stories will show these attributes or the lack of them in action.

The Authentic Leader in Action

A few years ago, I was working with a senior partner at a global firm who had been nominated to campaign for the role of managing partner for Europe, Middle East and Africa region (EMEA). The process for winning the 'election' was complicated and involved video and live appearances to audiences in locations around the world.

He came to me wanting support with his 'stump' speech and was sure about only one thing – that the best way to differentiate as a candidate and drive the business forward was to position himself as the 'character' candidate; the person who best embodied the firm's values and exemplified how integrity and character could be directly harnessed to drive revenue and talent recruitment.

He firmly believed that the strongest competitive advantage the firm had lay in how it was perceived by its clients and that increasingly clients wanted to deal with a firm that had a strong moral core and compass, was openly invested in what it believed in, took progressive stances on diversity and inclusion and put integrity at the core of the overall offering.

Character, trust and a values-driven approach was what he wanted to talk about and make the basis for his platform.

Where other partners campaigned on new approaches to revenue or services, techno-logical innovation or partnerships with other firms, his was a seemingly retropositioning, a back-to-the-future appeal that appeared almost old-fashioned.

But he set about showing the modernity of this approach – talking about the coming complexity of legal issues and how they would be inextricably linked to the great social and business issues of the next decade. He felt strongly that clients increasingly wanted to do business with a firm that stood for something and felt different to work with.

He outlined a muscular approach to using values and integrity as a differentiator and to putting substance behind commitments to diversity and inclusion, by actively investing in actions that would change how the firm hired, promoted and approached winning new business.

Out of almost a dozen candidates and after a whirlwind of different engagements that lasted over a month, he finished second.

I thought the result almost as significant as the stance my client had taken. An emer-gent leadership position, not quite strong or clear enough to carry the day, but plenty strong enough to move past the status quo.

The story has a happy ending. Securing second place allowed my client to actually advance his agenda, perhaps more than if he had been trying to do that in addition to having the responsibility of being managing partner. He is driving progress in this area – refashioning integrity and character as modern methods of driving competitive advantage.

The fact that a senior partner would campaign on such an overt platform of integrity and character shows *this moral core of authenticity is becoming more important and relevant to what employees and clients are looking for in their leaders*. His bet was that this would only increase as change accelerated and values and ethical issues became more commonplace as technology collided with concern for social values.

This growing awareness of the importance of values, integrity and character is prob-ably no more than nascent or emergent at the moment. It's coming, but it will be driven predominantly by the arrival of a new generation of millennial leaders for whom the 'whole values thing' will come far more naturally. At present, this kind of leadership is still dwarfed by the continuing penchant for old-style behaviour in many sectors.

Banking is everyone's favourite whipping boy, and of course there are plenty of signs of enlightenment and change happening in that sector. But for tales of poor, inauthentic leadership behaviour, it still takes some beating.

Looking back at the ten years I spent in banking, my impression remains that there was something fundamentally shallow, bereft of inner confidence and lacking in kind-ness, gentleness and generosity of spirit among so many senior banking leaders. I found it soul-destroying to see it played out so often in everyday actions.

The CEO who deliberately yelled at his senior reports on day one 'just to see how they coped and whether they could fight back'. The casual and utter disdain in which clients were held in the immediate aftermath of the global financial crisis when banks did not know how much exposure they had to sub-prime mortgages and were panicking. Suddenly the less profitable clients were ring-fenced and disparaged in meetings as talk quickly focused on how to 'exit' them.

Many of the leaders I saw in action seemed to conduct their relationships in a cold and calculating manner – very little humour, very little understanding of foibles or failure and very little 'hinterland' or interest in anything that couldn't be quantified, structured, sold or profited from.

This is of course a gross generalisation, but it was a strong view I formed over ten years of working closely with scores of c-suite leaders. A common attribute shared by poor leaders was not only a lack of emotional intelligence and awareness, but a more fundamental lack of interest in the commonplace things of everyday life, or indeed in anyone else but themselves.

They simply weren't interested in the challenges and tribulations faced by ordinary employees, the daily panoply of the human condition or the need to occasionally commiserate and comfort.

Everything seemed utilitarian and calculated on fault lines of weakness or strength. Among the most extreme, the level of narcissism was startling. Numerous studies of leaders in banking show that there is a significant over-representation of psychopaths and sociopaths among CEOs.

I think much of this behaviour is rooted in an existential lack of confidence and a vacuum or essential hollowness where normally you'd expect a moral core to be.

These two conditions when allied to a preening sort of misplaced arrogance makes for a lethal leadership cocktail, and marks these kind of leaders as incredibly poorly positioned to lead any organisation in the coming years. Values-driven leadership will certainly be the biggest challenge facing banking over the next few years.

But enough negativity. You get the point.

Let's return to the positive attributes and core qualities that will be crucial for the kind of leadership needed in the 2020s.

We've talked about vulnerability, generosity of spirit, kindness and emotional maturity. I think there are four other broad categories of qualities that will be important.

The first is a deliberative and consultative approach to leading: assembling a team of many talents, being comfortable hearing all views and acting in a proportionate manner by balancing competing interests and the need to be decisive with a clear commitment to fairness.

This brokering role – bringing many disparate views together – is a sign of strength rather than weakness and a signal that in dealing with complexity, mobilising a breadth of opinion constitutes wise leadership.

The second category revolves around track record. I think nothing really replaces the sense that a leader has been there, done that and got the t-shirt. That he or she has paid their dues helps to define a sense of genuineness and authenticity. Provenance of leadership is important – *the idea that leadership has been well earned rather than having been conferred for political or spurious reasons*. The ability to call on track record is invaluable in leading by example and role modelling the kind of behaviours that are needed to cope with change.

We saw a good example of this kind of leadership in the work we did with a client's business that was being sold by its parent company.

BOX 2.1 FINDING A NEW BUYER FOR THE BUSINESS

The CEO was well aware that the parent company was more interested in securing a smooth and profitable sale than in ensuring a commitment from any would-be buyer to save jobs or the operating structure of the business, which revolved around numerous specialist teams.

The parent company was willing to let the CEO drive the sale process. They allowed him plenty of latitude to hire specialist financial, legal and communications advisors to ensure the process unfolded smoothly.

The CEO had been in the industry his whole career, and now in his late 50s confided that his chief goal was to 'get as many of my people safely in the lifeboat as possible' and preserve as much of his business as was feasible under new ownership.

His leadership throughout the entire process was a study in grace under pressure and specifically in the benefits of having track record and provenance in the industry. Buyers, consultants, parent company and employees were all reassured by his knowledge and the way he went about balancing competing interests. Employees knew he had their best interests at heart and all parties took confidence from his humble but well-informed and straightforward approach that was deeply rooted in experience and track record. I've often thought that his authenticity was the prime creator of value in what ended up being a successful sales process.

A year after joining the new firm, he confided that he had lost only a handful of employees and had preserved the business structure. Of everything he had done in his career, he rated this as his top achievement.

The third category is courage, commitment and integrity. The ability to show physical, moral and intellectual courage when under pressure is the mark of a leader who is willing to put their values and beliefs on the line – something that will increasingly be on the agenda. The next story shows this kind of authentic leadership in action.

BOX 2.2 RE-ORDERING A CHINESE TAKEAWAY

When I worked for the Hong Kong Trade Development Council over the handover, we were lucky to have superb leadership in our top two executives: Dr. Victor Fung was the Chairman and de facto trade minister of Hong Kong and Michael Sze, the Executive Director who had been airlifted from the Hong Kong Government where as Governor Chris Patten's Principal Secretary he played a key role in dispensing political advice about handling China in the run up to the transfer in sovereignty.

Both men were adept at balancing robust messaging about Hong Kong's trade and economic capabilities and usefulness to China with more 'political' messaging about the importance of maintaining the rule of law, respecting private property and adhering to Western standards of transparency, honesty and freedom of expression.

They worked well together, with the Chairman's predominantly encouraging economic messages about Hong Kong's continuing value to China balanced by the more pointed political warnings of the Executive Director not to tamper with Hong Kong's special status.

On the eve of the handover, I witnessed a monumental act of leadership and courage. On hearing a final rehearsal of the handover speech that the Chairman was going to deliver at the historic event, Michael Sze stopped Dr. Fung in full flight and told him he would not be giving this speech That it was too sympathetic to Beijing and would be a historic mistake – it needed toughening up and re-ordering.

That one Chinese leader subordinate to another would tell his boss this in public, risking great loss of face or a huge political and personal standoff, was astonishing. That the recipient of this view would calmly accept and agree with the view and pivot to this new stance without any seeming discomfort was equally amazing. Both men showed maturity and an authenticity that came from a sense of integrity and deep commitment.

For me, this personal moment eclipsed all of the grander historic events that followed.

Patience and Humour

The final ingredients in our extra quartet of categories are two simple virtues that are hugely under-rated these days: patience and humour.

It has always struck me that patient and calm leaders are like great sportspeople, in that they seem to see everything unfold in a clearer, less frenetic way than other people. This gives them far more 'time on the ball' and a far better ability to see the big picture – where everyone is on the field and their interrelationships. This ability to be patient and show patience, I think, is a natural outcome of experience and track record, but also comes from the inner grounding that a values-driven belief set bestows on leaders.

And if all else fails, laugh. The ability to see humour even in a difficult and challenging situation is one of the clearest signs of authenticity and leadership.

To be able to laugh in the face of adversity is either the sign of a madman or someone who is able to get sustenance from deeper sources of knowledge, faith and confidence. The ability to both see the funny, human side in everyday events as well as laugh in the midst of danger can be hugely reassuring and a great relief to the rest of us.

The Teaching and the Unfinished Leader

One final comment on authentic leaders – the best impart their knowledge and wisdom and actively look to transfer competence. As we'll see in the last chapter on coaching, leadership and communication, there is an active dynamic among authentic leaders to give something back, to help the younger generation prepare for leadership and to pass on their observations and experiences. The very best leaders are adept at making this process very subtle; it is not directive teaching, but rather a case of encouraging you to learn and come to your own conclusions.

Looking back at the leaders I have learned the most from, it has always been those who posed questions, outlined scenarios, and then asked me what I thought should happen and challenged me to say what I would do and why. This selfless, awareness-raising approach lies at the heart of the coaching dynamic and is also a real marker of modern, authentic leadership.

This willingness to transfer the locus of control from them to you, making you the primary source of your own learning is the positioning of wise teachers. The leader as teacher, but not the traditional, hierarchical and directive teacher – rather a fellow companion on the road, interested in giving of themselves and helping you teach yourself.

This mind-set of passing-on rather than hoarding knowledge is complemented by the overall attitude to learning shown by authentic leaders. Again, the best acknowledge that no one is ever the finished product and that continuous learning is the only positioning that really makes sense in a time of disruptive change.

We seem to return time and time again when discussing authentic leadership – to that which lies within: values, trust, disposition, character, integrity, humility and kindness. There is something about this inner 'platform for good' that we are inherently drawn to and recognise as being nurturing, real and something to value. That is the real nature of authenticity.

A Father's View on Leadership

I'm going to give the last word in this chapter to my father, one of the most genuine people I have ever known. Among all the sayings he passed down to me, he had two that I think absolutely show authenticity in action.

He always said that the most important thing in leading or 'setting an example', as he called it (which itself is very telling), was the way you treated other people, especially when you disagreed or were in conflict with them. Rather like that line about being able to tell everything about a society from the way they treat their children and animals, he used to say two things are of primary importance:

First, you must never back someone into a corner, but always allow them some 'operating room'. And second, always allow someone to save face. Never destroy. Always be mindful of creating a way back.

I think these two sayings speak volumes about authentic leadership.

Part 2

A Framework for Authentic Communications

Chapter 3

Audience – The Primal Consideration

Overview – The Primacy of Audience

The place to begin with all communications should be the audience.

Effective communication is obviously a two-way street. But you wouldn't know it given the lack of attention paid to the audience in most people's preparations. And yet consideration of the audience is the primary ingredient in giving you the best possible chance of delivering an effective communication.

For leaders, the audience should be almost everything, certainly far more important than structure and content or engagement. What do they need, how will they receive my communication, what's on their minds that might be preoccupying them right now, what is the context for the communication, what type of an audience are they, what is the purpose of my communication and my desired outcome are all fundamental questions that need reflection before starting out.

Most leaders think deeply about what their intended audience needs if they are communicating upwards to shareholders, regulators or parent company boards. But communicating downwards or sideways to employees and customers is often a very different proposition. For these audiences, the weighting can tend to shift significantly towards content – what do I want to tell them?

But the other two parts of crafting a presentation, structure/content and engagement can wait. Your internal interrogation of what the audience needs is by far the most important part of preparing.

Engagement becomes a much easier proposition of aligning mode of delivery to what will work best, once you know more about what this precise audience needs here and now. An audience-focused presentation demands that you stay in 'engaging' mode. And working out what delivery mechanisms, like slides, stories, videos, demos and whiteboarding, will align best with what the audience needs will be a lot easier once you have a stronger picture of your audience and what's most important to them right now.

Some of the most powerful presentations I've prepared for leaders or seen them give have been simple conversations with few or no slides and little in the way of engagement techniques other than talking openly and honestly. Certainly, for highly emotive announcements, this and plenty of time for question and answer (Q&A) is what an audience needs most.

The same goes for structuring your presentation and developing content. Both are made much easier if looked at through an audience lens – what does my audience need to know, how much detail is appropriate, what do they already know and what are the key takeaways I want to leave with them.

Content is the most easily assembled part of the presentation and almost always the least memorable. No one ever says, 'wow that content was so interesting – don't you have one more slide you can show me'.

DOI: 10.4324/9781003198994-6

So what are the key questions to ask in order to evaluate your audience, to consider what they need and to get you started in preparing your presentation? Here are some initial questions you should consider (Table 3.1).

Initial Questions to Ask about Your Audience

The other practical piece of work you should do in considering your audience is to spend some time assessing what type of personalities will be in the audience. People's innate preference for how they receive information and what they think is important varies hugely.

There are plenty of different personality typology metrics out there – Belbin, DiSC, Meyers-Briggs – but for simplicity and basic insight, I have found the social styles or 'colours' typology as discussed by Thomas Erikson in his recent bestseller *Surrounded by Idiots – the four types of human behaviour*[1] to be the most efficient and immediately useful. The model was originally called the Social Styles model and was developed by David Merrill and Roger Read.[2]

Understanding and Adapting to Your Audience's Personality Type

The quadrants below help identify the four primary styles. Most people have one dominant and one supplementary style and this greatly affects how they process communications, what they are 'prewired' to look for and what kind of information and delivery mode they will best respond to (Table 3.2).

You can see the significant differences between these typologies and that it matters greatly what kind of personality you are presenting to. Everyone of course exhibits aspects of each of the personality quadrants at different times. But people prefer their innate or default positioning and this hugely affects how they process your communication.

This is a powerful concept because if you can get an accurate 'read' on the communications personality or preference of the person with whom you are communicating, you stand a much better chance of communicating with them in a way that makes sense to them, of appearing compatible to them and for leaders especially appearing accessible and empathetic to them.

Table 3.1 Initial questions to ask about your audience

Fundamental question	Supplementary questions
Purpose What is my purpose?	Why am I giving this presentation? What kind of communication is it? What am I seeking to do (inform, persuade, instruct, reassure, update, move to action)?
Importance Why is this important?	Is this important? How will they perceive this? What is in it for them, for the company, for this department or team? Is this more about them or about me?
Relevance Is this relevant for them?	What would be relevant for this audience? How can I make this more relevant? What is most relevant? What do they need?
Desired outcome	What do I want them to think, feel or do – each is a different type of presentation?

Table 3.2 Four primary personality styles

Blue – Analytical	Red – Driver
• Data-oriented	• Big picture-oriented
• Process and methodology-driven	• Actions and recommendation-driven
• Evidence-based	• Changed-focused
• Rational *not* emotional	• Rational *and* emotional
• Present-orientation	• Future-orientation
• Wants detail, facts and numbers	• Wants bottom-line recommendations
• Likes slides, Excel spreadsheets	• Likes few slides and concise information
• Conservative	• Realistic and tough
• Values 'proof', prep and order	• Values big picture backed up by details
• Time-rich	• Time-poor
• Factual engagement	• Directive engagement
• Favoured mode: spreadsheet	• Favoured mode: short verbal briefing
Green – Amiable	**Yellow – Expressive**
• Conversation-oriented	• Performance-oriented
• People-driven	• Passion-driven
• Focus: impact on/linkage to others	• Energy-focused
• Rational *and* emotional	• Emotional *more than* rational
• Present and future orientation	• Future-orientation
• Wants discussion and authenticity	• Wants inspiration and storytelling
• Likes pilot projects, demos, tests	• Likes videos, flipcharts, no slides
• Collaborative	• Exuberant
• Values developing a consensus	• Values a big idea and creativity
• Time-rich	• Time-poor
• Reflective engagement	• Energetic engagement
• Favoured mode: conversation	• Favoured mode: multimedia show

The importance of being perceived as compatible, accessible and empathetic is hard to overstate. Along with the person liking you, their feeling compatible with you is one of the strongest success factors in them forming a positive opinion of you as a communicator. Aligning to what they need and adjusting to their preferences – becoming more compatible to them – is absolutely fundamental to delivering a strong presentation.

Leaders ignore this at their peril. One of the most important aspects in assessing whether a leader's communication is effective or not is the effort they are seen to make to talk to people in the way they want to be talked to – in a manner conducive to the audience and to making a connection.

It is also fundamental to leadership. The ability to engender the feeling in others that you are open to their concerns, capable of understanding them and aligned to 'how they are' is the first and perhaps most significant step towards building trust. It is also a cornerstone of being perceived as authentic.

BOX 3.1 THE IMPORTANCE OF COMPATIBILITY

In the ten years I spent as a head of communications in four banks, this notion of compatibility was raised time and again by managing directors when asked what they wanted from mid-level subject matter experts who routinely presented to them.

Capability and credibility were taken as given. The managing directors genuinely valued and understood their expertise. But what these senior executives wanted were people who could deliver the information they needed *in the way they wanted it*. For the most part, the managing directors were all blue/red or red/blue personalities, and so they put a premium on the more junior colleagues understanding the numbers and getting to the point. Be brief, be bold, be gone was the mantra. The most common mistake made by the more junior people was either taking too long to make their point or not having a point to make; in other words, delivering the individual trees, not the entire forest. I remember one MD lamenting that a financial analyst gave her every conceivable piece of data except what the variance was caused by, what that meant and what she could do about it – the classic needs of a red personality type.

But I rarely saw this dynamic in reverse. Leaders wondering what adjustments they need to make so that they aligned to what more junior employees needed. The greatest adjustment that is commonly required is the need to slow down, take the time to explain what things means and allow for employees to reflect, digest and move forward. Too often the expectation is implicitly 'keep up or be left behind'. Not really conducive to building trust or authenticity.

A Deeper Look at the Model

Before we take a look at what adjusting to each typology involves, let's look more closely at what the model reveals about the different personality types. In the graphic below, you can see a summary of the key attributes of each typology, how they align to an issue or people orientation, their preference in terms of time pressure and professional job specifications each typology aligns to. Obviously, this is generalised and it is important to remind ourselves that everyone has aspects of all four typologies and is capable of functioning in different quadrants at different times. But as a tool to get a read on innate preference, it is powerful (Figure 3.1).

The blue personality describes a common workplace typology typified by expertise and mastery over the nuts and bolts of whatever the organisation specialises in. It is the most common route to the top – a pathway most senior management figures follow in the journey to the front office. This is why so many 'red typology' leaders often show very strong 'blue' attributes and in presentations demand both types of information. The pure blue typology gives you all the time you need to deliver your presentation and they are very welcoming of data and information in whatever form. These are the people that will actually read the budget spreadsheets you send before your meeting with them.

The red typology is reflective of a 'senior management' predisposition. Time poor and concerned with making decisions – they need the key information in as concise a format as possible. These are the people that scan through to slide 17 when the presenter is still on slide three. These leaders are pushed for time and intent on scanning for risk, bottom-line numbers and recommendations. Too much set-up or contextual information can be perceived as irritating. A wag in one coaching session suggested that red types only ever need three slides: (a) the issue we are discussing and why it is important, (b) what we found and (c) implications and recommendations. The key thing with the red typology is to hold your ground and not be blown back. Confidence and brevity are the two things you need most.

The yellow personality is found more in creative industries, retail, media or publishing and in the more traditional corporate, finance or manufacturing sectors can be a bit thin on the ground, especially at the leadership level. It is a less usual route to the top because their expertise tends to be based more on creativity than process or production. These

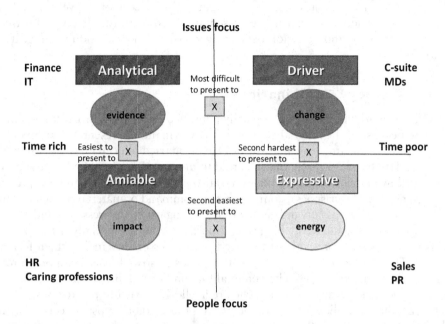

Figure 3.1 The four quadrants of the social styles model.

people thrive on energy, commitment, vision and creativity. They love big ideas, flights of fancy and the worst thing you can do in presenting to them is to be flat or disengaged.

If you are not passionate or at least invested in your own presentation, they will mark you down, switch off – or eat you alive. Yellow people are forgiving of prototypes, don't need the last detail worked out or even explained. They want the big picture painted for them and the big idea articulated. These are the people who love unusual slides or who use animated real-time whiteboarding techniques or only pictures in their slides. They often like no slides at all, the exact opposite of the buttoned-down blue personality.

And finally, to the greens. This typology is the only one that does not do what it says on the tin. Amiables are not happy-clappy. They are thoughtful, reflective souls who want to consider something before moving forward. They instinctively recoil at the CEO's action-orientated stance and are most concerned about impact on people and how issues are often linked. They want the information slowly and with plenty of opportunity to input into the process.

They are the calm figures you want in a lifeboat. Amiables often map to introverts in Meyers-Briggs and are likely to be kinaesthetic type learners in the visual-audio-kinaesthetic learning model (VAK). They don't like to be rushed and will often 'withdraw' from a presentation because it is going too quickly (and is off the rails) as far as they are concerned. They need to be involved in the process and want to talk and engage.

Multiple Typologies in One Audience

The question always comes up: 'what do I do if there are multiple different typologies in the audience?'. The answer tends to be that for good or bad, presenting with red and blue in mind is probably the default or safest option. The reds are the decision-makers and together with the blues will want to see impactful, accurate content. The irony is that it is the focus on engagement, emotion and meaning – the core of the yellow and green typologies – that is actually what make presentations come to life. It says a lot that we tend to opt for content and direction before engagement, emotion and meaning, if we're forced to choose.

Handling Typology Combinations

The blue/red or red/blue typology is typically perceived as the most difficult combination to present to because of the fairly abrupt swing they demand of presenters – from detail to big picture and back again. How many times have you tried to keep it big picture, only to be hauled back to 'prove' a point and then told to move on because 'I haven't got all day'.

The red/yellow or yellow/red combination is also perceived as challenging for presenters because you need all the crispness, confidence and command of material needed to present to the driver but with a passion and energy that will engage the expressive – and all this in double quick time. That's a really big ask for most presenters, especially if they are more junior. For most people, presenting to the red/yellow personality makes them feel really pressurised. This is probably the pairing that responds least well when both presenter and recipient are the same typologies. The potential for conflict and disagreement coupled with plenty of emotion and passion is higher when red/yellows present to red/yellows.

The green/yellow or yellow/green combination is the typology most concerned with the 'people factor'. Presenting to these people can be easier because they are prewired to react more to people concerns rather than focus on tasks and strategies. This people predisposition often manifests itself in an easier emotional wrapper to the conversation, with the performance imperative of the yellows being tempered by the valuing of consensus and harmony displayed by the greens.

The blue/green or green/blue combination is usually perceived as the easiest personality combination to present to. That's because of two things: time is usually not as big a factor and the overall tone is factual whether it is data or people that are being discussed.

It is interesting that in most companies, the workforce tends to be made up of more blues, greens and blue/greens than any other typology. These people have the propensity to want to get on with things in a straightforward manner. Neither particularly likes the internal politics that is often a hallmark of the reds and yellows.

This is only the briefest of introductions to this typology metric. The key thing is to remember that time spent thinking about what your audience is never time wasted. Arming yourself with some insight into how your audience may be prewired or predisposed to view your presenting is vital.

BOX 3.2 THE STYLES TYPOLOGY TAKEAWAY

The metric should serve as a reminder to leaders to be mindful of the 'amiable' needs of their employees. While most c-suite leaders are either red/blue or red/yellow, the most frequent typology for non-frontline staff is green/blue or green/yellow.

This means many employees will need time to adjust to and reflect on changes being put forward by a leader. They are far more likely to endorse the changes and get behind them if time is taken to engage and understand them.

And the 'people' quotient – the need to debate, engage, understand the impact and talk about any proposed changes – is something CEOs underestimate at their peril.

Emotional Awareness

Wanting to make adjustments for other people and understanding how you and your actions may be perceived by audiences are examples of the important role emotional awareness plays in good communications and leadership.

Most leaders strive for self-awareness and seek to be attuned to others' needs, preferences and emotional reactions. A leader's emotional intelligence (EQ) is far more important to effective communication than their intelligence quotient (IQ). This is a hugely important point and one that will be borne out as we look more closely at how engagement is perceived by audiences, what they find persuasive and what they remember and why.

IQ-driven communications that focus mainly on content and information transfer usually have only limited 'connective' power with audiences. People remember a presentation that has emotional power and is aligned to their emotional needs. The other drawback with focusing mainly on IQ-driven content transfer – rationally educating audiences – is that our ability to pay attention and to remember information is severely constrained. We have limited short-term memory or capacity in which to retain and process information. And our attention span – our ability to stick with an information-driven presentation – is remarkably low.

There is plenty of existing research and information on the relative power of EQ; Daniel Goleman's work is seminal here. Suffice for our purposes is the simple idea that to be a strong communicator and leader, you need to make a real effort to be aware of your audience's emotional needs and wants, their 'emotional ecosystem'.

What Audiences Need in a Leader

No one actually expects too much from presentations because we've all sat through hundreds of unfathomably boring ones. From the audience's point of view, *the benchmark for physical performance is astonishingly low*. No one expects good presenting.

If we're honest, the best we can hope for is someone who is 'normal', doesn't speak too long and makes a few useful points. We certainly don't expect someone too slick. We may even distrust leaders who appear too good at presenting.

Instead, the behavioural traits an audience wants to see are authenticity, passion and confidence:

- *Authenticity*: They want you to be yourself. To speak genuinely, act 'normally' and be congruent with how you regularly show up.
- *Passion*: They want you to convey the sense that you care about what you are telling them and that you respect them enough to be invested in your own topic. Passion in this case does not mean emotional presenting but an integrity and interest in your own presentation that is readily perceived by the audience.
- *Confidence*: Audiences want you to have the courage of your convictions. To be strong enough to make the effort to engage even though you may not want to do this or feel this way.

This is what the audience is asking of you. And their expectation is that you try rather than fully succeed. *For it is the trying that is noticed and valued, not subjectively how good you are.*

This is a key point. Audiences are hugely forgiving of a leader's physical delivery skills or behavioural traits. If you're being authentic, passionate about the topic and confident enough to try, *this signals to the audience that you value them*, and that you acknowledge and are addressing what they need. And in return, what the audience gives you back is significant.

Whatever anxiety you feel inside, they only perceive about 10%. And they perceive it as normal and understandable. They are willing you to succeed. A pause or 'lost moment' which seems like an eternity to you will be perceived as a welcome break in information flow by them. A hesitation here, a stumble there will be perceived far more negatively by you than them.

This supportive, 'willing-you-to-succeed' audience's view of you as a presenter is their 'contract' with you. If you are perceived to be trying to deliver authenticity, passion and confidence, effectively acknowledging what they need, what you get back in return is support and an audience 'willing' you to succeed.

It's when this 'contract' is not in place, when the audience perceives little authenticity, passion or willingness to try from the leader – when there is a fundamental lack of acknowledgement of what an audience needs – that things go wrong.

BOX 3.3 A NEW STYLE OF LEADER

Authenticity, passion and real confidence are often in short supply in our leaders. The traditional gruff, command and control archetype (predominantly men of a certain generation) may be fading away, but it has yet to be fully replaced with a different, generally recognised model.

I think a great example of this new type of modern-day leadership can be seen in Jacinda Arden, the prime minister of New Zealand. She has all these characteristics in spades – genuine and emotionally astute and not afraid to show emotion. Confident, but also willing to show vulnerability – she doesn't expect or pretend to know everything.

Expect to see more of this style of leadership emerge as millennials gain a stronger foothold in the boardroom.

When Things Go Wrong with an Audience

All presenters have one thing in common. Everyone thinks about what may go wrong. And the two things presenters fear more than anything else both involve the audience.

First is an openly hostile audience: catcalling, brutal Q&A, walkouts and interruptions. The second is the audience's anticipated reaction to you having a public meltdown: losing track of where you are, freezing, crying, physically being unable continue and falling off the stage. Both are the ingredients of our worst nightmare.

But they almost never happen.

Let's take the first scenario. Overtly hostile audiences usually only come about either because the topic is hugely emotive, the audience is fearful and the road ahead uncertain or controversial (a 'live' emergency, a town planning meeting or a political rally). Or the presenter has totally misjudged, not acknowledged or not even considered the audience. There is no attempt to be relevant. No attempt to be authentic, passionate and confident. Both happen, but rarely.

It is the second scenario that is far more common and the one most people cite as being their top fear. That they will lose face or suffer the emotional equivalent of a wardrobe malfunction. For most people, this manifests itself as a normal and natural unease at being in the spotlight.

Most people say, 'I just don't like being in the spotlight. I don't like the way I look. I can't stand my voice. I don't like presenting'. Even most extroverts don't cultivate the presentation spotlight. And for introverts, it can be exceedingly uncomfortable and anxiety-producing. In one training session, a female senior banking executive walked in and declared, 'I'd rather spend the morning having a root canal operation than do this training with you'. She went on to say that the root canal was easier because it was over in 45 minutes, she got anaesthetic and that this was 'three or four hours of real-time, unmitigated pain'.

This distaste for the spotlight is normal and applies to leaders just as much as everyone else. But the audience's response to this behavioural state is one of the most important insights you can have – *they are supportive*. They want you to succeed. You don't have to be perfect or even a 'good' presenter. You just need to be yourself and to offer this emotional acknowledgement and upfront contract of authenticity, passion and the willingness to try.

This is a huge tip for leaders – you don't need to be a polished presenter. The audience will cut you a lot of slack if they sense you are fully invested in the topic and them.

If this is the upfront 'contract' between presenter and audience – well known to every audience (if not every presenter or leader) – there are two other really important aspects of your relationship with the audience to take into consideration in planning your communication. Both are counter-intuitive and absolutely critical in optimising your chance of delivering a good presentation.

The first is the psychological bargain that needs to be struck with the audience in order for them to 'give you permission' to continue with your presentation. This is all about understanding the psychological landscape of the critical first five minutes of a presentation, the specific items that an audience needs to see and how supportive they are minded to be, based on what they get from you. Of course your presentation will continue whether this happens or not. But if it doesn't happen, they will struggle to engage with you and you will find it much harder to 'connect' with them.

For leaders, this may be a strange concept to understand as many will think 'I'm the leader and they need to listen to me'. But understanding and working with this dynamic separates authentic and effective leaders from those who elicit no connection with their audiences and for whom there is little empathy, connection or regard.

The second insight is more esoteric. It involves the second presenter in the room – and what you can do about them.

Understanding the Initial Psychology

It is completely normal for an audience to come to a presentation in a distracted and diffused frame of mind. They have their own concerns and hearing your presentation may not be top of mind for them. They can be worried about the mundane, thinking about their priorities for the day or haven't yet shifted into 'paying attention to you' mode.

Audiences simply do not care about your presentation as much as you do. They don't know what it's about, have not worked on it and are not invested in it. They have no 'skin in the game'. As employees or customers, they may be significantly affected by your presentation, but that is not the same as being invested in it.

And so it is important to recognise and make peace with this notion. Accept that they do not initially care and *making them care, giving them a reason to believe that your presentation matters to them (not you)* is your responsibility not theirs. They do not owe you anything, other than perhaps the common courtesy and ingrained impetus to be supportive and listen. Instead, the onus is on you as a presenter and a leader to do a number of things very quickly right from the outset.

Creating a Cognitive Map for Audiences – A Five-Point Plan

You need to:

Acknowledge the Audience

You need to be mindful of where they are and meet them there, not expect them to figuratively come to you. This means acknowledging how they may be feeling about the wider world, calling out any important issue or event that has recently had a shared impact on them, identifying or engaging with any elephants in the room.

In short, you need to have the courage and emotional awareness to comment on the common circumstances in which you are meeting and coming together. This may be difficult for you. Or it may be as simple and natural as the easiest human engagement can be. But it is certainly job one after accepting that it is normal for them to be distracted, inattentive and not invested in your presentation.

Acknowledging the audience may take the form of a story, a joke, some informal banter or even an initial Q&A. *What it doesn't involve is information transfer.* This is an emotional acknowledgement shared with the audience. It works best if it is collegial, observational and intuitive rather than unilateral, directive and analytical. This is hugely important and the first step in making them care and cutting through the clutter to command their attention.

Show Them Some Empathy

The next step is closely allied to acknowledging the audience. You need to show them some empathy. Show that you care about them before asking them to care about you and your presentation. Take that first step in making a connection. This can be self-deprecatory by acknowledging that you're asking them to 'sit through yet another presentation'. It can be you admitting to some foible or sharing a personal story that will resonate with their experiences. It can take the form of empathising about workloads, common challenges or difficulties. It is about you showing a willingness to care and think about them and where they are *in the human condition* right now.

Make a Connection

The overriding aim at this stage is to make an initial connection with the audience. Comics talk about getting audiences to 'eat out of your hand' as if they were zoo animals, but the analogy is instructive. You need to break down the natural barriers, speak in their language and cultivate that feeling that 'we are all in this together'. And encourage the audience to reach out to you.

One of the intangible gifts that people recognise in good leaders is their ability to make you feel as if they are talking directly to you and that you are the only person in the room. It is something about the power of undiluted attention and getting them to 'feel the love' or at least the connection.

Bill Clinton's oft-derided phrase 'I feel your pain' was a glib summation of what had been a very empathetic, authentic and natural effort to forge a connection with a woman in the audience at a presidential debate who had asked a question that revealed the toll on her of the economic downturn of the early 1990s. Clinton walked towards the woman, shrinking the physical distance between himself and the audience, effectively making it an intimate audience of only one person – and showed her some empathy.

So much of effective communications, at this stage of a presentation, is really about being human and relaxed enough to show your own vulnerability and reaching out and sharing that with others.

Make Them the Heroes of Your Presentation

Effective leaders always build this into the early part of their presentations. They are able to move the presentation from being something they are telling you to *something that you have agency in*, which is something you are being actively involved in and have the ability to shape – you are being called to have a view, take up arms or activate change.

This turning of a presentation on its head, so that it moves *from being a transfer of information* about something they want you to know *to a communal story of a shared mission or journey* along a pathway towards action, feeling, change or transformation, is what is happening here.

By *making the audience the heroes of their own story*, you are repositioning your presentation in two fundamental ways. First, *it is now about them, not about you*. And second, it has morphed into a story format and is not a presentation – and becomes something far easier to follow, get enthused about and remember. Presentations shared as a quest or story may seem somewhat facile or non-professional, depending on your perspective. But it is the secret elixir of the very best presenters, communicators and leaders.

Enter Bill Gates, the well-known innovator and philanthropist. It's a fairly well-known story and a popular YouTube video of Bill and his mosquitoes. And it illustrates all four of the points above. Here's a paraphrase of what he said at a malaria prevention conference in Africa on the efficacy of mosquito nets.

BOX 3.4 BILL GATES IN AFRICA

'Good morning everyone. Good to be here with you. Someone has kindly prepared some slides for me to show you – you'll be glad to know I'm not going to do that. Instead I want to introduce you to some friends of mine' (unscrews jar holding 50,000 mosquitoes and waves them about letting them fly into the audience).

Guards lock the door. 'I'll be back in about 30 seconds. Enjoy' (steps off-stage, camera picks up people laughing but many more looking disturbed, angry and scratching and waving the mosquitoes away). Bill comes back after 30 seconds.

'Guards unlock the doors. Bring in the big fans. Now that was uncomfortable right? Now you know they were not malarial mosquitoes but instead the plain vanilla types – otherwise you could have sued me if you got infected. But here's the thing. For these African children, those doors are always locked. There are no fans. And the mosquitoes are always malarial'.

'I've come here today to ask you to do three things: open your hearts; open your minds and open your wallets. And the equation is very simple. One net. One dollar. One life saved. When placed around a child's bed, these nets really work to keep them safe. One net. One dollar. One life'.

'Have a great conference and great day'.

Acknowledging the audience and showing some empathy – yes. He's not going to show slides but instead make a connection; the whole passage is designed to make an emotional connection.

And talk about making them the heroes of their own story. Suddenly they have the power to act. Rather than offer a worthy discourse on efficacy, Bill Gates speaks from the heart and directly puts the audience in the driver's seat. The best leaders do this all the time.

The last step in the five-stage guide or process is more straightforward and perhaps more easily explained.

Get Permission to Continue

The idea of getting permission from an audience to do anything will strike some leaders and presenters as bizarre and unhelpful. And yet, in a real sense, the above four steps are about getting 'permission' to continue and creating the right cognitive framework or emotional 'scaffolding' to support the subsequent parts of the presentation.

It is imperative that you do not jump too quickly to the detail or the content of your presentation. If you rush into the detail with barely a nod to what we have just discussed, you will be perceived as rude, peremptory and emotionally unaware.

Delivering a presentation is a bit like developing a relationship – there has to be some kind of getting-to-know-you stage where both parties set out the ground rules for how the relationship will develop and what will guide the later 'transaction' of delivering and receiving the communication or content. This applies even if the audience knows the leader well.

Getting permission to continue is the equivalent of that beloved BBC radio programme 'Listen with Mother' that ran from 1950 to 1982 and began with the immortal line 'are you sitting comfortably, then we can begin', since of course adopted by the BBC television children's television character Roly Mo before he starts reading a story.

Practically, what does it mean? Check in with the audience. Make sure they understand the main point of what you are trying to do. And make sure they understand the part they can play. It also means ensuring they have a good idea what they're letting themselves in for over the course of your presentation. And to do that, you need to make clear the roadmap for what lies ahead – what you are going to cover and how long it will take.

I call this whole five-point process 'building the cognitive roadmap' because it involves more than explaining the agenda or detailing the presentation segments or flow. It is really about making sure from a psychological point of view that the audience has everything they need to clearly follow and interpret or make sense of what is to come. It's more than a clear plan. It's a cognitive map.

The cognitive map consists of these five 'psychological' elements we have been discussing: acknowledging the audience, showing some empathy, making a connection, making them the heroes of the presentation and getting their permission. It is often very important to include other practical information, like telling the audience how long the session is going to last, what the main sections are and offering an executive summary near the beginning to manage their expectations.

Taken together, these elements are critical in bringing the audience with you. Not offering this to the audience, omitting certain elements or not being clear about them puts you at a disadvantage immediately.

BOX 3.5 THE COGNITIVE MAP TAKEAWAY

The entire acknowledgement, empathy and connection positioning at the beginning of an audience engagement speaks of a certain humility and humbleness that people attune to immediately. If it is not there, the emotional, connective wrapper for the entire communication does not exist – this is also felt immediately and acutely. This is what sets really good leaders apart and what people yearn for. But it is rare.

If it is present in a leader, it tends to engender loyalty and a willingness to go the extra mile. It can be summed up in that famous phrase from American poet and philosopher Maya Angelou: 'I've learned that people will forget what you said, people will forget what you did, but people will never forget how you made them feel'.

The opening three steps of the cognitive map are all about caring and feeling. The ability then to position employees and customers as the heroes of the story is pure storytelling magic. It transfers agency to the audience, as former US President John F. Kennedy did in his inaugural address by telling his audience to 'ask not what your country can do for you but what you can do for your country'.

Making audiences feel not just engaged but central to the story is a gift very few leaders have. Perhaps more than any other leadership imperative, this will be the crucial attribute in the years to come.

Finally, getting permission to continue – is again an act of humility – making sure people are comfortable and ready. This allows a leader to bring people with him or her and not set out alone.

Getting the Audience Onside – The Critical First Few Minutes

There is one other crucial element to making sure you have fully considered the audience – timing.

People's attention span is limited and you need to make good use of those times when it is naturally at its highest.

Remember we said that people are distracted at the beginning and that they are not yet invested in your presentation? Interestingly, although they are distracted, their inner 'wiring' is primed, and whether they know it or not, scanning the operating landscape. When you get up on stage or behind the podium or even begin speaking in a team meeting, the audience's disassociated state reduces – something new is about to happen and this boosts attention levels, even if only temporarily.

At precisely the moment we should be setting out our cognitive map, acknowledging and engaging and connecting, they are paying attention as they warm to the assignment and anticipate the road ahead. The problem is people so rarely receive anything new or of interest to warrant paying attention. Presenters don't normally deliver anything that causes audiences to reflect or feel something. And this massive opportunity to capitalise on the audience's attentiveness is squandered.

You only have a few minutes at the beginning of your presentation in which to get the various pieces of the cognitive map together before the audience's natural attention span deficit kicks in and their attentiveness begins to deteriorate.

This time at the beginning of a presentation is valuable 'real estate'. As you can see from the curve, the shape is like a giant 'U' with a kind of upward ramp in the first few minutes – while they're literally making their mind up about you – before attention plummets only to recover at the end when they are liberated by the conclusion (Figure 3.2).

This devastating 'U'-shaped curve describes the general trajectory of attention span, if presenters make no adjustments. If there is no cognitive map, no storytelling and no front-end loading of the most important aspects of the presentation, the audience's attention span flatlines. The squandering of the beginning of a presentation is a serious and common problem.

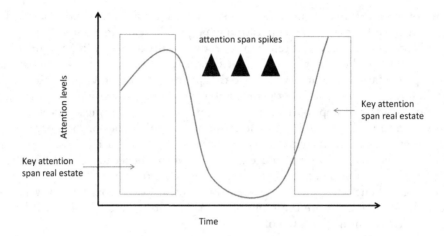

Figure 3.2 Attention span curve.

How Not to Squander Attentiveness at the Beginning

Instead of the usual boring introductory and almost fiduciary-type material we always hear at the beginning of a presentation, you need to cut to the chase and fire up the audience's imagination and attentiveness. As you mobilise your cognitive map, begin with something emotive, the most important point, a powerful story, a killer statistic, even the punchline. Just don't squander the opportunity.

This is hugely counter-intuitive.

Most presenters have erroneously been taught to save the best for last, like a bedtime story – the punchline comes at the end. In the business world, no one has time for this approach and best practice is to get some kind of summary up front so people get the most important information when they are paying attention. The idea is not to waste this fantastic 'attention-span real estate' when people are prewired to pay attention.

All the training I received in television constantly made this point. We had a formula in making television documentaries that mandated that you assemble the information in terms of visceral and emotive interest with the most powerful and important information placed first. The formula usually ran: 1–3–5-4-2 or perhaps 2–3–5-4-1, with the second best material placed first and the best last. Either way, the important material was placed at the points of maximum attentiveness from the audience's point on view – the beginning and the end.

The second imperative suggested by the attention span curve is what to do about the sagging middle portion. You cannot let your audience's attention span fall too low – typified by people bringing out their smartphones, talking, fidgeting or simply drifting away. You need to work diligently to keep them attentive. The best way to do that, especially accepting that the middle of the presentation is where the 'heavy lifting' and drier content usually resides, is to provide some variety and change the way you present.

Mixing up delivery techniques allows you to effectively reset attention span by *jarring them back to attention with a different way of presenting.* The actual change in presentation mode triggers their inner wiring. By changing things up you literally recapture and reset their attention span once again.

The good news is that almost anything qualifies as changing the way you present: a slower, faster or softer pace of delivery, moving from using slides to a flipchart or real-time whiteboarding, playing a video, telling a story, using a second presenter, stopping for Q&A. In television, we would work hard to build in different scene changes in the middle of a documentary to recapture attention.

The key takeaways in dealing with people's limited attention span are crucial – you need to use the valuable time at the beginning and end of the presentation effectively and frequently change the way you present.

The Cognitive Map – What to Include in the Critical First Five Minutes

So in the first few minutes of a presentation, what are the key components to include? They're laid out in the next graphic which includes the crucial 'cognitive map' elements we've discussed, but also other ingredients and options. Certainly, creating engagement and impact at the very beginning can be very effective. Equally a short executive summary of what you plan to cover and brief credentials (if needed) can help meet audience expectations.

The different components are coded by star, triangle or square to indicate if they are predominant strategies that involve audience interaction, physical delivery and engagement considerations or content/structure techniques. You may not choose to use all these techniques. But you need more of them than you might think (Figure 3.3).

As you can see, there is a lot to consider in the first five minutes and a lot to get right. The stakes are high. Get the initial impression right and you will put your audience at ease and forge common ground with them, getting their permission to continue. They will be more inclined to pay attention and actively invest in a presentation they now care about and are anticipating.

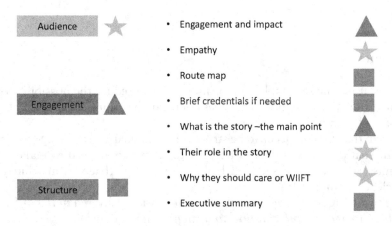

Figure 3.3 The critical first five minutes – what to include.

Understanding the Second Presenter in the Room – The Parallel Presentation Being Constructed

There is one more challenge that you face right off the bat – understanding that there is a second presenter in the room and what you can do about that. This mysterious second presenter is actually the audience themselves. The very act of communicating involves accepting the idea that *the audience's computation of your presentation actually represents a second presentation. A parallel presentation is being constructed in real time, as you deliver your information.*

No matter what you do, the audience will construct their own interpretation of what you are saying. So it's probably more accurate to say that there is not just one second presentation common to everyone in the audience, but rather as many different versions as there are people in the audience.

What good looks like is that these multiple interpretations of your presentation align closely to what you have actually said and meant. You always have to expect that people will remember different parts of your presentation and internalise it differently depending on how they reacted to the information.

What you don't want is to confuse or complicate your transmission so much that you leave them on their own to try and navigate your content or discern your meaning. If you do this, the audience will punish you with impunity by blithely constructing their own 'fantasy' parallel presentation that doesn't bother to track yours for accuracy at all. If you are confusing, you give the audience licence to stop paying attention, stop trying to follow what you are saying and instead to make their own understanding of what you are saying.

Some of this will happen anyway. Audiences are human. Minds stray. Points are not heard. Difficult points are open to debate and misinterpretation.

How to Combat 'Second Presenter' Syndrome

To give yourself the best possible chance of not wasting your carefully constructed opening five minutes, you need to work hard at ensuring your content is three things above all else:

1   Concise
2   Simple
3   Meaningful

If your material is concise, simple and meaningful, you reduce the possibility of it being misconstrued and misunderstood. This does not mean the information has to be simplistic and cannot deal with weighty matters.

It does mean that content needs to be structured, chunked and presented in a particular manner, one that aligns as closely as possible to what people need to make sense of it. And minimises the bad habits we all have as presenters that will absolutely kill any chance of clear communication.

What we're aiming for is user-friendly communication delivered *in the order in which people expect to receive information and aligned with how they process and make information meaningful.*

That's the subject of the next section on content and structure.

BOX 3.6 SECOND SYNDROME TAKEAWAY

Being aware of the 'second presenter' syndrome should act as a powerful cautionary tale for leaders. And a reminder about the importance of keeping it simple and focusing on meaning.

As a leader, you have so much invested in making sure that employees and customers do not misunderstand what is happening (or needs to happen) and are able to articulate it for themselves and others. Keeping the narrative lean and focused on what is most important is imperative to ensuring clear communications.

Notes

1 Erikson, Thomas, (2019), *Surrounded by Idiots – The Four Types of Human Behaviour*, New York, Macmillan.
2 Merrill, David and Reid, Roger, (1999), *Personal Styles and Effective Performance*, New York, CRC Press

Chapter 4

Structure and Content
Why Simple Is Good and Less Is More

Overview – Less Is Always More

The central conundrum of content is that *the less you offer, the more people understand.*
It is a truism that communicators almost universally offer far too much content. Most
audiences prefer to receive only the key information and some core proof points. They
want a handful of takeaway messages that are tied to the core narrative and support the
presenter's 'bottom-line' conclusion.

What they don't want is what almost all presenters tend to give – way too much
information.

It is another truism that we live in an age of information overload. We are bombarded
by thousands of messages a day. The line has it that we get information when we really
crave knowledge. This is wrong – we don't crave knowledge, we crave meaning.

What we actually want is illumination. Less heat and wattage and more light. This is
in short supply these days.

The Key Content Challenge – Restrict the Information Overload

Information overload is the number one content problem for communicators. We know
we don't want too much when others present. *So, why do we forget this when we are
putting together our own presentations?*

I think there are three main reasons.

The first is that we *fear the minimal being perceived as vacuous.* We are anxious not
to reap the reputational damage and shame of being perceived as lightweight or not fully
understanding our subject if we cut back to what is essential. And so we take refuge in
the 'haven of detail' to make sure our expertise is clear, to bolster our self-esteem and
strengthen our chances of being taken seriously.

By displaying mastery over subject, our hope is that we have our expertise and by extension ourselves validated. We know in our heart of hearts that this isn't true, and still
we do it constantly. Of course, there is a balance to be maintained – you do need strong
and evidence-based content, but *it's the telling detail you need, not the exhaustive detail.*
Preoccupation with unnecessary detail can signal a more junior orientation. It is a sign of
presentational maturity when the *value of content eclipses the volume.*

This is what the best leaders do all the time – get to the essence of things quickly and
efficiently.

The second reason is that we seem to have a *disdain for and distrust of more emotional
and less rational methods of communicating.*

DOI: 10.4324/9781003198994-7

We have been inculcated through the formative years of our education, through university and college and then as we climb the corporate ladder, to deliver a hypothesis-driven and empirically grounded treatment of the relevant facts. We are taught to leave the emotion behind, to be objective rather than subjective and to be exhaustive in our plundering of 'proof'.

How often have we been told to leave the tall tales, pictures and stories behind and to focus on what can be seen and above all proven?

And finally, we labour under the insidious confirmation bias that *our own information is different and more worthy*. The positioning seems to be 'I think: therefore it's important'. This is seen by how difficult it is to edit your own material. Once we begin, it can be almost impossible to cut things out. Instead, we succumb to mission creep – just one more slide, one more graphic, one more example. And so, content grows rather than being judiciously edited.

In my job as a producer at the Canadian Broadcasting Corporation (CBC) radio programme 'As it Happens', I had a boss who said, 'what you leave on the cutting room floor, they never knew existed'. With the pointed directive, that editing would make the programme tighter, punchier, clearer and more meaningful to the listener.

The younger ones thought she was mad and tried to cram it all in with the telling excuse: 'but it's all great content'. To which, with a sage shake of her head, she responded: 'everything's always good – by choosing and editing – you make it better'.

This is less is more writ large. And still we don't listen.

We applaud when presenters are brief. We love it when they 'give us back time' (the greatest gift you can give a client or an audience, by the way) or promise not to show any slides or say 'so in summary....' Why? Because the interminable slog is coming to an end. The real existential dilemma of our lives is not wading through the slough of despond, but the slough of instruct. The weight of listening to content that is not invited and not welcome is like a form of Chinese water torture – seemingly inevitable, inescapable and immutable.

And so what is good? The awful beauty of the answer is that we already know: clear and intuitive structure, a few concise points, funny anecdotes and 'killer statistics', an easy-to-follow storyline and a few memorable sound bites and takeaways.

The Key Structure Challenge – Getting the Information in the Right Order

If this is the key *content* challenge, *the great structural challenge is to get the information in the correct order*. Too often, what happens is we overemphasise different parts of a presentation and underemphasise or forget other key sections. *Audiences broadly need four different types of information in any presentation. But they are lucky if they get three of the four.*

It is more common for one or two of these critical chunks of a presentation to simply be omitted or forgotten rather than for them to appear in the wrong place in the structure; but either way, the damage to audience understanding is significant as clarity is undermined.

As communicators, and especially as leaders, we owe it to our audiences to deliver concise information in a clear structure. And to signpost clearly when the structure is changing – that is when we are entering a different phase of the presentation.

The best place to start examining content and structure is with two cornerstones templates or concepts that delineate the underlying structure for all presentations and which audiences intuitively crave. The first concept helps us discern the order in which people expect to receive information – the psychological route map people follow in their own mind when they are trying to make sense of what you are communicating. This is called the 'Imaginary Dialogue' because it tracks the internal 'conversation' the audience has in order to make sense of your communication.

The second template looks at the typical trajectory of a presentation. This is the shape drawn by presenters when asked to trace the highs and lows *of their own presentation as it is perceived **by them** after delivery*. This trajectory is hugely illuminating in determining the key portions of a presentation, the different stages and what is needed in each stage.

Together, the two templates give insight into how to structure for clarity and understanding and what type of content to put where.

Template One: The Imaginary Dialogue – Delivering Information in the Correct Cognitive Order

I first saw the Imaginary Dialogue in action in Sydney about 25 years ago. The trainer asked me to take part in an experiment. She handed me a piece of paper that would be a proxy for 'her communication to me'.

She instructed me to ask her four questions to make sense of her 'communication'. And then she startled me by saying: 'I already know your four questions and in what order you will ask them'.

She explained that the Imaginary Dialogue works the same way for everyone, no matter gender, culture or creed, because it tracks the same cognitive pathway that everyone uses to make sense of what is being communicated. And it is called 'imaginary' because it takes place internally in the recipient's mind.

So I dutifully answered my four questions:

1 What is it?
2 Why are you giving the communication to me?
3 Can you tell me a bit about the communication?
4 What do you want me to do with it?

These simple four questions are magic. They are gold dust. It is probably the tool I have used the most in all the journalism, corporate communications and PR work, consultancy and presentations coaching and training over the past 25 years.

As you can see in this graphic, the four questions align with different types of information. Three are best delivered in an emotional manner, detail in a more rational way (Figure 4.1).

The imaginary dialogue helps simplify very complex topics and keeps them from becoming overwhelming by reminding us that we need to take people on a cognitive journey of understanding by answering clearly the key question of each stage. This model describes a simple conversation of clarity where the recipient is seeking to understand what you are talking about.

The information (in order) people expect to receive when we communicate

Question	Type of information	Best delivered with
What is it ?	Title Main Point Sound-bite Setting out your stall	Emotion
Why me?	Relevance Context Background	Emotion
Tell me more	Details	Reason
What do I do now?	Call to action Value and Benefits Meaning	Emotion

Figure 4.1 The imaginary dialogue.

The Four Stages of Information Delivery

Stage 1 – What Is It?

The first stage – 'what is it' – is crucial. In this stage, you need to clearly name the topic or subject of your communication – this is a presentation about X, Y and Z. It can be very factually stated – 'we're here to talk about climate change' – or done in a more engaging manner – 'scientists now believe we have only 30 years before we reach a tipping point in our ability to effectively control and reverse global warming'.

Job one as presenters is to be absolutely crystal clear with our audiences about what we are talking about. This doesn't mean you have to preclude creativity or drama. Quite the opposite. The best presenters often will introduce a topic in a dramatic way aimed at creating instant impact and engagement.

For instance, in a documentary the reporter will often appear on screen at the beginning to tell you what the film is about. So a film about failed corporate governance is made instantly more compelling with the headline statement from a reporter that 'this is a story about corporate greed, venality and hubris – and how many died because of one firm's utter incompetence'.

The point is people have to be clear about what you are talking about or they will not come on the ride with you. They expect to have to work harder in the middle of the presentation, when the complexity and weight of detail create some psychological 'heavy-lifting'. They don't expect or react well to being confused at the beginning.

And don't misunderstand this basic human *need for clarity at the beginning of a communication* with *how* that is done. There is a fascination right now with *beginning with the why*. Communicator Simon Sinek has had a great deal of deserved success getting people to understand *the power of why* – that, in his words, 'people don't buy what you do, they buy why you do it'.

Sinek suggests that by starting with 'why you do what you do', people will be more motivated, energised and attentive. This is undoubtedly true and a powerful notion that encourages us to communicate more about our values, beliefs and commitments – the 'why' of what we do.

But Sinek is effectively using a 'why' construct to introduce the 'what' he is going to talk about.

His example in his TED Talk 'The Golden Circle' is about Apple.[1] He says they put the 'why' first in appealing to customers. And it goes like this: 'everything we do we believe in challenging the status quo. We believe in thinking differently'.

But he is saying this in the context of how Apple markets itself. He has already set that up so that we know what he is talking about. If he began his famous TED Talk by just saying the Apple line – this would be a great impact and engagement line – which he would then have to explain.

At any rate, this fundamental need for clarity around what you are talking about is profound.

Stage 2 – Why Me?

The second step follows very closely. Articulating to people why they should care and what's in it for them is crucial.

Again, if the 'why me' is not clear, people shut down and turn away. They lose interest. Their 'old brain' perceives that there is no newness or danger, nothing relevant for them here and they switch off.

Relevance, context and background are absolutely critical to deliver right up front, right after you are clear about what you are talking about. Effective communicators build the 'what is it' and 'why me' stages into their cognitive roadmap – their early efforts to acknowledge the audience, show empathy, create a connection before they continue. In most cases, these two steps need to happen in the first minute or so.

People believe that most presenters are quite good at answering the 'what is it' question – scoring them seven out of ten on average. The consensus on the 'why this is important to me' question is brutal and unanimous. *Presenters almost never do enough to address why audiences should care.* The worst don't do it at all – blithely progressing down the track of their own presentation, not caring or being aware of the need to 'sell the story' by making it relevant to people.

Some make an attempt at it, but get muddled and talk about why it is important to them. Very few reach out to really talk to audiences about why they should care – a key attribute of good leadership communications. That's what the Simon Sinek method does very well – it gives people a 'reason to believe'. This is the time to make the audience the heroes of their own story.

The scoring for presenters in this stage floats between two and three, with some battle-hardened audience veterans delighting in scoring presenters zero.

There is one more important consideration to cover before we move on to the third stage of detail.

A funny thing happens to most audiences if you powerfully deliver a clear sense of 'what is it' and 'why you should care'. Audiences relax and 'give you permission' to continue to the detail. This exactly mirrors the stage in the cognitive map (discussed in the previous chapter) where you should be asking for their permission before you jump to the detail.

If everything is done clearly and powerfully and in alignment with audience rather than presenter need, *the asking and granting of permission to continue comes together at the same time*. And this alignment is a really powerful send-off into the land of detail.

Both presenter and audience are ready to move on. The ground has been prepared.

And so, into the land of detail.

Stage 3 – Tell Me More

The first thing to say is that the permission to move on to the detail doesn't give us carte blanche for overloading on detail. Permission is withdrawn very quickly by audiences if you overstay your welcome in detail land.

This stage is the most familiar for presenters and the one in which they pick up the highest marks. Audiences usually grant a score of nine here, acknowledging people's proficiency at communicating expertise, data, detail and information. Some say that morphs into a two or three because almost all presenters go on too long. But suffice to say no presenter forgets or underplays this stage.

And this stage is the easiest for presenters. It is best done rationally and audiences don't expect too much engagement or performance here – they want to focus on the key information.

But many presenters get lost in the jungle of detail and are figuratively never seen again. Some lamely emerge from the jungle with the immortal line 'so in conclusion'. This is the signal for weary audiences to recover their attentiveness to 100% in their anticipation of rapidly being liberated from the jungle.

Stage 4 – What Do I Do or What Does It Mean?

The fourth stage rarely happens.

Addressing and articulating 'what do I do now' or 'what does this mean' is often done in a perfunctory manner, where the presenter simply summarises the handful of key points he or she has made in the detail stage or else offers an uninspiring call-to-action or directive. But very often presentations simply come to an end – they collapse under their own weight – as the presenter finally tires of their own detail.

The summary is abrupt, quick and over.

Instead, what should happen is that presenters should recognise they have arrived at an astonishingly valuable part of the presentation. As we've seen, the end is a critical time where audiences are near 100% attentive and are craving a closing or summation that focuses on meaning.

What audiences most want at this stage is for the presenter to aggregate up their information to what it all means. *This is not at all the same as simply summarising points that have gone before*. It requires *shifting from rational fact-driven mode to a deeper type of communicating* about what the audience is meant to take away, remember and feel.

My worst nightmare as a television reporter, working to extremely tight deadlines, was an interview subject who gave me such great detail, information and sound bites, but then did not prioritise and tell me what was most important – what was most meaningful or worthy of being the focus of the piece.

This is a seminal point. We tend to feel that any indication we make as presenters to tell audiences what they should think, feel or do or what the presentation means is unnecessary, because we have laid out all the facts and it is up to the audience to decide what they mean. Or that trying to discern meaning for them will be perceived as grossly patronising.

And yet, this is what audiences want us to do. They crave meaning. They want you to summarise not by recounting main points, but by aggregating up to meaning. It removes the burden of deciphering complex content from the detail stage, but more importantly *it allows us to think about the information in a qualitatively different manner.*

It is only by focusing on meaning that audiences move what they have learned from the rote accumulation of facts to something that will be remembered. In effect, *we all need to create the 'story' of what we have just learned in order to simplify and remember it.* If we do not get guidance from the purveyor of this information – telling us what it means – many of us simply will not create that story for ourselves at all. *And if that story, focused around core meaning, is not created, it is simply not remembered.*

Presenters should not be wary of offending or patronising audiences by talking about meaning. Knowledge is relatively ephemeral and easily degrades over time. Meaning is more powerful and has a longer shelf life.

BOX 4.1. IMAGINARY DIALOGUE TAKEAWAYS

The Imaginary Dialogue is a reminder to leaders to articulate the why and not to rush too quickly into the detail, but instead, like the five-point cognitive map, make sure enough time is spent at the beginning articulating why things are changing so that people understand the 'burning platform' or context for change.

Equally, leaders should not shirk from the responsibility of communicating about meaning at the end of their presentation. This aggregation of detail up to meaning is really a 'clarity gift' for audiences – you are making sure they get the main points and are being clear and prescriptive about what they are.

Leaders should not feel burdened by the need to deliver the weight of detail in an important communication. That is for others to focus on at a different time. Yes, the telling detail is needed, but for leaders the main job is motivating and mobilising around meaning.

This happens predominantly in steps two and four of the Imaginary Dialogue. Having a template that shows the direction of travel helps leaders (and those who prepare their communications) to remember this.

Using the Imaginary Dialogue to Structure a Presentation

You can use the Imaginary Dialogue to help structure any kind of communication. Put the four questions in the column on the left, your key points that correspond to each stage in the middle and then some performance or engagement notes in the third column.

A table focused on climate change and global warming might look like this (Table 4.1).

Another example is work we did a few years ago with a firm that wanted to announce the launch of a new performance-related pay scheme and explain how it would work. We discussed this with the CEO and Head of HR for a long time and the pending announcement became too long and complicated, groaning under the weight of evermore information.

This is often what goes wrong in many presentations and communications when detail and information is the primary driver rather than meaning.

We suggested using the Imaginary Dialogue to help us order the key information. We came up with something that looked like the table below. There was no engagement information since this was an all-staff email.

Table 4.1 Climate change warning

Questions	Type of in formation	Engagement ideas
What is it?	*Topic/headline* Presentation about 'the tipping point' after which action to combat climate change is likely to fail	Story, testimonials, video 'killer' statistic Montage of photos
Why me?	*Relevance* The most important issue for everyone because we are talking about the survival of the planet and our species. This is literally our 'burning platform'	Deliver direct to audience
Tell me more	*Key points* 1 Each degree raised has significant consequences 2 Where efforts to quantify and combat global warming have had some success and what remains to be done – it's challenging 3 A game plan and the key levers of change	Slides Graphs Photos Videos Scientific evidence Statistics
What do I do? What does it mean?	*Meaning* We need to make significant changes now before we reach the tipping point	Deliver direct to audience

Performance-Related Pay Announcement

Table 4.2 Performance-related pay announcement

Questions	Type of information
What is it?	*Topic/headline* We are strengthening the link between compensation and performance and intend to implement a performance-related pay system for all employees.
Why me? Why is it important?	*Relevance* This will affect every employee in how they get paid, promoted and retained. As we move from a product to customer-focus, it is important that we focus more on performance. We need to strengthen our positioning in a very competitive market and aligning pay directly to performance rewards and incentivises this change.
Tell me more	*Key points* 1 Bonuses will vest over a long time period, have more weighting towards shares than cash and be more directly tied to performance and (where possible) customer satisfaction metrics. 2 Pay for the top 25% of staff will increase by an average of 5% annually. 3 The 10% lowest performers each year will leave the firm.
What do I do? What does it mean?	*Meaning* This will mean a renewed focus on performance for every employee. We recognise this is a major change and one that will explicitly reward performance. We need to align our compensation programmes to fully reflect our need to strengthen performance, competitiveness and customer satisfaction. Please understand and support the change.

By using the template, we helped cut through the clutter to what was truly important. Of course there was a need for a lot more detailed follow-up information as the changes began to be implemented. But we got this first announcement out in a relatively clear and succinct manner

Crafting a Short Sound Bite or Elevator Pitch – Cutting Through the Clutter to Deliver Meaning

The Imaginary Dialogue also works very well to help you structure a short message, elevator speech or sound bite for the media. In the graphic below, the order and flow of the Imaginary Dialogue remains unchanged, but has been chunked into three distinct phases that each last for 10–25 seconds.

The first two stages – 'what is it' and 'why is this important' – are represented by the first box, where it is imperative that you clearly set out what you are talking about and why that is important to the audience. The detail and content of 'tell me more' is the middle of the statement or answer (where it would normally reside in a longer presentation) and the last box represents the summing up on meaning that is so crucial to driving understanding and memorability (Figure 4.2).

For a short, powerful message – a statement of intent, a call to arms or simply used as an executive summary of a much longer presentation – this structure is very effective because it aligns to what an audience needs to receive to make sense of what you are talking about.

So, for instance, our climate change example, from earlier in one-minute verbal form using this structure, might look like this:

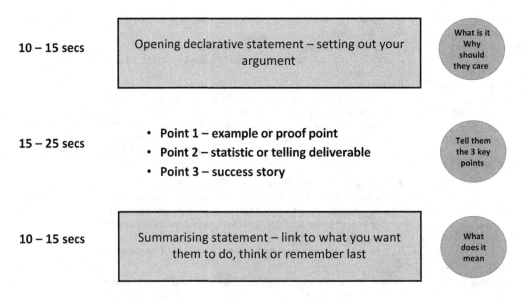

Figure 4.2 Template for delivering a message.

BOX 4.2

We are fast compromising the earth's own resilience – our planet's ability to absorb carbon emissions and cope with global warming.

There is broad scientific agreement that we have perhaps 30 years before we reach a 'tipping' point beyond which action to combat climate change is likely to fail.

This is important because we are talking about the survival of the planet and our species. This is literally our 'burning platform'.

Here are the three key things we know so far:

1 We've got about 1.5 degrees left to work with – and 30 years.
2 Politics as usual won't work – the Kyoto Protocols and Paris Agreements are worthy, but woeful.
3 We need a global game plan.

BOX 4.3

What all this means is that doing nothing is not an option. Doing everything may only just be enough. We have to act now.

Most of all, we need common purpose, commitment and behaviour change.

Now. Before it's too late.

This structure deliberately simplifies. It works best to deliver a message, offer an executive summary or give people an overall favour of what your presentation is about. It is high intensity and you cannot talk like this for too long – it can sound glib and shallow.

But used in the right way and at the right time, the Imaginary Dialogue in verbal form can help you:

1 *Deliver a clear and powerful message,* because it follows the cognitive order in which people expect to receive information.
2 *Cut-through-the-clutter* by allowing you to focus only on the most important information.
3 *Get to the point,* because it gives you a GPS system for understanding when and why you have reached your destination and should stop.

A GPS System – How to Know When You've Reached Your Destination

Let me explain that last point. Timing is important in using this structure.

You can see the suggested time range down the left of the graphic. This provides guidance in *getting through the four stages in under a minute.* This is important because studies show that in a one-on-one conversation, where the audience expects to speak or answer in response, the communicator has a bit less than one minute to make his or her point. Much beyond the minute mark and the recipient of the communication will start feeling it is 'their turn' to speak. They get agitated and stop paying attention rendering continued information flow increasingly worthless.

More importantly, *at about the one-minute mark in a one-on-one conversation, the listener has received about all the information they can handle.* The density of the information received thus far means that it is no longer easy for the recipient to trace back to the beginning of the message or to fully follow the thread as it has been delivered. Once people lose track of where you have come from and see no sign of the information flow ending, they begin to drift. At that point, they lose attentiveness and crave closure – they want what they perceive as a 'wall of information' to stop.

Try it for yourself sometime. Try speaking to a business colleague, loved one or friend for more than a minute. And give no sign of stopping or slowing down to let them in on the conversation. Your listener will usually not react well at all.

Understanding the Emotional Wrapper or Bookends of the Imaginary Dialogue

The verbal structure using the Imaginary Dialogue also mirrors what is sometimes called the emotion-logic-emotion sandwich – where to catch the audience's attention, you begin with an emotional appeal in explaining what you are talking about and why. Then, you segue into the more rational middle of the sandwich – the 'filling' – where you give three 'proof' points or key pieces of fact or substance. And then you return to emotion when you sum up on meaning.

Again, it is worth reminding about two points here. First, the emotional wrapper – the first and last boxes in the structure – is what 'sells' or convinces. Second, we need to remember to deliver the second box information and get over our feeling that if we talk about meaning that will be misconstrued as patronising.

First, here is an example of the power of the emotional wrapper. I've taken Martin Luther King's famous 'I have a dream' speech[2] and reduced it to a one-minute elevator speech. In poor taste, possibly – but it helps to illustrate the point.

BOX 4.4

So I say to you today my friends that even though we face the difficulties of today and tomorrow, I still have a dream. It is a dream deeply rooted in the American dream. I have a dream that one day this nation will rise up and live out the true meaning of its creed – 'we hold these truths to be self-evident that all men are created equal'.

I have a dream my four little children will one day live in a nation where they will not be judged by the colour of their skin but by the content of their character.

---

1   I have a dream that one day on the red hills of Georgia, the sons of former slaves and the sons of former slave owners will be able to sit down together at the table of brotherhood.
2   This is our hope. This is the faith that I go back to the South with....
3   So let freedom ring.

BOX 4.5

And when this happens, when we allow freedom to ring...we will be able to speed up that day when all God's children... will be able to join hands and sing in the words of the old Negro spiritual: 'Free at last, free at last, thank God Almighty we are free at last'.

The emotional wrapper (the two boxes in the template above) is hugely powerful in communicating. In a short message, it is powerfully evident. In a longer presentation, the emotional wrapper delivered at the beginning and end of the presentation is hugely important.

The rational middle or the 'filling' of the emotion-logic-emotion sandwich acts as the evidential proof that we need to trust our instincts, and this is absolutely needed for us to believe whatever proposition the communicator is making.

But *it is the emotional instinct that is by far the more powerful driver*. Emotion is quicker, more visceral and more memorable, and as such is often the crucial 'missing ingredient' in many presentations.

Let me explain this in another way in a wonderful story from my university days.

My girlfriend and I were discussing whether to travel to India after graduating. We were going round and round in circles, getting into evermore detail but not making the key decision about whether to go or not. Finally, she cut the conversation short, looked me directly in the eye and said, 'are we going or not?' To which I replied, 'of course'. As soon as this fundamental was clear, we dealt with the detail very quickly.

Afterwards, she explained what had happened by saying: 'the heart always knows much faster than the head'. She went on to say that learning to trust the initial soundings of our heart is hugely important because it can actually speed up the decision-making process by more quickly recognising and ratifying what it is you really want to do.

The rational check is needed so that we feel comfortable that we have covered specifics and important realities and that our decision is not simply based on a flight of fancy. But this rational stage is essentially 'backfill', that is, *we already know what we're going to do, we're just checking*.

Trusting the emotional underpinnings of our decision-making is very similar to trusting our emotional reaction to a communication. It is the internalising of how we feel emotionally about what is being said that stays with us long after the rational facts have faded.

Our second template is directly linked to the Imaginary Dialogue, but shows how this plays out directly in a presentation.

Template Two – Understanding the Trajectory of a Typical Presentation

One thing I often do when working with leaders on their presentations is ask them to sketch out what they perceive to be the highs and lows of their presentation. I first used this technique a few years ago with a senior leader who was rightly anxious about presenting to a room full of potential investors. He had developed an impressive piece of technology and together with the CEO was trying to raise seed money to scale the business.

He practised his presentation a few times, and like many people was proficient at conveying the detail and general information transfer. He felt particularly comfortable in the middle of his presentation where he was going to demonstrate how the technology worked.

He was very concerned about his engagement skills and connecting with the audience in the opening part of the presentation. He wanted to leave a strong final impression – in this case, a call to invest – and was worried about the question and answer (Q&A) section.

I asked him to sketch out what he felt were the highs and lows of his presentation. Here's what he drew (Figure 4.3).

We then spent about 30 minutes talking through what each high and low point represented in his presentation. That produced a sketch on the whiteboard that looked like this (Figure 4.4).

The key insight from the exercise was that the low points all involved a performance imperative and emotion. The leader intuitively felt he needed to 'connect' with the audience at these points, but he wasn't sure how to do that and wasn't confident. He admitted his expertise was analytical and that he was a blue typology.

His analysis of his own presentation was intuitive, accurate and powerful.

Figure 4.3 Trajectory of a typical presentation.

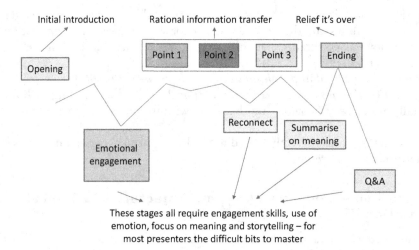

Figure 4.4 Focus on the 'performance' parts of the trajectory.

It went like this (Table 4.3):

Table 4.3

Beginning	1	**High point** – I feel nervous at the beginning, but then quickly feel more comfortable as relief kicks in that I'm actually doing this now. The anticipation and worrying is over.
	2	**Low point** – I know I should engage and make a connection with the audience, but I don't know how to do this or what that looks like and that's not my sweet spot. I'd rather get into the detail.
Middle	3	**Three high points** – Delivering the detail feels comfortable. I invented the product and I can talk about the key aspects. Showing a demo is a bonus because all eyes will be off me and I can 'read' from my script. I'm confident presenting this part.
End	4	**Low point** – I know I need a strong ending, but I thought I would just summarise the main messages I've already given. I'm not sure what else to do as the demo is surely what will sell the idea to investors. I know a lot is riding on how I conclude.
	5	**High point** – I feel considerable relief when this is over.
Q&A	6	**Low point** – I'm dreading the Q&A. What if the investors ask me a question I don't know the answer to or I give information that is not to their liking? The CEO will take the 'business' questions, but I will need to handle the proof of concept questions.

As I listened to his explanation of what he felt at each key part of the presentation, it occurred to me that I had heard this many times before. He was describing a trajectory and associated feeling for each stage that was common to almost all presenters.

His tour of his own highs and lows was illuminating and valuable for a number of reasons.

First, it made the work we were doing together much more personal. We were able to discuss:

1   What he felt at each key stage.
2   Why he felt that way.
3   What he could do about those feelings to strengthen his overall presentation.

Second, it provided a focus to the work and effectively identified and scoped out the size of the task ahead in an analytical way – which is exactly what senior executives crave.

And third, it solidified the realisation that what was needed was not a 'complete make-over' of the content or him as a presenter, but instead a targeted session focusing on the 'performance' aspects of the presentation.

For leaders, this focused approach comes as a profound relief. Their content is usually in fairly good shape. What is mainly needed are suggestions to:

1   Thin the volume of information
2   Bring more shape and focus to the storyline
3   Chunk into clear sections

This can progress quite quickly and often is taken offline. In person, they are now eager to work out how they can, in very identifiable moments, make the telling emotional intervention, connection or engagement that will help drive understanding and meaning for the audience and make the presentation memorable.

Table 4.4 Comparison of ordering and structuring tools

Trajectory	Imaginary dialogue	Cognitive map	Logic sandwich
Emotional engagement	What is it + why me?	Cognitive map	Emotional wrapper
Points 1–3	Tell me more		Logic filling
Summing up on meaning	What do I do + what does it mean?		Emotional wrapper

Using the Trajectory Template to Strengthen Presentation

Back to our senior leader.

He wanted to work on three things: the initial emotional engagement, summing up on meaning and his confidence during the Q&A. This felt like a doable assignment that could be done in a couple of hours.

So we set to work. The first thing I did was point out to him how his trajectory, which we agreed is common to all presenters, maps almost exactly to the Imaginary Dialogue (Table 4.4).

This helped us recognise the importance of the 'emotional engagement' part of the presentation. We came up with a short exercise that helped him identify what he wanted to say during this part.

I asked him to list the three things he was most proud of and the key benefits the technology would deliver if made operational, and then to talk about that. He spoke for about 90 seconds in a powerful, authentic and engaging manner, telling me clearly how the technology worked, what the benefits were and what that would mean to users.

His pride was evident throughout and helped him 'connect' with me. He ended with a clear call to arms saying that his work would count for nothing if investors didn't help mobilise the design.

He realised he had just written the content for his 'emotional engagement'. The informal back-of-the-envelope scribbling of his key points and then the conversational manner in which he delivered the information undoubtedly helped. There is something about forgetting slides and graphs and simply talking to one other person that liberates both our thinking and performance skills.

Using Conversation and the Story Format to Craft Emotional and Meaning Content

This kind of approach involves two old lessons from television land. The first is the producer's trick of getting a reporter who has become entangled in their own detail to in a minute or so tell the producer what the story is about. This is the equivalent of getting presenters to summarise in elevator pitch style what their presentation is about.

It works almost every time. The reporter or presenter can hear what they are saying and this is a powerful catalyst for clarity. *To hear in your own words what is important or what sounds like mumbo jumbo is revelatory* and helps us understand what information to put first, second, in the middle and last.

The second lesson is that telling the information as a little story liberates the performer within us. Most people recoil at the challenge to be engaging and don't like being told to perform. But everyone can talk and no one minds explaining what they are trying to communicate.

Both lessons revolve around telling a story. Stories are the best vehicles for conveying emotion and meaning. They are in our DNA. Everyone with a little encouragement can tell a story.

So our leader's 90-second story exercise gave him the basis of his emotional engagement, allowing him to powerfully preview what everyone was about to see.

We addressed the ending on meaning in the same manner – by looking at what his three key points actually meant. And he agreed that the Q&A no longer looked so daunting because he could focus on the technology questions with confidence and leave the business queries to his CEO.

The key insight in this entire session had been driven by the leader illuminating the trajectory of what he was experiencing. We then used this as a guide to help strengthen the portions he felt most concerned about.

One of the key takeaways about this story is the importance of recognising that the key phases that need improvement usually involve performance or engagement skills, which is the subject of the next chapter of the book.

Before we turn to engagement, it's worth taking a closer look at four key aspects of crafting compelling content: storyboarding, articulating the 'burning platform', telling a big story and the importance of differentiating and having a point of view.

Storyboarding – Understanding the Five Main Storytelling Stages in any Presentation

Storyboarding refers to exactly the same process that is used in film-making and speech writing, that is, chunking the content and flow into a linear structure from beginning to end.

Storyboarding is a great way of plotting out the key points or 'scenes' you want to cover.

The graphic below shows two different templates that can fit any kind of presentation. The first you've seen our leader use. The second is adapted from Tom Bird and Jeremy Cassell's work in their excellent book *The Leader's Guide to Presenting*[3] (Figure 4.5).

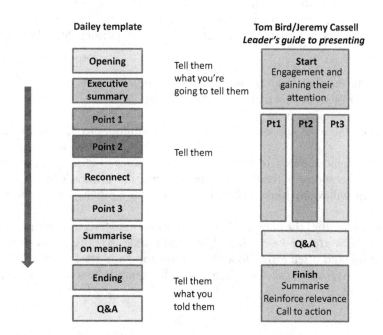

Figure 4.5 Storyboarding a presentation – two templates.

Most storyboarding templates have a critical beginning portion that focuses on gaining the audience's attention and engaging and building a connection.

The middle portion of most templates revolves around information transfer and is almost always based on three different chunks or scenes. Most people have heard about the power of three – the fact that three is normally considered the optimal number of items of content that can be included in one presentation. This doesn't just mean three pieces of information, but three substantive heading or points, each of which are backed up by different smaller 'proof points' or examples.

BOX 4.6 THE POWER OF THREE

The providence of this theory is often traced back to an experiment conducted by a Professor Miller in the 1960s, where he found that the range of items students could reliably remember in under 40 minutes was three to seven items, with the number skewing closer to three if the information was detailed.

Short-term memory (what's at work in under 40 minutes) is generally understood to mean that which we can retain easily without resorting to longer-term brain mechanics that filter, sort and recall.

A good way to think about it is that it is like the difference between 'recent activity' and 'file folder' search on a computer. Or, what is referred to in advertising as 'top-of-mind' awareness, information that is easily recalled because it has just been presented. The key takeaway is that we cannot remember much in any one go.

Our two templates above have endings that focus on summarising meaning or relevance and a call to action.

It is the similarities that are interesting in storyboards rather than the differences. There seems to be a broad agreement on the optimal structure and the fact that storyboarding is useful.

The key thing about storyboarding is that it is a device that clarifies what should be important by playing your story back to you – a bit like an elevator pitch. With storyboarding, the process is visual. Using storytelling it is auditory. Storyboarding is best used to help you:

1   Minimise the number of scenes in your presentation
2   Get the order of scenes correct
3   Understand the segues needed between scenes
4   Think about the most appropriate engagement techniques to be used in each scene

The following graphic shows a technique we use with a lot of clients who want to storyboard a key presentation for their management teams, but acknowledge that each member of the team will want some freedom to deliver the presentation in their own way (Figure 4.6).

The template identifies the core 'rail' of information or key 'scenes' in the presentation. The first two slides are the beginning. The middle slide is really a placeholder for the core information (and often grows to a number of slides) and the last two slides focus on meaning and an overt call to action. These five slides remind clients of the key scenes they want to talk about.

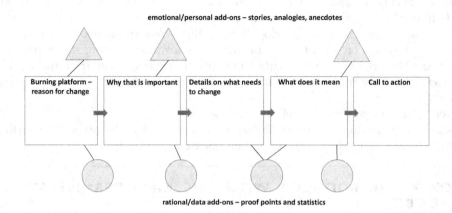

Figure 4.6 Storyboarding template.

The triangles above the slides indicate where presenters temporarily have the freedom to go off-piste, away from the core rail to inject some stories and personal reflections adding more emotional information. Likewise, the circles underneath indicate moments to show more data or 'killer' statistics before returning to the key scenes.

This gives clients enough latitude to make the presentation bespoke for whoever is presenting while following the agreed rail of information.

Articulating the 'Burning Platform'

The first two slides focus on what is often called 'the burning platform' or reason for people to believe.

Perhaps more than any other part of a presentation getting people to buy-in to *why it is important* is crucial.

Articulating the 'burning platform' is a sure-fire way of capturing attention, driving relevance and making the audience the heroes of the presentation. In planning a presentation, leaders often make this their very first stage of planning. Is there a 'burning platform' I need to talk about? Can I articulate one that will explain the change I am seeking?

And if there is no burning platform to articulate, do I need to make this presentation? Or can this be done a different way and perhaps by someone else?

Telling a Big Story

Even if there is no 'burning platform', presentations really benefit content-wise if presenters tell the biggest story that is possible and credible. So many presenters tell timid, small and internally focused stories. And then they wonder why no one is inspired.

They make no effort to locate their stories within the zeitgeist of the times, to identify how what they are discussing ties in with or is emblematic of the challenges and issues the business is facing.

This impetus to tie a particular story to a wider, bigger and more meaningful setting is hugely important. This is how people become mobilised, motivated and inspired. Again, television provides a critical clue in how this is done.

Television is built around the premise that as we tell the story of one, we are telling the story of all.

That by elucidating and showing the telling detail of one person's story, we are shedding light on the generalised condition that affects many other people.

This is one of the genius hallmarks of storytelling. You are invited in hearing about one person to reflect on what that means for you – how do you compare? What do you think about this? But also to implicitly and explicitly make the leap from the specific to the general, from the time-bound to the timeless, from one person's situation to a bigger truth and bigger story.

In telling the story of one, we tell the story of all.

Consider my opening to a documentary I made more than 30 years ago in Alberta, Canada, for CBC Television, the national broadcaster.[4]

BOX 4.7 REPRODUCED WITH THE KIND PERMISSION OF THE CBC

April 1988. The tumbleweed pile high against the fences.
Or else scud across the earth, mocking the land early this year.
For one, the solitary journey ends, caught on a barb of wire.
Bill Herman knows the feeling.
He too is caught.
He can only watch and wait and hope.
For a rain that will give him back not only his land, but his livelihood.

It was important to capture people's attention and their emotions in the story of Bill Herman. But we went on to tie this to the wider story of drought and despair in oil-rich Alberta.

It's one of my relentless mantras told in almost all coaching and training settings – Life is short. Tell a big story.

The Importance of Differentiating and Having a Point of View

Finally, we could not finish a section on content and structure without discussing the critical importance of differentiating and having a point of view. There is little point in delivering any information that is bland, opinion-neutered and undifferentiated. It simply won't be valued or remembered.

The vast majority of the content we see and hear every day is just this – boring. Labouring mightily to confirm what everyone already knows or suspects. Or else acting as a compendium, pulling together information around the consensus view.

Most presenters actually say very little although they talk a lot. Their presentations are careful and cautious in how they impart their information. It's almost as if someone out there decrees that they need to steer clear of actually saying anything of value, of committing to a point of view.

But it is exactly this act – of taking up a definitive position, of having a point of view and of deliberately focusing on what is different about your presentation – that will set you apart as someone who delivers great content.

Your last great task as you begin to set out your content, in addition to thinking about a possible 'burning platform' and 'big story', is to see if you can tell a *different* story or hold a *definable viewpoint*, a story that hasn't been heard before or heard *in this way* before or a viewpoint that provokes debate and discussion.

Content has a hard enough time being remembered in a presentation without labouring under the burden of being boring. Remember the Chinese water torture of information overload. It's made much worse if the problem is not just volume but value as well. *Boring and voluminous is the nightmare scenario.*

Instead, think different and opinionated in a good, provocative, 'give them something they don't know' way.

If your content is strong, it makes being engaging so much easier.

Notes

1 Excerpt taken from Simon Sinek TED Talk, delivered at the TEDx Puget Sound event in September 2009 and referenced from https://www.ted.com/talks/simon_sinek_how_great_leaders_inspire_action?

2 Excerpt taken from the speech on the website of the Martin Luther King Jr. Research and Education Institute at Stanford University, https://kinginstitute.stanford.edu/

3 Bird, Tom and Cassell, Jeremy, (2017), *The Leader's Guide to Presenting*, London, UK, FT Publishing International.

4 Script reproduced with the kind permission of CBC television.

Chapter 5

Engaging to Create Impact and Meaning

Overview – Communication Is Engagement

All communicating and presenting should be engaging. After caring about audiences and aligning to what they need, *ensuring that we are communicating in an engaging manner should be our second most important priority.*

On one level, all communication does start off being engaging. *The very fact that another human being is drawing attention to themselves engages our attention.* There is something innately compelling about watching someone making him or herself vulnerable and beginning to impart information or meaning.

But as we saw in the section on audience, this initial, almost voyeuristic attentiveness that is hard-wired into us is squandered by most presenters and communicators.

That propensity to squander attentiveness by not engaging really begins even before the presentation starts, with the operating mindset of many presenters. *Presenters often think engagement is something to be added to a presentation to make it come to life,* after the more important work of crafting content is completed.

Be honest with yourself. How often have you done just this? Completed the content of a presentation and then set aside a small amount of time to work out what bits of engagement you can deftly insert into the presentation – and where – that will relieve the tedium of the information transfer. At the same time seeking to keep to a minimum the performance anxiety that usually comes with delivering in an 'engaging mode', something that is not your sweet spot anyway.

In other words, the hunt for engagement usually means adding in a bit of video, maybe showing a couple of slides with pictures or builds and then showing a bit of emotion in the right places.

But this is exactly the wrong way to approach engagement. As something that can be added-in, once the presentation is complete, to modestly 'spice-up' delivery.

In fact, effective commentators and leaders know that *all communicating by its very nature requires engagement.* Or else it's doubtful whether any real communication has taken place at all.

Even looked at in purely transactional terms – has that piece of information made its way from the communicator or leader and been accurately understood and taken on board by the audience – there is plenty of reason to query whether, even with this lowest of benchmarks, effective communication has actually happened.

Transactional, content-driven communications that is low on engagement is also correspondingly low on effectiveness, low on the value we internalise and ultimately not very effective in driving meaning and memorability.

Rather, it is **engagement** that takes this 'transactional' communication and changes it into something *transformative*, something that will mean something to us and which we will remember. This is the nub of what authentic leaders do in their communications.

DOI: 10.4324/9781003198994-8

It is by engaging the audience and playing to their different senses, different ways of processing information and deliberating activating their neuroscientific pathways that drive meaning and memorability that we succeed in communicating. All else is merely masquerading as information transfer.

This rather sober assessment is not meant to denigrate the content in our presentations but to remind us about *how presentations are actually processed, what actually works for audiences.*

Wanting to ensure that a presentation is interesting, high on the engagement quotient and interactive for the audience is not the hallmark of an 'information-light' leader or someone more interested in spin than substance. Rather, it is an indication that the leader has understood the fundamental truth – that *content is the least effective conduit and driver of impact, meaning and memorability.*

The key realisation is that 'we are all animals at heart'. We are swayed far more by the more rudimentary elements of voice and body language than we ever are by content. As an animal species, we simply have a more immediate and far stronger reaction to these elements of communication. Deciphering content is predominantly rational and its power is ephemeral. Reacting to voice and body language is instinctive, intuitive and immediate, and first impressions last a long time.

There are two stories that help illustrate this fundamental 'animal' point that all good engagement rests on.

The Much Misunderstood Professor Mehrabian

You may have come across the much misunderstood Professor Albert Mehrabian, who took up a teaching and research position at the University of California in Los Angeles (UCLA) in 1964. Mehrabian was interested in calibrating the role played by non-verbal communications in face-to-face exchanges.

Across a number of controlled experiments using 17 female participants, Mehrabian wanted to test the impact of tone of voice, the spoken word and facial expressions on the participants' ability to discern liking.

The experiments were very specific and were conducted in a face-to-face environment. Participants were asked to focus on what they believed and what created impact for them and to factor in incongruence between words and emotion: a complicated experiment with specific caveats.

What resulted was Mehrabian's famous formula that 55% of people trust facial clues to discern 'liking' or disliking; 38% verbal (voice) cues; and only 7% take direction most from the words themselves.

These findings routinely get misinterpreted to state that:

- Ninety-three per cent of effective communication is non-content. Or
- Fifty-five per cent of effective communications is body language, 38% voice and 7% words.

Both are gross generalisations. Mehrabian spent years cautioning people not to generalise and reminding that the results were derived from very specific conditions.

Nevertheless, the general takeaway has caught people's imaginations and is definitely useful. That facial expression and body language cues in general, and voice and tone tend to be more powerful in creating impact than words or content.

This rings true. We tend to react first and foremost to a presenter or leader's general confidence level, their overall body language (warm and welcoming or stand-offish), their eye contact (shifty, direct) and their relative ease and comfort in physically engaging an audience.

We then notice the tone, pace, volume, projection, timbre, quality and confidence of voice, and we make a quick judgement on whether this is a voice to which we can listen.

Way down this animalistic checklist is content.

This order of impact – body language, voice, then content – is seen time and again in the order in which people give feedback. People comment first about the overall impact or confidence level of the presenter and the response they had to the effort made to engage them. Whether it is commenting about lack of nerves, smiling, eye contact, confident voice, nice pacing, the initial feedback is almost 100% about either body language or voice.

We are moved first by what has created impact on a physical level and only then do we turn our attention to how our minds were engaged.

This is the real lesson of Mehrabian.

His 55-38-7 formula is often used indiscriminately and inaccurately. Left unchecked, it masks two important truisms – that although content would never be as low as 7% in overall value, it is the least impactful part of a presentation. And the even more important point – that it is physical impact – that visceral engagement of our senses – that is the first and by far the most powerful driver and determinant of engagement.

The Montreal Manifesto

When I worked at CBC Television in Montreal, the network commissioned a survey asking people to identify what they saw on television that had the highest impact on them. What created the strongest impression, highest rate of recall and most meaning? What were they moved by most?

However we asked the question, the result came back the same way: 'another human being talking about something emotional and powerful that I feel passionately about and is relevant to me'.

This is the Mehrabian principle in action.

Body Language

The Power of Body Language – What Good Looks Like

Just as we are all animals at heart and respond first to physical cues in communication, it is also true to say that *most people intuitively recognise what good body language looks like.*

It can be difficult to describe good body language and most people find it easier to articulate how it makes them feel – that is at ease and comfortable. But most discussion around body language focuses on three elements: authenticity, confidence and a sense of deliberateness.

The first two are the same ingredients that audiences want from a presenter – and this is no surprise. We want body language that is first and foremost congruent to the presenter – that is they are acting in a way that we recognise as being authentically 'them' – natural and normal.

'Be yourself' may be perceived as one of the most unhelpful pieces of advice ever giving to presenters and communicators, but it is actually one of the most valuable. This applies to leaders as well. Under no circumstances try and 'put on a persona' that is not

you. People see through it a mile away and it makes them feel very uncomfortable. We see this occasionally with news presenters or leaders who occasionally put on a 'corporate' or 'presenting' voice and demeanour, presumably to appear more in control and powerful. It looks fake, undermines that goal and is very difficult to sustain.

Strong, positive body language comes across as congruent. It has a settling quality and does not leave you wondering what is going on or whether you can trust the person. Quite the opposite: it is both self-enhancing and puts others at ease, leaving them with a strong sense of confidence and that everything is in control and will unfold as it should.

People want to see a presenter or leader 'comfortable in their own skin', at ease with their foibles and confident in their own ability, but also aware of their vulnerability and weaknesses.

Good, strong, positive body language is inherently open, inclusive and generous of spirit. And so the universally understood arms held wide open signalling 'welcome'. A smile that breaks the ice. Eye contact that lasts the 'correct' amount of time – two to three seconds. More and you look like an axe murderer, less and you come across as shifty and untrustworthy.

How you walk and talk is important. Both need to be motivated. Deliberate and declarative.

The key body language takeaway is that people need to sense that what is happening is congruent to your overall personality and it is not random but deliberate.

The core idea here is that audiences need to see the link between deliberateness and motivation. We need body language to appear to be motivated by something that is rational – 'okay he is walking there now, that makes sense to do'. If it is random, either because there is little deliberateness or declarative quality in the presenter's physical comportment, then that gets perceived as unnatural, unsettling and weak.

One of the most frequent questions I ask in a physical rehearsal is exactly that – 'what is your motivation for doing that'? If there is a rational answer, chances are the movement will look congruent and strong. If there is no motivation, it will come across as unmotivated, random and thus weak.

And so, what does good look like? Well, here are two contrasting views of body language (Table 5.1).

Table 5.1 Two contrasting views of body language

Effective body language	Poor body language
• General congruence with emotions and behaviours	• Little congruence, particularly with facial expression
• Authentic emotion	• 'False' emotion
• 'Expected' behaviours	• Unusual behaviours/trying too hard
• Ease of physical comportment	• Self-conscious
• Deliberate/motivated movement	• Swagger or random movement
• Appropriate/expected hand movement	• Choppy hand movements and pointing
• Open and expansive gestures	• Closed and inhibited gestures
• Generosity of spirit	• Intimidating approach
• Straight talk	• Braggadocio
• Normal voice	• Corporate voice
• Normal range of modulation	• Theatrical modulation
• Slower more deliberate pace	• Faster more uncontrolled pace
• Optimal eye contact – 2–3 seconds	• Poor eye contact – too short/long

General Predisposition and Attitude

It's probably worth saying at this juncture that people are influenced in a positive way by general disposition and attitude. We've all sat through team meetings, pitches, presentations and events, where you can almost instantly discern the mood of the person presenting or leading. The 'tells' seem very telling. Whether it's the smile, warm and inclusive tone of voice or confidence – these positive expressions of disposition often 'leak-out' naturally and are difficult to manipulate and manage, which makes them reliable indicators.

Equally, the same thing happens in a negative way. We've all been in sessions where you can cut the tension with a knife. The unease is palpable, people talk about 'walking-on-eggshells' and being wary of saying the wrong thing.

General predisposition is one of the signals people pick up on fastest and one of the indicators they trust most. Precisely because it is difficult for people to mask, change or manipulate and therefore it is deemed by audiences to be very useful in forming first impressions.

Another way of saying this is that we often take an instant like or dislike to someone and we don't really know why. I think there are three reasons which may be helpful in explaining this more.

The broadest reason is to do with attitude. Some people exude a helpful or 'willing' attitude. An HR director once told me that if all candidates are equally strong, then attitude and general disposition is the game changer. Do they come across as supportive, welcoming, willing to help and not precious? And does this attitude translate to a sense of energy and agency?

Likability and Compatibility

The second thing at work here is illustrated in the seminal work of Robert Cialdini in his classic book called *Influence: the psychology of persuasion*.[1] Cialdini makes the strong case that *we ascribe credibility, find more persuasive and are willing to be influenced more by those we like and are compatible with than those we are not.*

If we believe and like the general disposition and attitude being shown by a leader, we are far more likely to 'allow' ourselves to be influenced by them. This ability to project and cultivate likability can of course be manipulated significantly. But when it is sensed innately by an audience in the first few moments of interaction, it can be a powerful example of positive body language in action.

Primary and Secondary Signals

Third, this general disposition or attitude is a powerful part of body language because it involves primary body language signals. We have the ability to decipher these primary signals of body language quickly, efficiently and accurately.

That's because some aspects of body language are universally understood. They involve primal emotions – joy, fear, happiness – and are often shown through first order signals like smiling or scowling. We rightly feel confident in our ability to decode these signals and understand what they mean. In fact, this tends to happen instantaneously.

When we've used facial recognition tests, where the audience is asked to guess the emotion being displayed on the subject's face, the results are very instructive. For these primal emotions like happiness and sadness, people score almost 100%.

But try discerning coyness, shame or indecision. It's much more difficult.

These secondary signals are more subtle and require real de-coding and interpreting. They may be mixed, nuanced or open to interpretation or only decipherable if we examine the context far more closely. So, for example, someone wrapping their arms around their chest may be perceived as being a bit standoffish and distancing, but it could also just be that the person is cold.

Wide Range of Body Language Signals

Another complicating factor in addition to deciphering nuance and context is the wide range of what qualifies as body language:

- Facial movements – both primary gestures (smiling) and secondary tells (tics)
- Physical movements – like opening our arms for a hug or waving hands in front of our face
- Involuntary responses – such as breathing, sweating and blushing
- Eye movements – including speed, direction and focus
- Body positioning – like the so-called 'power position' where feet are shoulder width apart and shoulders held back
- Spatial proximity to people – how much space is between people, who is facing where and what position is spatially most influential

To really get a handle on body language, you'll need to delve into specialist literature. One of the best books I have seen is from ex-FBI profiler Joe Navarro called *What Every Body Is Saying*.[2] It is filled with great tips and provocative insight into body language.

For example, who knew that the most honest part of your body is your feet – they never lie. And where they point is what you're interested in. As Joe says: 'look at where the feet of the person you are speaking to are pointing – if it's towards you: they're interested. If not: sorry: not interested'.

Body Language Matters

So the key point for audiences seems to be of a dual nature. First, rely on your instincts and intuition and your reaction to the presenter's primary body language signals. But also don't be too quick to ascribe meaning to the more nuanced body language you see – there may be a different interpretation to what you're seeing and feeling. Consider the context.

For leaders, the message should be simple. Body language matters. Be aware of the impression your body language is creating and the power it wields. Be mindful that during your initial interaction with audiences, they will be making these calculations based on your general disposition and attitude and the primary signals you are displaying.

And remember our friend Mehrabian with his important message that for any audience, the physical nature of our communication is the primary conduit of impact and meaning.

Voice – The Window to the Soul

People talk about the eyes being the window to the soul. But it really should be the voice. Voice is the single communications ingredient that moves people the most and provides the biggest insight into the communicator.

The primary attributes of voice are well known: pace, modulation, projection, tone and timbre.

Pace – the speed at which people speak. Audiences usually perceive pace fairly straightforwardly, as being too fast, too slow or just about right.

Pace is the vocal area that affects most people. Simply put, most people speak too quickly. There are two reasons for this: people are nervous and want to finish their presentation as soon as possible. They also have a lot to say and want to 'cram it all in'.

Pausing between chunks of content slows down the overall delivery pace, and although it may not actually alter the speed of speaking, it can certainly help in our ability to digest what the speaker is telling us.

Pausing and slowing down also helps to cut down the number of 'ums' and 'ahs' the presenter delivers. These 'filler words' happen because the speaker is talking faster than his or her brain can process. The brain is inserting these words to force the presenter to talk more slowly. The fact that the brain is doing this is a powerful indicator of the need to slow down in a way that is beneficial for the audience and the presenter.

Such is the power of voice in the overall equation of delivering effective communications – that 'slow down' is probably the second most useful piece of advice any communicator can receive after 'less is more'.

'Slow down' is the magic elixir because it confers so many benefits on both presenter and audience (Table 5.2).

It is hard to overstate the case for slower-paced delivery. It is absolutely critical to the overall delivery of a good presentation or a meaningful communication.

Modulation – the amount of 'up and down' in the presenter's voice. Do they vary the pitch and frequency or is the signal constant or 'flat'? Next to pace, this is probably the second most important vocal area.

Most people have fairly 'flat' voices – that is the range of variance in their voice is narrow. They do not move up or down much.

I often use this short exercise to illustrate what is needed. Imagine the two graphics are monitors in a hospital room (Figure 5.1).

The patient attached to the monitor on the right is dead – they've flatlined. The person on the left may be having a heart attack, such is the wild fluctuation in their signal. Both represent extremes and what we should be aiming for is the territory in the middle, some modulation, but tempered.

What good looks like varies because modulation is so personal. But there is very broad agreement that a decent amount of modulation is good and an absolutely crucial tool in being an effective communicator.

Table 5.2 Benefits of slowing down

Presenter	Audience
• More time to think about what you are saying • Builds confidence • Reduces 'ums' and 'ahs' • Reduces 'glitches' and 'clicks' in your delivery caused by uneven pacing and breathing • Puts more breath in your lungs – deepening your voice and further slowing your delivery • Confers sense of 'gravitas' on presenter • Allows presenter to more easily build pauses into their delivery flow • Is the primary facilitator in pacing your delivery – building in pauses and shifts in tone and volume • Keeps information flow from seeming like a 'wall of information'	• Allows the audience to 'keep up' • Gives the audience more time to digest and understand meaning • Provides a respite from the 'wall of information' • Allows audience to connect with the presenter • Is a prime facilitator in the audience forming a strong initial impression • Helps the audience ascribe to the presenter the key attributes of authenticity, passion and confidence – if the presenter is speaking too quickly, this positive assessment is less likely to happen

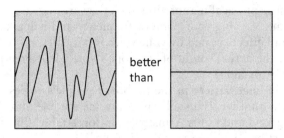

Figure 5.1 The importance of voice modulation.

Voice is so personal to who we are and such an important part in creating overall impression and impact – that we must beware the radical makeover. There is nothing that undermines a presenter or leader's credibility more than to be seen to be changing their voice too significantly.

'Modulate your voice' can be a really irritating and potentially embarrassing piece of feedback for a leader to receive because the natural level of modulation in a person's voice is more personal to them than say volume or pace. People can quickly and without much fuss or effort make changes to their volume if they are speaking too loudly or softly.

Altering your pace is more difficult but a very understandable assignment.

Changing the modulation in your voice is different because it is closely tied to personality. Being told to add more modulation to your voice is like being told to swim better – imprecise and unhelpful.

And so the approach that I have found works best is to reposition modulation as energy.

People don't know how to add modulation to their voices and may resent being encouraged to do so. But *change that to energy and it becomes more of a neutral challenge, not freighted with the implication of personality.* Most people seem to know intuitively what 10% or 15% more energy feels like, and the way they do this most frequently is by modulating their voice more. It's easier for most people to 'add more energy' than to 'add modulation'. They know how to do that.

Projection – the ability for a presenter to 'deliver his voice' to the entire audience, to project across the room in a way that is audible to everyone. Few leaders have any issues in this area because this is one aspect of voice audiences are not afraid to give feedback on. If they cannot understand what you are saying, if you are mumbling or not projecting, they tend to tell you.

Volume – the relative loudness of your voice. Like projection, this is not often a problem for most people. Because they will have been told enough times in the past to 'speak up' if people couldn't hear them, this potential issue usually will have been addressed early on.

Tone – strictly speaking, tone refers to the pitch or frequency of the voice, so we often speak of someone's voice having a shrill or harsh tone. In reality, when we talk about the tone of someone's voice, we are often referring to the much wider concept of their overall 'tone' in communicating.

So when we comment that he or she is an 'empathetic communicator', an 'accessible speaker' or lovely to listen to or perhaps is rather declarative, straight-talking or even harsh in her overall tone, then we are thinking in general about how their voice is a key component of the entire physical manner in which they are engaging. Either way, tone is exceedingly important. Varying your pitch or frequency and being aware of and paying attention to the overall effect created by your voice is critical.

Timbre – refers to the actual sound of someone's voice. Is it breathy, silky, resonant, 'smoky', mellow, heavy or light?

There is obviously a huge variety in the timbre of people's voices and no one quality is deemed better than another. Unusual voices are memorable and the timbre of some voices, like Ella Fitzgerald and Louis Armstrong, unforgettable. But the real indicator of quality is how did that presenter's voice make you feel?

Think of Barack Obama or Nelson Mandela. Their voice is a huge part of their overall communicator's persona. And here I think we are back to that idea of the voice as being the window to the soul. Voice is so much easier to decode than body language, so visceral and powerful in its ability to elicit emotion and meaning.

My mother still had my father's voice on her telephone recording system two months after he had died. Every time I called in that two months and had to leave a message – even though I knew what was coming – I was still shocked and moved at how powerful a reaction I had to hearing his voice.

Such is the power of voice.

Listening and Questioning – Key Skills in Building our Ability to Engage

After body language and voice, two key skills for any communicator are the ability to really listen to people and the ability to ask useful, clear questions that clarify and illuminate understanding.

Listening and questioning are integral skills in enabling us to engage. They are the primary vehicles through which the receivers of information interrogate, evaluate and clarify what is being transmitted. Strong presenters and effective leaders know that they need to constantly 'check in' with the audience to check understanding 'against delivery'. Has what has been said been understood in the manner that was intended?

Strong listening and questioning skills lie at the heart of this 'checking against delivery' – of making sure that the message has been received clearly. And this of course is essential in laying the groundwork for any meaningful further discussion and debate over the transmitted information; if it is not clear to start with, things will only get worse.

Once understanding has been secured – and this can often be an iterative process that takes multiple rounds of listening and questioning – moving on to acting on the information where that understanding is mobilised and activated almost always requires further listening and questioning.

If body language and voice are the two prime pieces of the engagement puzzle that have to do with how the presenter or communicator is received and perceived by the audience, then strong listening and effective questioning are probably the two key skills needed most in order to move on and do something with the communication.

Listening – The Art of Listening

Really good listening is a rare talent. It is something most people are not blessed with. Most of us go through life far more willing to speak than listen. We are not encouraged to listen in the same way we are encouraged to speak. Good listeners are often written off as introverts who sit on the sidelines and can't be bothered to engage.

Good listening is perceived more as a personal attribute that some people have and can bestow as a gift on others rather than as a key communications skill that we should all aspire to and cultivate.

We are very forgiving of those who are not good listeners (that's most of us) making excuses about how difficult it can be to be truly attentive or to set time aside. We feel it more important to 'cut through the clutter' (other people speaking) to stake a claim in the crowded marketplace of ideas and conversation.

And we often assume *there will always be a time when we can listen* – that we can always row back and check in with that person we knew wanted to say something, but whom we were too busy to listen to at the time.

How many of us have come to regret that impulse? When a father is no longer here to listen to or a loving relationship withers – simply because we couldn't make listening a priority.

The poignancy of listening, its power and ultimate redemptive value was brought home sharply to me during an interview in Quebec with a very elderly woman.

BOX 5.1 THE POWER OF BEING REALLY LISTENED TO

I cannot remember the topic of the interview, but towards the end, she simply stopped speaking and began to weep. I was mortified and felt that I'd caused offence with something I'd said. (Always the impulse is to think of ourselves and what we may or may not have done.)

Instead, she composed herself and said very gently to me, 'I'm crying because this is the first time in twenty years that someone has truly listened to me'.

Such is the power of listening. Far more than talking, voice quality or any gesture or body language – real listening with undivided attention is a powerful, life-affirming act that is never lost on the recipient.

Nancy Kline has written a seminal book on listening called *Time to Think*.[3] It is written from a coaching perspective and makes the big point that the most important job coaches have is to listen, to hold the space for the client and help co-create with clients a reflective 'time to think'. The exact same thing could be said of leaders, and this ability to encourage reflection and shared understanding will be a key leadership communication skill in the years to come.

Modes and Levels of Listening

There are three basic modes of listening:

Combative listening – which is not really listening at all, but instead simply waiting for a break in the conversation, when you can jump in and make the points you want to make.

Passive listening – which is when we try and pay attention but are easily distracted and give in to those distractions.

Active listening – where we give our full attention to the speaker, maintaining good eye contact, being supportive, engaged and interested in what is being said.

This 'acknowledgement' of the speaker is similar to the acknowledgement that needs to happen with the audience at the beginning of a presentation. Those who are very good at this active listening have an edge and are often spoken of as having the ability to make the speaker feel special and that they are being focused on completely.

There are also three predominant levels of listening:

Distracted – where we are simply not paying attention for whatever reason. Or attention is fleeting and not sustained.

Attentive – where we are making an effort to stay with the speaker and listen for information and for meaning. Attentive listening includes 'regular' paying attention but also deliberately being vigilant listening for those important moments.

Transformative – *this level of listening is something that happens to us rather than something we can adopt or engineer. Transformative listening happens when we are willing to pay attention with our whole bodies and minds.* When we keep ourselves in a vigilant listening mode, we are more likely to discern feeling and meaning to transcend the mundane to grasp fundamental truths. What we hear in this stage is the telling phrase, the slight crack in the voice or quaver due to emotion – and we glimpse perhaps unintended meaning.

In coaching sessions, people report not being able to avoid being distracted much of the time and they have to make an effort to stay attentive, and that transformative listening is rare. This all feels about right. It is difficult to stay attentive, our ability to concentrate and remember is poor and our attention span is limited.

The transformative impulse is triggered by a transmission of meaning from the leader or presenter or it happens because the audience is being moved to reflect on their own condition and experience. Either way, transformative listening is a key skill for leaders to hone – to be able not just to dispense meaning but to listen for it as well.

Listening between the Lines

Most people intuitively know what 'listening between the lines' means. This is the ability to 'read' what is really going on. To listen for tone, be sensitive to extra pauses and to the real import of words that may be understating the issue.

This is what mothers famously do after only seconds of listening to us; they intuitively know what you are really saying and what is really going on.

We get better at being able to do this – the more we listen to people and the more we 'check in' with them to see if the information we are picking up is accurate. This technique of playing back to the speaker the feeling you are getting from them is a classic coaching technique, whereby asking for clarification of what you have heard and seeking a deeper understanding of what they meant gives them 'permission' to open up and engage on a deeper level.

Journalists and reporters get a lot of experience listening between the lines. I did hundreds of interviews as a television journalist and you develop a 'second sense' about what people are really saying.

Some specific techniques include listening for incongruence between words and emotion, words that are powerful but delivered in a very understated or flat manner and vice versa. This is often indicative of something happening between the lines or outside the bounds of what has actually been said.

Another thing to look for is evasive eye contact and body language – a speaker who is telling you something but not looking at you or avoiding eye contact and whose body language is not congruent with what is being said. Often, this incongruence indicates someone feeling dissonance or being in conflict with themselves.

Often, it can be as simple as hearing someone say something and expecting an emotional wrapper around the statement that is simply missing. If your feeling is that there is more here than meets the eye, pay attention to that sentiment. A reluctance to explain further can also be very telling.

These are all attributes of a leader's communication skill set that are rarely talked about. But they will be essential for the authentic leader who will need to articulate direction in a sea of disruptive change and not be thrown by the power of our emotional responses.

Listening for What Is not Being Said

Sometimes, what does not happen or what is not said is very telling, especially if you would generally expect it to have happened. Checking in to see why the comment didn't happen or wasn't said can be very illuminating. Often, this is an indicator of repressed emotion, of bottling something up or of a very different opinion being held in the room.

Leaders know not to take silence for agreement. Overtly asking for other views or eliciting views from quieter members of a team can pay real dividends in developing a much more accurate view of what is actually being sensed or felt.

Pointing out that someone did not comment on a certain thing can open up a conversation. The key thing is to be vigilant. Listen and watch and do not be afraid of 'naming it' and asking if this is important. Very often, this willingness to 'call things out' to verbalise feelings, emotions or undercurrents can take a meeting, Town Hall, presentation or Q&A session to much deeper and more useful ground.

Surfacing these ideas and holding them in a neutral, non-judgemental way is the mark of a good communicator and a good leader.

'Holding the Space' for Someone

This idea of 'holding the space' for someone or doing this in a team meeting is crucial. It refers to the act of 'giving permission' or making it possible for the person or room to be reflective. To allow silence and reflection and to resist the impetus that is ingrained in us to fill the silence or move on in a linear, progressive, 'get-things-done' manner.

Giving people time to think by simply being quiet and recognising what is happening is the key here. Honouring what has been said and what is being felt by not adding to it and not seeking to further interpret it. Letting things sit and settle before being in a hurry to move on – all of this can be very powerful. It is also very counter-intuitive in the world of business, where time is money.

But this act of pausing and reflecting, making it okay not to move forward yet, can be hugely productive. It can clarify and shed light rather than more heat, enabling you to move faster once you start up again because something fundamental has been recognised.

The Value of Listening

Listening is hugely underrated. Done well, and it elicits deep pools of information that can help you connect better and be perceived as an effective and emotionally aware communicator or leader. Not done well or simply not done at all, and you seriously undermine your own effectiveness. Listening is an art. It requires slowing down and thinking about the other person or people. Taking yourself out of the equation and putting yourself in someone else's shoes.

Once you have listened, then it's time to move on to questioning

Questioning

The Power of Questions

I am always amazed at how much mileage effective leaders, communicators and presenters get out of questions. Questions are often perceived as the poor relation to statements, and principally used by those who don't know and don't have power.

But I'm convinced that the equation is fundamentally the other way round. *Those who know ask, so that those who don't know discover.*

Wise communicators speak very little. And when they do, it is often to ask the pertinent or 'killer' question – the question that cuts to the heart of the matter, making everyone feel engaged, involved and valued, the question that repositions the audience from mere listeners to the heroes of the presentation, discourse or speech.

The best questions convey far more information and meaning than a statement ever could. And they are not merely vehicles through which to gain or disseminate information or wisdom. In their many guises, questions perform a multitude of functions and can be deployed in a myriad of different ways. Here are some.

BOX 5.2 HOW QUESTIONS ARE USED

1 To elicit information.
2 To clarify understanding.
3 To summarise key points.
4 To signal a change in direction.
5 To encourage consensus.
6 To prevent groupthink.
7 To provoke innovation or new thought.
8 To brainstorm.
9 To open up discussion.
10 To close down or confirm actions.
11 To build rapport and empathy.
12 To stake out common ground.
13 To prick pomposity.
14 To encourage emotion.
15 To inspire and motivate

Questions are the often the key tools for enlightened leaders, where the primary dynamic is not to instruct or direct, but to encourage reflection self-awareness and learning.

In settings where the chief aim is to manage a process of discovery, questions like listening are usually at the heart of what is happening. Questions that clarify, probe and summarise that are rooted in understanding past performance and imagining future states. And questions that help forge a shared agreement on a way forward. Here, the role of questions is very different from their primary role as gatherers of information.

What Does Good Questioning Look Like?

Across this wide spectrum of questioning there is broad agreement among journalists, coaches, facilitators and teachers – those who use questions the most – about what works, what doesn't and what good looks like. Here are some of the most frequently mentioned ingredients of good questioning.

BOX 5.3 TEN TIPS FOR GOOD QUESTIONING

1 **Short** – no more than one sentence and avoid asking two or three questions at once.
2 **Simple language** – no fancy words or multiple sentences.
3 **Concrete and pointed** – ask what you mean to ask, do not beat around the bush.
4 **Open-ended questions** – use to elicit information and open up the conversation.
5 **Close-ended questions** – use to confirm, summarise and agree action.
6 **Follow-up questions** – ask questions to get to the heart of the matter. Don't be afraid to dig and don't let unanswered questions go by.
7 **Funnel-shaped** – start wide and then get progressively more specific.
8 **Focus on meaning** – audiences want meaning. Ask questions to elicit this.
9 **Use emotion** – often a more emotional question will bring a more powerful answer.
10 **Use simple metaphors** – simplifying a complicated situation via metaphor can produce a memorable answer.

A little bit more about this from a personal perspective. Working as a journalist, coach and facilitator for years, the importance of good, succinct questions is hard to overstate.

From journalism, I learned the power of making questions clear and simple. There is a fashion these days for news presenters and interviewers to build so much context into questions and to ask double- and triple-barrelled questions – and I think this comes from that eagerness to show expertise and knowledge that we discussed in the chapter on audience.

In coaching and facilitating, the same principle is at work. Simple questions are universally welcomed. Questions that allow for a clear exchange of information invite personal examination or reflection or help summarise work and encourage participants to move on to the next stage of the process. *The 'light-bulb' moment should come from the answer not the question.*

The first key principle should be to aim for simplicity. Questions should be light and succinct. Not weighed down by carrying too much context or information themselves. They are meant to get other people talking, not to give you a licence to talk.

The second key rule is timing. Often, ***when*** *a question is asked is every bit as important as* ***what*** *question is asked.*

Knowing when to ask a pertinent question is allied very closely to listening between the lines and for what is not being said. This ability to ask the insightful question that cuts to the heart to the matter is largely based on your listening skills.

When you sense that they've arrived at a key moment, asking that simple question is imperative. This is the time to encourage people to speak and to push them, if need to be, to confront the issue in play. At these times, a leader can often be more effective by acting as a catalyst for the distillation of others' views and feelings, not as the prime commentator.

Asking the Question in a Positive Manner

How you ask the question – how it is actually phrased – play an important role in whether the question is perceived in a positive way or negative manner. And this, of course, can be crucial in determining what you get from the question.

A positively phrased question will invite debate, encourage learning, facilitate open dialogue and generally be perceived as being supportive, affirming and welcoming to the audience. Conversely, a negatively phrased question will tend to be perceived as judgemental, restricting debate and constraining further dialogue or follow-up questions.

The 'Heavy-Lifters' and the Dangerous Question

What and **how** questions are perceived in a much more neutral manner than **why** questions.

What and how questions are perceived as being functional type questions that are asked simply to gain a better understanding of the factors or emotions in play. So questions like:

- What is important here?
- How are we going to do this?
- How do you see this happening?
- What has caused this?
- How can you do this better?

These are all perceived as straightforward, non-judgemental fact gatherers. And as such, they should form the lion's share of your questioning lexicon.

What and how questions are heavy lifters that gain information efficiently because they are perceived as 'honest', 'no-agenda' type questions. People are usually eager to answer these kinds of questions because they perceive them to be 'externally focused' on the real, sensory world of events, factors, processes and timelines.

The contrast with the other hard-working question why is startling and powerful. **Why** is almost universally perceived as more personal. It is concerned with internally focused things like meaning, responsibility and culpability. **What** happened and **how** it happened feel qualitatively different than **why** it happened. And people sense this right away.

Look at the difference between these two examples. Imagine you are a 17-year-old and your father is doing the asking (Table 5.3)

The **why** sentences feel more personal and judgemental.

The takeaways are important:

1   *Use **what** and **how** questions as much as possible when framing your questions* – They are by far and away the most positively perceived from your audience's point of view.
2   *Use the **why** question judiciously* – Either wait until enough trust has been built to allow the use of the more personal 'why' question. Or if using it at the beginning of

Table 5.3

Example 1	Example 2
Sentence 1 – What caused you to be late last night?	Sentence 1 – What is it about the London dance club scene that you like so much?
Sentence 2 – Why were you late last night?	Sentence 2 – Why do you like the London dance club scene so much

the process, be aware of its power. This may allow you to short-circuit and get to the essence of the issue and what can be done about it very quickly. Equally, it can seriously disrupt efforts to create engagement and build rapport and may slow things down by not allowing for more neutral information sharing initially

3 *Why questions can always be reconfigured as* **what** *or* **how** *questions* – This is hugely important because it allows you to ask the power of a why question using the wrapper of the less provocative how or what question.

This packaging of **why** questions as **how** and **what** questions is a key skill for leaders. So 'why did this happen' becomes 'how did this happen' or 'what caused this to happen'. Both of the latter two sentences defuse the sense of potential culpability, *turning the exercise into a postmortem about process rather than responsibility.*

The Role of Emotion in Engagement

Before we wrap up the framework section of the book, a word on the central role emotion plays in fostering engagement.

We've already looked at the importance of communicating with emotion and how it is a far better conduit of meaning and memorability than rational information. It is less dense and more easily remembered. Emotion helps drive engagement.

It is sobering to realise that it is the oldest and least complex part of our brain that makes the final decision or on whether we are persuaded by something or not.

Behavioural economics is many things, but essentially posits the same sobering theory – that we are simply not as rational as we think we are and that plenty of everyday decisions big and small are driven by a mixture of the rational, emotional and primal.

The stem or reptilian part of our brain looks for a few influential signals to make up its mind about something. This is scandalously oversimplified, but for our purposes here, the key point is that only a relatively few number of ingredients play a disproportionate role in engaging our decision-making processes and that list is led by emotion.

First and foremost, we remember and are persuaded by emotion, by things we feel emotional about and to which we ascribe meaning.

We are influenced by rational, concrete information like data, margins and price. But we tend to ascribe outsize influence to that which we can see, hence the seminal role of pictures in driving decision-making. More people are visually oriented and so a picture is usually worth at least a thousand words. Another visual aspect at play is that we are overtly influenced when we can clearly compare and contrast to see impact. Think about the power of Al Gore's before and after pictures of the snow cap on Mount Kilimanjaro in his climate change documentary *An Inconvenient Truth.*

How we feel about what is being proposed, how it aligns with our personal value system and beliefs is also a very powerful driver in influencing our ability to remember information and transform those impressions into something lasting, memorable and meaningful. If a business proposition or presentation passes our personal litmus test, this is disproportionately important to us.

The key thing to remember is that *it is the emotional component that most powerfully drives engagement. We remember that which we are moved by.*

But the other really important realisation to make is one that we don't hear as frequently. *The shocking truth is that emotional components of decision-making work much faster and more powerfully than the rational components.* The heart always knows what the head is just waking up to as my girlfriend taught me in our debate about going to India.

This is the last point to make here. We must try and include emotion not just because it engages audiences, *but because it is central in how people make decisions about our communications.*

The Criticality of Storytelling

The most effective leaders understand that storytelling is the best vehicle or conduit for the conveying of emotion and meaning – the twin pillars of building true engagement. Stories are bred in the bone, part of our DNA and how we are hard-wired to take in and remember information. They are the oldest form of communicating and have been unfairly and naively disparaged over the years as too lightweight for business purposes, for illustrating the complexity of the situation and – as we discussed in the chapter on audience – showcasing our expertise.

But it is the very act of embracing vulnerability and agreeing to open up – of risking reputation by speaking at a simpler and more fundamental level – *that is both the core ingredient of authentic communication for* leaders *and the core requirement of good storytelling.* The best stories come from the heart and are delivered with emotion. They have an effect far beyond, and precisely because of, their simple framework.

The power of metaphor, the moral of the story, the invitation to find yourself in the story, the ability to tell the story of all through the story of one – these things are rarely lost on people and speak volumes in a way that detail simply cannot. In the end, *the simple act of opening up and telling stories is the pathway that starts building trust in a way that mere information transfer never does.*

Authentic leadership is built around this dynamic of forging trust and then acting in a manner that honours that trust. Stories are the ultimate way to engage.

The Power of Engagement

Engagement is communication. There should be no reason to treat engagement as a nice-to-have extra that can be added in at the end to spice up a presentation. Engagement is either present and is happening between a leader and their audience or it is not present and not happening. The former makes for powerful communication. The latter is one-way information and often falls on deaf ears and infertile ground.

Truly engaging with audiences is exhilarating and exhausting, but it is absolutely central to delivering strong communications. If we don't take the audience into consideration and plan to engage with them, we are left relying only on our content to deliver the human interaction and engagement that sits at the core of all effective communication.

It is simply too heavy and unrealistic a burden for content to bear. No one's content is that compelling. But more importantly, content-only communication is simply not how human beings are wired. People yearn for meaning, for passion and authenticity. They want to hear stories and to be engaged.

We undoubtedly need information, but we are able to internalise and remember only if the information comes in a powerful, engaging, audience-friendly wrapper. Otherwise it simply passes us by.

BOX 5.4 THE ENGAGEMENT TAKEAWAY FOR LEADERS

Leaders face such pressure to drive concrete deliverables like strategy, policy, growth, profitability and recruitment that there is a completely natural predisposition to focus more on content, less on audience and far less on engagement.

But it is precisely this equation that needs to change. With complexity and uncertainty increasing exponentially, with the three specific 'reset' challenges of control, trust and connectivity and with businesses facing the two mega trends of accelerated technological change and rising concern for social values – leaders simply have to focus more on their ability to engage.

Far from being 'soft' skills, authentic body language, acute listening, wise questioning and emotional literacy is emerging as the new lexicon of enlightened and effective leadership.

Put another way – gone are the days when a supremely talented but disengaged leader can cut it. No matter the expertise in play, it will increasingly be the skills of the shepherd, the motivator, the coach and the muse that leaders will need.

None of the other requirements will lessen. But they will increasingly be marked down as hygiene factors, as the need to engage and empathise, understand and motivate audiences and lead and articulate change comes to the fore.

Notes

1 Cialdini, Robert, (1984), *Influence: The Psychology of Persuasion*, New York, William Morrow and Company.
2 Navarro, Joe, (2008), *What Everybody is Saying*, New York, William Morrow and Company.
3 Kline, Nancy, (2000), *Time to Think*, New York, Cassell.

Part 3

What Authentic Communication Looks Like – A Toolkit

Chapter 6

Optimising Presenting

PowerPoint presentations

Death by PowerPoint

The phrase 'death by PowerPoint' is common knowledge. What began as an interesting and much improved way of presenting information has morphed into the ubiquitous and dreaded default way of presenting to any audience.

It's amazing to think PowerPoint was released by Microsoft on May 22, 1990, now over 30 years ago. When it came out, PowerPoint was a huge improvement on those old acetate templates that you would draw on and then project onto a screen. Nothing about that mode of delivery ever worked well and so PowerPoint was an instant godsend.

Now, everyone decries its overuse. But it is still by far and away the default vehicle for making a presentation or transmitting information. For all the attention heaped on social media, whiteboarding, technical platforms like Slack, Jabber and Teams that allow you to share information and techniques like Prezi and Miro that help you add movement and make your presentations 'come to life', PowerPoint is still the dominant vehicle.

What can we do to lessen our reliance on PowerPoint, so that we don't risk alienating audiences before we even begin, with them dreading yet another slide deck presentation? And if we decide to use slides, how can we use them in a more audience-friendly manner? These are the two key questions.

Who Is in the Driver's Seat – The 'Dual Focus' Problem Inherent to Slides

The first issue to confront right off the bat is whether to use slides at all. There is an inherent weakness or challenge in using slides, in that *they divide the audience's attention between you and the slides.*

It is a little bit like the 'second presenter' syndrome we talked about earlier, where the audience constructs a presentation in parallel to the one you are delivering. This happens as they digest and internalise what you are saying and transform that to a form they can remember. Remember we suggested that you can minimise the difference between the presentation you are presenting and the one they are creating and internalising by being super clear, signposting major points and not being afraid to be directive on what it means.

When you use slides, another 'second presentation' process is happening. In addition to the audience creating a presentation in their own minds, you now effectively have two sources of information competing for the audience's attention – in effect, two presenters: you and the slides.

DOI: 10.4324/9781003198994-10

One of the most telling questions that can be asked of a presenter is *who is in charge of driving your presentation – you or your slides?* Many people will sheepishly admit that it is the slides that are in the driver's seat and they are merely coordinating the advancement of the presentation and offering colour commentary – with the slides and the information they carry performing the chief 'narrator' role in telling the story.

This feeling of being 'out of control' and that the slides are in control is symptomatic of the wider issue at play here: the division of focus inherent in using slides.

By using slides, you are inviting the audience to focus on the slides and not focus on you. This automatically cuts down on your potency as a presenter and your ability to engage with your audience. To minimise this effect, you need to regain control over your own presentation by relegating the slides to a supporting role and recapturing the primary presenting role for yourself.

You need to be the one making the main points, not your slides. To do that, you need to reduce the complexity of your slides, use the **slide titles** as the major story signposts of your narrative and use the **slides themselves** to highlight one key point per slide. Take information out of your slides and use the slides as a pathway to direct the story in outline form. This allows **you** to fill in the detail and drive the storytelling or narrative, which puts you back in the driver's seat.

This fundamental storytelling role or function should never be relinquished to slides. Control over delivering the meaning cannot be outsourced to slides; otherwise it never happens. Giving up control over slides fatally undermines the presenter by removing them from the equation almost completely.

Unfortunately, we all know what this looks like. The presenter loads up on slide detail and then reads the material to the audience, often turning and facing the slides as if obediently paying them homage. Audience engagement sinks to rock bottom because the audience can read so much faster than the presenter can speak and there is nothing for the audience to engage with or anticipate. Their old brains remain dormant – there is nothing new here.

Keep the primary role of presenter for yourself. Never cede this responsibility to your slides. This is especially critical for leaders.

Keeping It Simple with Uncluttered Slides

The companion piece of advice here is to keep the slides simple – declutter them so they are the supplementary agent in the presentation and not undermining your authority, agency and effectiveness.

Over the course of my career, I have seen some amazing slides. Gant charts with so many step changes as to be indecipherable. Excel spreadsheets transferred verbatim to PowerPoint and rendered in font size three to cram all the numbers on to one slide. Mindmaps of mystical complexity. Always and everywhere too much information.

This recalls the point made earlier that we worry about being taken lightly if we don't showcase our knowledge and information.

But *it is also a very practical problem in those cases where the slide deck also has to serve as the document of record.* In pitches, where the presentation deck is the final document left for the client to evaluate; at conferences, where the presentation deck is submitted as the presenter's official contribution; at investor sessions, where the numbers are everything. And internally, when angling for a positive business decision, we are loath to leave out the detail. In all these cases, it is a really gutsy and risky decision to underplay the need for detail.

There are a few ways around this particular challenge.

First, include *telling not voluminous detail. Focus on value not volume.*

Second, use an appendix to gather together the detail that underpins the main points you are making. This makes it easy to access and user-friendly for the audience.

Third, if possible, separate your 'presentation slide deck' from your 'official document of record slide deck'. The former is built around driving engagement and helping you perform and present. It can be shorter, more visual and include only the biggest points and telling detail. The latter, in addition to all this, often includes case studies, finer detail, supporting statistics and scenario examples.

There are ways around the problem of how much detail to include; but the key point is to ration yourself so that the detail is understandable and the slides visually appealing. This last point is critical. You know your reaction when you first see a slide filled with too much information. It's the same reaction you have when you see a really crowded agenda slide: a sinking feeling of dread.

People react viscerally and visually to slides. Clutter or too much detail is a big turn-off.

We once worked with a client that requested a session at their corporate strategy away day devoted to decluttering slides. The slides were of mind-blowing complexity and used small fonts, multiple arrows, charts within the slide and lots of numbers.

The in-house analysts were reasonably comfortable with them because they understood all the information, but they recognised that for their clients, the bottom line message was not clear and that the slides were off-putting. They included important information, but looked like brain dumps and had not been edited to showcase the really important information.

Of course, the amount of detail should be tailored to the audience's knowledge level and their need to know the detail – and some rather complex technical information may be entirely justified and even desired by the client. But even then, the fundamental points are:

1   Are you de-coding the detail and being directive on meaning? This cannot be left up to the slides.
2   Even experts get tired of reams of detail. Our brains rebel at undifferentiated, dense information.

This issue of overcomplication is widespread and can have serious consequences that undermine your presentation. Overly dense slides are really the reverse problem of outsourcing control over your slides.

When slides are too dense, the not-so-subtle message to the audience is aren't you glad I'm here to help you understand this information – let me help you. We are meant to be humbled by the presenter's mastery over granular detail and pathetically grateful that they are now going to help us navigate our way through the slides.

This is not a good position to put your audience in – that of helpless and cowed supplicant. Unless the audience are technical experts and will welcome the detail and presenter de-code, the positioning for a regular audience needs to be different.

Aim to involve them, have them intuitively understand your material, become interested, get involved and be invested in the presentation. If it's all too difficult – and you're spending too much time explaining everything – they simply give up, withdraw permission and build their own negative view of what is happening.

How Many Slides

How many slides is enough? It depends and in all cases will be different. But a rule of thumb that works for many people is to roughly align the number of slides with number of minutes presenting using a maximum ratio of approximately 2:3, so 13 slides for a 20-minute presentation. This rough guide will give you time to present your slides without racing and will allow you time to engage and do the question and answer (Q&A).

Earlier, we discussed storyboarding and talked about using five core slides to tell a story. Once you have the basic structure laid out, you then need to make a call on how many supplementary slides you need in each key area. Just remember, the answer from the audience is always the same: the fewer the better.

A Word on Structure and Order

The other key structural consideration is to *pay attention to the order of your slides*. Ideally, this should track the order in which people intuitively receive information (covered previously in the Imaginary Dialogue).

I have seen many presentations jump too quickly to the detail with little or no 'cognitive map' that helps build audience connection and engagement. Time spent setting up a presentation at the beginning is never time wasted.

Another way to think about this is to try and start with the general and move towards the specific. Do not go too quickly to the detail before setting up the general idea or thesis.

BOX 6.1 WHAT DEVELOPMENT COMPANIES GET WRONG

We do a lot of work with construction and land development companies. They often send people to practice presentations to local authorities or town councils focusing on a particular development site.

Presenters come equipped with about ten slides for an eight-minute presentation (too many), but almost invariably do not show a site map until well into the presentation. This gets pointed out in the feedback after their first practice round, and the difference in clarity is astounding when the slides are reordered so the overall location map appears at or near the beginning.

People need the big picture, both figuratively and literally, before you get too far into the detail.

There are three other pieces of feedback that are offered very frequently to these presenters from their peers and all are instructive:

1 **Sell us the subject** – Have something in the beginning that tells us what the opportunity is or why we should care and that summarises the ask or offer.
2 **Delete slides** – We get what you are saying and fewer slides will help you be clearer.
3 **Show a summary slide** – Bring your key points together in one place.

There is a kind of cognitive direction to slides that people innately feel comfortable with: an overview at the beginning, a summation of what that means at the end and the denser proof points in the middle. It is interesting that even when done well, PowerPoint handles the middle rational transfer of information more efficiently than the more emotive and engaging bits at the beginning and the end.

That's why it is so important to think about how you integrate using PowerPoint with other modes of communicating so you can create the most optimal mix for your particular presentation.

Using Slides in Conjunction with Other Modes of Delivery

Slides work well with video. Embedding video in your slides can help you make a more emotive point at the beginning, explain clearly a more detailed point in the middle or underline a persuasive 'selling' point near the end. Video gives you and the audience a break from each other and a much needed change of pace. It is relatively easy to pick up where you left off and that few seconds of communicating in a different way really helps with attentiveness and engagement.

Slides work well with flipcharts and whiteboards. Many presenters like to integrate these modes by illustrating an important point in real time in a more engaging way. This point then is often left sitting on the whiteboard or printed out and distributed. Or, if it's on a flipchart, it can be tacked up somewhere in the room.

This physical act of creating something, sharing it with the audience and then keeping it around as a visual cue to aid memory is powerful.

Slides can work well with stories, although they tend to sit at opposite ends of the engagement spectrum. The key thing with moving from PowerPoint to stories is to be aware of the 'lunch-bag let-down' feeling that audiences often get when the story is over and you are returning to showing slides. For many presenters, telling a story acts better as a segue to another mode of communicating such as a Q&A session, a breakout discussion or coming back to a video. No one will ever turn down the chance to hear a short, well-delivered and relevant story – it's what comes afterwards that is important.

Actively think of how you can use slides with other modes of communicating. Anything you can do to take the pressure off slides as the second conduit of presentation – after you as the presenter – is a good thing to do.

BOX 6.2 WHAT THIS MEANS FOR LEADERS

I think PowerPoint is one area of communications where leaders can make a real difference, leading by example and encouraging an organisational culture that pays attention to the quality of its presentations and empowers its employees to take back control.

Leaders can encourage a change of emphasis, so the premium is placed on engagement and experimentation on a physical level and storytelling and the articulation of meaning on the content side.

Leaders intuitively do not like PowerPoint presentations as they instinctively understand that the spotlight is being shared and potentially diffused in effect. Most leaders do not outsource control over the presentation to the slides and tend to err on the side of simplicity and 'big picture' messages rather than regale employees with too much detail. One leader I worked with in banking was famous for only having a picture of an animal on each slide for whatever point he was trying to make – one picture and no words.

I think it is this intuitive understanding of the power of theatre and presentation – of connection and making a few points well – that many leaders intuitively grasp and this is partly what makes them such difficult audiences for more junior employees to present to.

Encouraging employees to restrict the number of slides, get to the point and tell an engaging story around the most important idea is something that leaders get for themselves, but could do far more to encourage at the individual and organisational level.

Pitches

Life's a Pitch

Pitches are set-piece events that are inordinately influenced by the communicators on both sides of the divide. They are short time-bound showcases or microcosms of everything that is important about communications. They throw into sharp relief the power of engagement, the importance of being likeable, the need to get to the point, how to show detail and expertise to address rational concerns, but balanced with delivering that sense of trust and value that allows us to buy or be persuaded. Throw into the mix close proximity body language, the need to adapt quickly to different personality typologies and do all this in less than 50 minutes – and it's easy to see why *pitches are the most fraught of communications.*

Pitches are the stage where most everything that we can talk about that is important in communications can be seen writ large. They test rational and emotional skill sets and tend to have definitive outcomes – even if the most frequent, ironically, is deferral or delay.

Creating Differentiation by Getting to the Conversation Faster

The key traditional driver in a pitch environment is the expectation on both sides that *certain proscribed information is delivered in a predictable order and to a preset time-line.* For both sides of the pitch divide, these expectations dictate a very linear and templated process.

But what if to create differentiation and engagement you set out to deliberately subvert that order and timeline?

A few years ago, we were working with a financial services firm. The process that governed their pitches to institutional investors and pension fund trustees is laid out in the key building blocks shown in the graphic below (Figure 6.1).

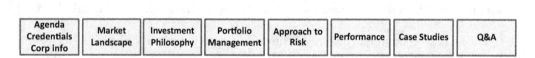

Figure 6.1 Regular pitch process for financial services firms.

The process should be recognisable to just about any organisation. Begin with credentials, discuss market landscape and general opportunities and then describe how your product or service is the right one for the client, offer some cases studies and do a Q&A.

Our client had a problem and saw an opportunity. The problem was they felt they were not able to differentiate from all the other firms pitching for investment mandates. They felt the typical pitch length of 45 minutes was far too long to go without interaction and drove mediocrity and boredom. They were losing mandates because of a process that constrained their ability to do something different.

They were already working with us on simplifying and decluttering their pitch decks, building a stronger opening and more of a storyline into their presentations – and aligning everything using the Imaginary Dialogue. They had a couple of senior fund managers who were strong communicators and willing to do something different.

The opportunity crystallised when the *Harvard Business Review* published an article suggesting that the vast majority of CEOs actually hate presentations and want to get to the conversation as fast as possible.

The thesis is that CEOs usually know most of the relevant information already and are far more interested in assessing credibility, scanning for risk, probing for reasons to trust and calibrating value and opportunity costs. For them, all this is more efficiently done in a conversation where they get to intervene when they want to.

This struck our client as instructive and was the catalyst for change, the light-bulb moment that helped drive a radical makeover of their pitch process. They made the following changes:

BOX 6.3 THE PITCH PROCESS MAKEOVER

- Appendix document sent to the client prior to pitching.
- Presentation slide deck reduced in size from 60 to 15 slides.
- Actual 'pitch' lasting 7 minutes instead of 45 minutes.
- Talked about the client's situation with insight, knowledge and context.
- Played a short video highlighting key ideas.
- Summarised in story form.
- After seven minutes, stopped and engaged in conversation with client.
- Client invited to 'direct' rest of pitch and focus on any aspect that had been presented or sent to them.

Their reworked pitch process looked like this. The appendix consisted of the six tiles immediately after the Q&A box (Figure 6.2).

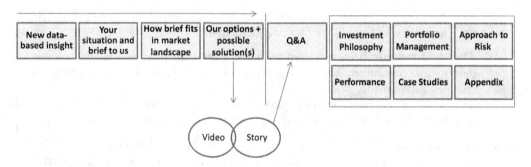

Figure 6.2 Reworked pitch process.

The results were startling: increased sales, better interaction, engaged clients and brand differentiation.

This kind of radical makeover is uncommon. But the story highlights some key issues pitch leaders need to think about. And they are counter-intuitive because they seem to fly in the face of what should be needed and preferred:

1   How can you get to that critical conversation as quickly as you can, *while still covering all the necessary detail*?

2   How can you build-in interaction and not drone on for 45 minutes in directive mode, *even though that is traditionally what a pitch has required?*
3   How can you vary how you present and differentiate, *but do this in a professional manner?*

The feedback was that, in this case the right balance had been struck. The client got as much information as they normally would have, but it was prioritised and sequenced very differently. Increased interaction was welcomed *especially because it focused on the client.* And the presentation was still crisp and professional – the video and story elements short and relevant.

Balancing Detail with Keeping It Simple

Another key issue is the need to balance detail with keeping it simple. Traditionally, this issue has never really been considered in a pitch because detail was deemed to be what the client needed most. Detail equated with 'substance', while keeping it simple sounded suspiciously like 'style' or an excuse to be lazy and not do the hard yards.

But as we saw earlier, this is simply not how people are persuaded. They do not find complexity reassuring. They need to know you understand and have command over the detail, *but they also need to know what matters and how you're going to make a difference.* And have this delivered in a relatively simple storyline.

We lost a pitch recently that shows the perils of over-preparing and loading up on detail and of not getting the balance right between detail and keeping it simple.

Here's what happened:

BOX 6.4 LOSING THE PLOT – A CAUTIONARY TALE

We were pitching to a financial services company who were looking to raise their profile. The brief was complicated by two elements:

1   They had recently been acquired by a big European firm and needed to undergo some rebranding and clearly explain to employees and stakeholders the changed relationship.
2   They wanted a communications partner who would eventually help them extend their presence to Europe working with their new parent company.

We delivered a fairly traditional pitch and included a lot of information on our 'integrated approach' offering media relations, insight research, rebranding expertise and lots of case studies.

We lost the pitch on a unanimous and unflattering decision:

1   Too much detail.
2   No storyline or clear idea of how we would add value.
3   Came across as disparate elements, not one team.

They chose a firm with a much narrower media relations track record but a simpler story of how they saw the challenge and what they would do.

This balance between needing to show detail but not overdoing it is an important lesson. In our case we felt sandbagged a bit – penalised for commenting on all the elements of their situation. But it was a clear lesson on the perils of overcomplicating the brief and of not having a clear narrative line and showing value.

It's About Chemistry more than Credentials

One area where overcomplication is constantly seen is credentials. The plain fact of the matter is that once you are invited to the final round of pitches, you have already passed the credentials test.

They've done their due diligence and, broadly speaking, are amenable to working with you. In others words, they believe you can do the job.

The pitch that you think is about detail, credentials, track record and expertise *is actually about evaluating chemistry*. While you're delivering beautiful detail, case studies, graphs and credentials, they're actually scrambling to figure out if they can see themselves working with you, not debating whether you have the knowledge.

This is hugely unsettling. And another counter-intuitive knock. *Who knew that pitches are really emotional beauty parades?*

If what they're most concerned about is this intangible feel-good factor, maybe it is important to cut back on the detail, get to that conversation more quickly and pay attention to personal chemistry.

I think you have to be judicious in how you reduce detail, but certainly when it comes to credentials less is more. Don't forget, everything you're going to tell them, they almost certainly already know.

Making a Personal Connection – Trust and Likeability Still Play a Crucial Role

This notion that it is chemistry that is perhaps the most important thing being tested in a pitch is unsettling. It changes your set of assumptions about what is important.

In a pitch, this is particularly problematic because the entire process is set up to convey information.

Finding opportunities in that process to do the softer stuff is difficult. Forging connections, asking insightful questions, putting yourself in their shoes, listening carefully, smiling and making eye contact, offering concise observations and showing a positive disposition – all can seem quite counter-intuitive to attempt in such a proscribed process.

And yet, this is often what ends up helping you win the pitch. It's that personal element again, as we saw in the chapter on engagement. How you make people feel has a powerful effect on whether they hire or are persuaded by you. People buy people or as Simon Sinek said, 'people don't buy what you do, they buy why you do it'.

Allowing yourself to engage rather than transmit, to listen rather than talk and to question rather than declare are weird ideas for a pitch. I think we've all grown up with the notion that a pitch is the ultimate rational 'clearing house'.

But the emotional reaction is more primal than the rational one, and likeability and trust are the most powerful indicators of influence. It really does help if they like you.

Aiming to co-create in a pitch rather than instruct is the most counter-intuitive idea of all.

BOX 6.5 THE PARENT COMPANY

We were pitching to an employment law firm and an interim management team, who together had been asked to ensure the smooth removal of a UK management team that had lost the confidence of its parent company.

We were up against one of the leading crisis communications firms in the UK. The pitch was low tech and consisted of us submitting a paper and then talking about it with them.

We had a lengthy conversation and engaged well with both firms during the talk.

When we won the assignment, they explicitly told us that we'd probably scored a bit lower on expertise and track record, but they both strongly felt the parent company would much prefer working with us rather than the more high-powered but brittle crisis experts. The likability and compatibility factor in action.

Indecision in the Driver's Seat

The final counter-intuitive idea is that after all the work preparing for and delivering the pitch, a frequent decision is 'no decision'.

The status quo is a powerful default positioning and inertia, even in the face of what may be a seemingly obvious need to change should always be considered a possible and perhaps likely outcome. Change is difficult and comes with many hurdles to overcome before it can be set in motion.

Sometimes clients or internal senior executives are not yet in 'buying mode'. Or the 'burning platform' that drives the need to change is not yet clear or clear enough to overcome inaction.

Pitches that create need, sell from a point of view and say how they are different from others tend to do best.

A Willingness to Take Risks and to Change

Change is difficult and risky. Moving towards a more interactive, conversationally driven dialogue that allows the 'receiving' team to calibrate chemistry, likability and trust and the 'pitching' team to reduce detail by focusing on meaning should be liberating and differentiating for all.

It's my guess that this process will gather steam exponentially. But at the moment, we're still in the early stages of change.

BOX 6.6 TIPS AND HINTS FROM THE COALFACE

Keep it short – get to that conversation as soon as you can.
  Frame everything around their need.
  Have a simple narrative thread and storyline.
  Clearly show your value.
  Be mindful of the 'chemistry' requirement – try and interact all the way through.

BOX 6.7 WHAT THIS MEANS FOR LEADERS

The main takeaway for leaders is to mobilise the powerful insight they intuitively have into what they like seeing when they are pitched to, and strongly encourage their organisations to make these changes in the way they pitch to clients.

A handful of changes can have a volcanic effect, producing more client-centric, compelling pitches that are far more attuned to what a client needs and less to what the pitching organisation wants to sell them or do to them.

Pivoting to get to the conversation faster, spending more time talking with the client about what is valuable and moving rote information to an appendix allowing for clients to prioritise and customise what they want to discuss are all changes that are very difficult to make without support from leaders at the top of an organisation. I've seen it happen once at an organisational level and the effect was profound.

Virtual Presenting

The Trade-Off between Performance and Process

The advent of Covid-19 has seen virtual presenting grow exponentially.

The key observation about what this means for presenters is probably one that will cheer most people. *The biggest change with virtual presenting is that the balance moves away from engagement and performance and to process and professionalism.* That is, people understand that the format constrains how performance-oriented a presenter can be and are willing to trade interaction and engagement – the physical side of communicating – for a clear process that, with all the technology involved, is run in a smooth, professional manner.

Yes, voice and body language are still important in virtual presenting, but the premium is on process and clarity. And so things like *'signposting', expectation and time management and having a clear agenda are far more important.* Because the presenter is not there face-to-face and in the room, the cues that an audience normally get are vastly reduced. The presenter's verbal and non-verbal cues are constrained and the audience vibe, which often helps signal that something needs to be clarified, is totally absent.

Of course, this also works in reverse. For presenters, the cues received from the audience are not as strong either. The psychological backdrop to the presentation is more subtle and harder to read. And the entire dynamic can feel far more like a one-way street where feedback can be very difficult to gauge.

The ability for both presenters and audiences to organically react in a face-to-face setting does not work as well virtually. Both sides are forced to acknowledge the greater importance of process and clarity.

Clarity over process is part of the bigger issue of ensuring a professional experience for the audience. *There are more 'moving parts' to a virtual presentation and making sure they all come together smoothly is a big requirement.* There is a lot to juggle, if you think of sharing slides, enabling Q&A and the 'chat function', handling technical issues and keeping to time. All of this is more important in a virtual environment because the worst that can happen – a total technical malfunction – does not really have a counterpart in face-to-face presenting.

Certainly, every time I have presented or moderated a virtual event, it is the technical aspects that concern me most. They are of sufficient importance that if the event is important, large or public, you should consider separating the presenter function from the technical and/or moderating function. *This emphasis on professionalism is the virtual counterpart to the emphasis on engagement in face-to-face presenting.*

The Changed Presenting Dynamic

In addition to the need to ensure a professional experience and to be clear about process, there are three significant differences to the presenting dynamic.

More Tolerance for a Directive Approach

The first difference is that *audiences tend to react favourably to a more directive approach* to information than during a face-to-face presentation. Normally, downloading information and transmitting to an audience would be marked down as not engaging. But *in virtual land, there seems to be far more tolerance for a more directive approach.*

Partly, this is a function of virtual fatigue. Unlike face-to-face training sessions which can last a whole day, our ability to take in a screen-bound experience seems to last about 90 minutes. It is exhausting looking at a small screen, being on screen, paying attention without the rich panorama of visual and physical cues and trying to keep up with the thread of what is going on.

Because of this 'fatigue,' audiences seem to welcome a more directive approach where categoric, information transfer is the focus. The caveat to this is that the information needs to be less dense, less controversial and less debatable. Again, we are making a trade-off here: 'I'm willing to have you as the presenter be more directive and in transmit mode, as long as you agree to keep it short and relatively simple'. This trade-off is similar to the one that gives up engagement for professionalism and clarity over process.

A Diffuse Spotlight may Create Distance and Dissonance

The second major difference is that while the presenting or performance spotlight is more diffuse, *more responsibility rests on the presenter than in a face-to-face environment.*

This more diffuse spotlight may make some presenters feel more comfortable – they are literally sharing the spotlight with the audience. However, many people have commented that the in-your-face nature of these video calls is such that everyone – presenter and audience alike – are being looked at directly and constantly.

The diffuse nature of presenting virtually is important to adjust to. On the one hand, you do not have the immediacy of face-to-face presenting which some liken to being on stage. Virtual is far more like radio or television in that regard, in that there is a technical gulf between the presenter and the audience.

On the other hand, as we've said, the responsibility is ramped up which makes the virtual role somewhat dissonant. Distanced and diffuse on the one hand, but directly responsible and *supposedly in control* of the entire process on the other. This dissonance that may come from being 'in control' of a process that is reliant on technology platforms out of your control is another reason to outsource the technical role to someone else. That way, some of this dissonance or anxiety diminishes and you can concentrate on presenting.

A Need for Authenticity and to Respect Vulnerability

The third major difference is the strange trade-off between emotion and authenticity. We have looked at how the virtual presenting environment constrains the ability of the presenter to engage, perform and modulate the emotional quotient of their presenting. This seems accurate, reasonable and fair.

But there seems also to be a growing requirement for virtual presenters to make up through authenticity and genuineness what they cannot deliver by way of engagement and emotion.

This is another trade-off that may go something like this:

> I know the format constrains your ability to engage and frankly I don't need that in a virtual setting as much, but I do need you to be genuine and authentic. I don't want to waste my time or feel like I'm being manipulated or fooled and with this distance between us, I just need to know you have my best interests at heart.

I think this is a real issue in virtual presenting: the idea that audiences are a bit more vulnerable in a virtual setting and are looking for transparency and honesty in all communications. *The very distance that is at the heart of this type of communicating counter-intuitively means that audiences need reassurance that the presenter is going to be straightforward and genuine.*

What this means practically is even less tolerance than usual for overt marketing or virtue signalling. Sharing is in and selling is out. Tone of voice needs to be calmer and less robust.

Taken together, these three changes describe quite a changed psychological framework for virtual presenting.

BOX 6.8 WHAT THIS MEANS FOR LEADERS

The 'new' virtual presenting landscape gives leaders a real opportunity to try out for themselves what a more genuine, vulnerable and empathetic style of leadership looks like, without feeling like they're undergoing a complete makeover.

Because there is such a premium placed on process, professionalism and directive content, the more traditional 'command and control' type leaders who keep communications short and to the point will feel comfortable that the overall shape of presenting virtually is sympathetic to this style.

But adding little bits of empathy, emotion, awareness, authenticity, humour and audience acknowledgement goes a long way and is really appreciated in the disruptive times we're living in. Presentations are for the most part time-bound and functional; so this effectively becomes a great landscape to practice a bit more of an open approach within some safe parameters.

Again, the leaders I have seen being most effective so far in virtual land are the ones who keep things quite straightforward, but manage to mix in a little humility and vulnerability at the same time.

BOX 6.9 PRACTICAL VIRTUAL PRESENTING TIPS

Speak more slowly than usual and use more pauses.

Pace yourself and frequently check in for audience understanding.

Regroup and summarise before moving on.

Signpost and make sure people know what is happening and what is coming next.

If the audience is small enough, consider asking people questions by name.

Accept there may be technology issues and stay cool in handling them.

Chapter 7

Performing in the Spotlight

Overview

Speeches are the great cornerstones of communication: the most elevated and personal forms of individual communication in the business world and often the calling card of great leaders; memorable, moving set pieces that sketch out a vision, strategic direction or an unfulfilled dream.

They can be prosaic and mundane, but the best speeches have the power to move people and make history. For leaders, speeches are intensely personal, reflective of who they are and by definition idiosyncratic in nature and delivery.

A speech by its very nature carries weight, elicits expectation and confers gravitas. Many books have been written that collate great speeches from down the years. I haven't seen one book that collects great PowerPoint presentations.

Speeches have a wide spectrum or range in which to operate. There are speeches for celebrating, for exhorting, for stiffening resistance and for explaining change. There are speeches that are warnings, calls to action, declarations of intent, strategic blueprints. And there are different genres: the eulogy, the convocation, the oration, the commemoration and the official welcome or goodbye.

In the business world, most set-piece speeches tend to be delivered at strategy or corporate away days, at internal milestone celebrations or external industry events. The less exciting may accompany the launch of a new product or service or explain a change in compensation or structure. But many business speeches are fundamental to recalibrating corporate actions, reassuring employees or selling the case for change.

A Speech-Writing Carousel

I spent four years as a strategist and speechwriter in Hong Kong, writing speeches for the Chairman and the Executive Director of the Trade Development Council, effectively the Trade Minister and Deputy Trade Minister of Hong Kong.

The key speech themes were about Hong Kong's role as China's services supermarket and gateway to international capital markets and financing, the need to ensure the continued competitiveness of Hong Kong, the green agenda and the need to protect 'the goose that lays the golden eggs'.

Most speeches were a fine balancing act, because the message needed to be about trade and economics and could not be overtly or ostensibly political. But the entire raison d'être for the communications campaign in 1996–1997 was to reassure investors, foreign businesses and governments about the sustainability of Hong Kong, primarily because China needed Hong Kong intact and functioning. This special status had been enshrined in the 'One Country, Two Systems' idea, something that looks increasingly precarious now.

DOI: 10.4324/9781003198994-11

The speeches I have written since then have covered a wide range of business sectors and leaders. If anything, these speeches have been more challenging to write because the Hong Kong speeches were articulating the case for 'no change', whereas the business speeches have almost always focused on the 'burning platform' and the need for change.

These speeches had to take into consideration behavioural aspects like trust, credibility and motivation, aspects that were not key features of the 1996–1997 political speeches.

Important business speeches usually feature most of the following themes:

- Explaining corporate strategic direction
- Identifying challenges that lie ahead
- Explaining the need for change
- Laying out the path forwards
- Identifying milestones on that journey

Core Elements of a Speech

There are four core structural elements that leaders need to make sure are present in the speeches they write for themselves and/or are written for them:

1   The classic storytelling structure and narrative arc
2   Emotional and intellectual engagement
3   Clarity of structure
4   Physical engagement and energy

Using the Classic Storytelling Structure and Narrative Arc

Good speeches follow the classic storytelling structure – beginning, middle and end.

In stories, the first part sets the scene, introduces the protagonist and the challenge, sketches out the qualities needed to reach a successful end and perhaps outlines an initial setback, key issue, doubting or daunting moment that needs to be overcome. By the end of the beginning, we are clear about the task ahead and the type of story we are going to hear.

The beginning is where the speechmaker or leader must strive to get the audience's attention and to engage them in the story. Using a story structure helps leaders do this because of our innate understanding of stories and familiarity with them – *we expect to be engaged precisely because we find stories easy to follow and they resonate so deeply.*

The middle is where all the action happens. For speeches that adopt a storyline structure, this is the place to develop your thesis, to surmount individual issues with specific ideas and then as the plot thickens, to deal with deepening complexities and scenarios as well. Good speeches lay out progress in story form and good communicators, as we saw earlier, make the audience the central part of the story – the protagonists and the heroes.

In both a speech and a presentation, as in a story, *the middle is where the heavy lifting resides.* But it can be made much more engaging by being told like a story, with scenes, setbacks, villains and heroes.

The end brings catharsis, resolution and denouement – everything is tied up and all the threads of the story are explained. This doesn't necessarily mean everything is sorted out – the end of the story may be a stark warning or call to action. *But the meaning is clear. As we saw in the overall communications framework, the key dynamic in all good endings is to impart meaning.*

Eliciting Emotional and Intellectual Engagement

Following the basic story structure indicates the primal importance of the beginning. It is crucial, when our expectations have been triggered by the storytelling, to use the opening to elicit emotional and intellectual engagement.

It is absolutely fundamental, while the audience is primed after the introduction of the story, to be absolutely clear about why the audience should care. What is the issue at stake or the challenge in play that we need to address together and why is change needed now?

You need to elicit this emotional and intellectual engagement in this crucial portion of the speech – it is the most important part of the speech and the biggest determinant of success or failure. If the issue or challenge is clear and compelling, you will get off to a good start.

Ensuring Clarity of Structure

Right behind in importance is the need for clarity. We have said that the story structure provides an innate clarity because it maps to something we all intuitively recognise and value. But the story format only gives you the exoskeleton of structure – you have to do more than simply follow this structure to ensure clarity.

In following the various twists and turns of your storyline, audiences need signposting, foreshadowing and signalling. And they need you to stay true to the story format by following the storytelling or narrative arc.

The narrative arc ensures that *the story is delivered in a linear development through time and space, so that charting progress and knowing where you are at any one time in the story is easy.*

If you deviate from this arc, or make it complicated with too many asides, off-piste sideshows and extraneous issues and characters, then the structure starts to crumble and the speech becomes confusing. Because the storytelling arc is hard-wired into our consciousness, any deviation from this anticipated direction of travel can be deeply disruptive for an audience. Upsetting our storytelling expectations by subverting the narrative structure or by not clearly signposting acts as a cognitive shock to the system and undermines the innate power of story structure to help speeches be powerful and clear.

Encouraging Physical Engagement and Energy

Finally, speeches are written communications, but *delivering a speech well requires performance skills and an overt effort to engage all our senses.* What an audience wants in a presenter: passion, authenticity and confidence are even more true of a speech-maker. In a presentation, there are other vehicles that help the presenter engage like slides, videos and whiteboards. A speech is entirely dependent on the interplay between the speaker's words and their whole body performance.

With a speech, it is just the speaker. And so, positive and inclusive body language, natural use of hands, congruence of movement, energy levels and quality, pace and tone of voice are all critical.

This overall projection of persona as the speech-giver commands the stage is every bit as important as the words being delivered.

But how can a leader be confident that the speech writer will ensure that the speech can be delivered in a way that will engage the audience?

Speeches need to be written in a way that makes it easy for the speech-maker to engage and indicates what he or she should do physically at key portions of his or her delivery. Here are some examples of how to do that:

- Phrases that cry out to be delivered with energy or empathy
- Short sentences that make it easy to alter pace and pause
- Paragraphs that bucket certain types of information together, so that performance can be focused in delivering the right feeling for each section
- em lines' that fire our imaginations
- Funny lines that can be delivered with humour or a smile
- Big ideas that allow the speaker to be inspirational
- Using 'we' or 'you' language which helps builds rapport and accessibility

Think of Mandela, Obama, Churchill – they all have their own definable style and all are very different. What they have in common as great speech-givers is their ability to use their whole body to deliver the speech, not just rely on the words. And so we are treated to Mandela's gentle wisdom and soothing cadences, Obama's soaring rhetoric and energy and Churchill's growling defiance.

Remember Maya Angelou's priceless observation: 'I've learned that people will forget what you said, people will forget what you did, but people will never forget how you made them feel'.[1]

All of the great orators know this: at the end of the day, no matter how good the words, it is the feeling that engages most.

What Leaders Need to Know about the Speech-Writing Process

The Briefing

It is imperative in preparing to write a speech that leaders give a proper briefing to the person who will write the speech. The briefing needs to come not from a chief of staff, head of research or corporate apparatchik, but from the actual deliverer of the speech. *Speeches are intensely personal and have to be crafted for the taste and style of the person delivering the speech but also for their character, values and beliefs.*

This is not something that can be done by proxy. That is not to say that ideas given by a host of people cannot be woven into the speech. In Hong Kong, over the handover, we had a special think tank convened amongst government departments to source and savour ideas, to do research and put together position papers testing various lines-to-take in speeches.

But nothing beats hearing from the leaders themselves. In my experience, the brief from the deliverer of the speech is crucial. They always have plenty of ideas to bring to the conversation. They have special insight into what they want to say, what is different this time or what they feel has to be said.

The briefing fundamentally provides a vehicle through which to develop that special relationship between leader and speechwriter that lies at the heart of a good speech. Writing a speech is an iterative process – it often proceeds in fits and starts with rewrites, pilots and the testing of certain language, only to go back to the drawing board with a fresh approach. And that's even before the final editing, sense checking and proofreading stages.

This iterative process of writing one speech extends to writing all speeches for the same senior executive. The briefing allows this particular speech to be located within the firmament of all the speeches that the leader has given that the speechwriter has written. This institutional knowledge of the process – what has worked and what hasn't and how the speeches were received – is invaluable in understanding the permutations and changes that are needed for the latest speech. This is why most leaders work only with a handful of core speech-writers and sometimes only one.

It is very analogous to the coaching process, where a coach and client work together to improve performance and deepen awareness. This process reveals wisdom and progress and helps build a shared understanding of how best to work together for results.

Nothing can take the place of a personal briefing. Do not let yourself be talked out of having this happen.

Storyboarding

Just like preparing a slide presentation, the use of a storyboard can be very helpful for leaders in agreeing the main scenes or points to be made in the speech. Building a speech around key scenes helps to keep it clear and prevents any one scene from being weighed down by too much detail or expectation.

In the many briefings I have taken, often the information the leader imparts comes to you in scenes. They will say that they want to talk about X, Y and Z themes and make these key points. A key part of crafting a speech is taking these themes and constructing a series of scenes that are linked together by the overarching story arc or narrative – the main thread or proposition of the speech. The speech-maker then can easily review this narrative and make changes efficiently.

The Criticality of the Beginning

Leaders need to create empathy and build a connection right from the start. Be clear about what is to follow, and in most cases give an executive summary or preview of your main points. Audiences are more forgiving of waiting to hear the key points as the speech unfolds than they are of waiting to hear the main points in a presentation; but the same dynamic of cutting to the chase, setting out your stall and being clear about the proposition that we saw earlier still holds true.

The engagement factor revolves more around being crystal clear about the emotional and intellectual engagement of the 'burning platform' that we've just talked about.

The beginning is where all of this is laid out in front of the audience. Like a presentation, this is when they make up their minds about you as a leader, when they decide to give you permission to continue and pledge to try and follow what you're going to say. Leaders should pay particular attention to making sure the speech has enough emotional clout at the beginning – this is where the connection with the audience is sealed.

That second presenter syndrome we discussed earlier is a factor in speeches as well. But it is more difficult for the audience to construct a second parallel narrative that they imbue with meaning because, unlike a presentation, they only have the leader's words to work with. In a presentation, they have all the visual and auditory content as well – there is more to work with to create this parallel presentation – but with a speech, this material simply doesn't exist.

What does tend to happen is that if the speech is poor, complex or not engaging, the audience gives up even faster and just drifts off.

The Art of Speech-Writing

The three key imperatives that drive a speech are:

1   **Congruence with the speaker** – Words, phrases and language that match the cadences, character and style of the speaker.
2   **Simplicity of execution** – Elegance, short and simple sentences that are absolutely clear.
3   **Lines that are meaningful and memorable** – This will allow the audience to retain key concepts, feelings and content.

First, it is imperative that the person who is writing for you, knows you: how you speak, your rhythms and mannerisms, when you pause and for how long.

Second, insist on keeping sentences short and simple as the best way to convey clarity of thought. Convoluted structures are difficult to get both tongue and brain around and end up undermining the overall performance. Leave caveats and codicils behind.

Third, it must be your intention as a leader to tell a big story and to leave audiences with a memorable line or meaningful thought. A few years ago, we worked with an insurance firm whose CEO was desperately trying to shift the firm from a product to customer focus. I wrote a keynote address for him to give to an insurance conference, where he initially poked fun at how boring insurance is and then repositioned it entirely in one passage. It had a startling effect on his audience and his company.

BOX 7.1 REIMAGINING INSURANCE

There is a view that insurance is actually the most boring product in the world. No one in their right mind looks forward to buying insurance. It is a commoditised product and is a perfect candidate for automated selling online.

The logical extension of this viewpoint is to automate the entire process, so that a customer's computer can simply order a renewal of the policy from a web engine and no human contact is needed at either end.

But here's an interesting equation. The typical insurance policy is indeed the least interesting and least valued product in the world, *until it is needed. Until it is activated. And then, it becomes perhaps the most valuable product in the world.*

There is a conundrum at work here. *It is only commoditised if it is never used. The moment it is used, it becomes hugely valuable and the personal interface or wrapper around the product is everything.*

One of the very sad aspects of the rush to embrace the technology channel and to rationalise everything else is that we have created a very siloed industry. We have effectively outsourced exactly those parts of the value chain that contribute a disproportionate part of the human value.

What Makes a Speech Memorable?

Plenty of things make a speech memorable: big ideas, boldness, freshness of vision, wry comments and biting humour. Newness, beautifully constructed phrases and of course emotion.

The best speeches cause us to think and feel. They challenge us to look inward as well as outward, answering the age-old question 'what then must we do'. They renew, refresh and reinvigorate.

Some of the accepted masterful speeches are particularly instructive.

Ted Kennedy's lyrical call-out of his brothers' vision, using beautiful words from Tennyson but then tying this to his ceding The Dream, but only temporarily – because the bigger causes all three espouse would live on. There is poignancy here – the realisation he will never be President, the ache of two tragedies still not healed and the possibility of a new promise, now not to be fulfilled.

There is the wonderful simplicity and defiance of Churchill's first speech after becoming prime minister and the quiet graciousness of Reagan's salute to the crew of the *Challenger*.

The best speeches have lines that are gems – incorporating wisdom, truth and insight. We recognise these lines when we hear them because they go beyond being emblematic – they speak to the human condition in all of us.

Think of George Floyd in May 2020. 'I can't breathe' sums up better the pain felt by so many than perhaps anything written over the last 400 years. Leaders should look for every opportunity to deliver these gems. They are what people remember and are moved by (Table 7.1).

Table 7.1 Excerpts from famous speeches

Reagan – 1986 Challenger explosion	Winston Churchill – 'Blood, toil, tears and sweat'
The crew of the Space Shuttle *Challenger* honoured us by the manner in which they gave their lives; we will never forget them, or the last time we saw them, this morning, as they prepared for their journey and waved goodbye and 'slipped the surly bonds of earth' to 'touch the face of God'.[a]	I have nothing to offer but blood, toil, tears and sweat. We have before us an ordeal of the most grievous kind. We have before us many, many long months of struggle and suffering. You ask, what is our policy? I can say: it is to wage war by sea, land and air, with all our might and with all the strength God can give us; to wage war against a monstrous tyranny, ever surpassed in the dark and lamentable catalogue of human crime. That is our policy. You ask, what is our aim? I can answer in one word. It is victory: victory at all costs, victory in spite of all terror, victory, however long and hard the road may be; for without victory there is no survival.[b]

Ted Kennedy – 1980 farewell

And someday, long after this convention, long after the signs come down and the crowds stop cheering, and the bands stop playing, may it be said of our campaign that we kept the faith. May it be said of our Party in 1980 that we found our faith again. And may it be said of us, both in dark passages and in bright days, in the words of Tennyson that my brothers quoted and loved, and that have special meaning for me now:

I am a part of all that I have metThough much is taken, much abidesThat which we are, we are – One equal temper of heroic heartsStrong in willTo strive, to seek, to find, and not to yield

For me, a few hours ago, this campaign came to an end. For all those whose cares have been our concern, the work goes on, the cause endures, the hope still lives and the dream shall never die[c]

[a]https://history.nasa.gov/reagan12886.html
[b]https://winstonchurchill.org/resources/speeches/1940-the-finest-hour/blood-toil-tears-and-sweat-2/
[c]https://www.emersonkent.com/speeches/address_to_the_dnc.htm

Panel Discussions

If the ROI is Good, Why do They Feel so Bad?

Panel discussions should be a leader's best communication friend. They are relatively easy to do, do not require a lot of preparation and give you a good amount of positive exposure and return on your investment.

So why, for many leaders, do panel discussions seem like the worst kind of public presentation? For many, it is because of a perceived lack of control on the panellist's part.

A presenter has almost complete control over the presentation (subject to timelines and logistics) and can directly influence the audience's reaction and response to the presentation. The common view is that a panellist can do neither of these things and is instead exposed to the vagaries of the moderator's questions and the ensuing audience question and answer.

For these people, the fear of the spotlight is far outweighed by this lack of control. This is hugely interesting because I think it speaks volumes about what people actually fear when presenting – it is never about the spotlight per se, but always about *appearing* to lose control.

The other key turn-off is that many people worry about saying something too provocative or opinionated in an unscripted moment that will get them into trouble with their firms, or conversely feel they have little to say and worry about feeling exposed as a fraud on stage.

To be fair, not many c-suite leaders will feel this way, but it is a real factor among senior managers and potential leaders in business.

It's not so much *imposter syndrome* – most people contemplating being on a panel discussion know they have the expertise to do it – rather, this is *ghost syndrome*, where what is causing anxiety is the idea that they either don't have a worthwhile opinion or they will have to constrain what they can publically say.

Perversely, this concern about content being either too fiery or too bland is not something people worry about presentations. There is something about the structure of a panel discussion – where it is not in your control – that is off-putting for many people.

The reality is almost the exact opposite. *It is far easier to ensure you feel 'in control' and your content 'correctly positioned' in a panel discussion than in a presentation.* The main reason for this is that there is safety in numbers. You simply won't have the time to feel really out of control or exposed and your opinion will be conveyed and digested within a discussion of multiple points of view. *This leavening of focus means the spotlight is shared and that should be liberating.*

But perhaps even more importantly, in a panel discussion, you have far more control and power than you might think. In everything from preparing content to attending the moderator's planning call, from identifying your comments and crafting your messages to delivering them in real time you have a significant amount of control. And there is far less work and risk involved than preparing and delivering a presentation.

Not All Panels are Created Equal

Panels vary widely in two main ways: number of panellists and style of panel. Most panel discussions barely qualify as panels. These are the ones that ask each guest to make opening remarks. Then there is a moderated discussion based on the collected comments. No cut and thrust. No controversy.

Then there are the panels where each panellist is asked to comment on the same question. This is a bit better as the top-heavy portion has been removed. But the dynamic is all wrong. Since each panellist gets the same question and all questions and comments go through the moderator, the panel is constructed to deliver conformity.

Best by far are the news-style panels, where the moderator invites panellists to jump into the conversation and not wait to be invited or instructed. These panels have the best chance of delivering the back and forth debate and comments that audiences want to see. You need to think on your feet and be skilled at sensing when to jump into the conversation.

These panels often include some preparation and 'scripting', so that what seems natural and off-the-cuff has sometimes been agreed beforehand. There is plenty of room for preparing and commenting in only those areas of the debate you have suggested you will take part in – and rehearsed beforehand.

The news-style panel, where the moderator encourages the free flow of debate and comments do not have to go through the moderator, has the best chance of delivering a lively conversation, which is what all panels should really aspire to. This is also the best format for enabling panellists to perform at their best and be perceived that way by the audience.

Preparation

You probably need somewhere between 45 and 60 minutes to prepare for the average panel discussion. The first thing to do is very practical and will keep you from wasting time preparing too much information. Find out how long the panel segment is meant to last and divide the number of minutes by the number of panellists. This will give you an idea of how much content you need. So a typical panel discussion lasting 40 minutes with four speakers will mean you need to prepare a maximum of 10 minutes' worth of material.

But it's actually not as much as that. Deduct time for the moderator to introduce the session and for time between questions and you're probably down to about 36 minutes – so about nine minutes to prepare. Each question and answer takes on average about one minute, if the moderator's questions are about 10–15 seconds long and your answers are about 45–50 seconds.

Using this math, you now have nine comments of about 45 seconds in length to construct. And in a news-style panel, it will likely be far less than this, as between a third and half the time will be spent nimbly reacting to other's comments, not simply delivering your own.

In a 40-minute panel with four guests, you might realistically expect to have to prepare five or six comments of about 45 seconds in length. Not anything like a presentation.

To do this, you need to have a few key points to make and some supporting proof points and statistics. But most of all, *you need a point of view* about the main topics that the panel will focus on. This requires not being afraid to take a view and have an opinion and then be prepared to present the information in a differentiated manner.

In terms of preparation, joining the moderator's call pre-panel is one of the smartest things you can do. Moderators share their questions, participants meet, trade views and work out who feels strongly about what and who will talk to what question.

The moderator's call often serves as a short 'rehearsal' for the actual panel discussion. Trying out your views and gaining assurance on the likely reaction they will provoke makes the actual panel discussion so much easier.

Key Dynamics

The key dynamics in a panel discussion are threefold: getting used to being in the spotlight, identifying a view or an opinion and delivering your messages.

Getting Used to Being in the Spotlight

Being in a panel discussion is nothing like delivering a keynote presentation where you are the sole focus of attention. Here the spotlight is shared between the other panellists and the moderator.

Although audiences focus mainly on whoever is speaking, quite a bit of the time is spent scanning the entire panel. There is far less focusing on the speaker in a panel discussion than there is in a presentation. In a panel discussion, the focus is more on the overall dynamic – who is reacting to whom.

However, while the actual spotlight is not glaring on you as an individual so much, you have to remember that you are always in the spotlight. You are always within the audience frame of reference or 'viewfinder'. The key takeaway is that although the spotlight is more diffuse, you are always on. You cannot afford to let your guard down and daydream.

In reality, most people forget about the spotlight within moments of the panel beginning. It is a little like the performance adrenaline athletes feel anticipating the start of the match, and then as soon as it starts they are engrossed in playing the game and forget their anticipatory worries.

Like any presentation, it is important that you feel comfortable and act naturally. *The best source of confidence is usually your own knowledge*; it is highly unlikely the audience will know more about the subject you are debating than you do.

Another source of confidence is knowing that you have some worthwhile points to make. Rich content delivered in a concise manner is a really effective antidote to the ghost syndrome discussed earlier. Having something to say will boost your sense of credibility and leave you far less likely to feel exposed.

Identifying a View or an Opinion

Working out your point of view should not be difficult. The key thing is to try and tell a big story, as we discussed earlier. Finding a trend in your industry and having a think about what that trend means for customers, clients, stakeholders and the general public is what is needed here.

As a leader, the idea is to push yourself about what's happening in your business, where that's leading and what it means in a wider context. And you should be able to do this without risking any comment too incendiary for your firm to handle. *Think of it like a dinner party, where you want to put an interesting view out to the table – that is the dynamic you are aiming for.*

An important point to make here is that you can allude to or identify a view or an opinion without owning it. That is, you can raise it as a subject worth exploring without being seen to endorse an explicit view.

This 'honest broker' role is one of four different roles you can adopt without necessarily committing to a point of view. In these roles, you are bringing focus to bear on an issue without taking up one side or another. This is perceived very positively by the audience as helping turbocharge the conversation rather than prevaricating and not taking a view.

The other three roles include devil's advocate, conscience-of-the-audience and the summariser.

The devil's advocate does just that. Brings up the counterpoint, focuses on the weakness of an argument or why something may not be the way a speaker has said. Done occasionally and diplomatically, this can encourage really lively conversation.

The conscience-of-the-audience is a role that some panellists feel very comfortable performing and can be a godsend for the audience. It requires you to put yourself in the shoes of someone in the audience listening to the panel discussion. What is the burning question that no one has asked or discussed that the audience wants answered or the audience wants to raise and have acknowledged? Being able to presuppose this question and then pose it to the panel is a real skill and is perceived as you adding value to the debate.

The summariser uses the same skill that you see in team meetings. *The person who pulls together the different threads of the conversation and summarises where the discussion has led to has inordinate influence in a meeting.* This is generally perceived in a positive light because summarising allows for meaning to be discerned, action taken and for the meeting to move on. Often, you can engineer this same dynamic in a panel discussion.

Identifying rich content and interesting views should be relatively easy on a panel discussion – there is no requirement to buttress your information with slides or other audiovisual aids. Engagement is important, but there is a limit to what you can do when you are seated and interacting with a number of other people.

Having a few strong points and delivering them in a concise manner is the key dynamic at work and for most leaders contemplating being part of panel – it should not be that difficult.

Delivering a Message

What is more challenging is that having settled on a few cogent points to make, you are able to deliver them in a concise manner. Here, our work with the Imaginary Dialogue earlier comes in useful. Delivering your comment in three portions and in under one minute is really advantageous in a panel discussion, where a premium is put on interaction and sharing viewpoints, not hogging the microphone.

In the structure for delivering a message with clarity and power (discussed in Chapter 4), it is the last summary statement focused on meaning that is the key. That is what the other panellists and the moderator will remember and play off. That is where the most important information should come from.

Psychology of Panel Discussions

There is basic psychology and body language involved in panel discussions. Where to sit, where to look and how to ensure you can interject to get the air time you need without appearing pushy.

Where to Sit

Generally, the 'power' position is thought to be the seat in the middle of the panel. It's almost akin to chairing a meeting where the person in the middle is seen as the pivot point for the conversation and through whom much of the discussion will flow. The middle seat has disadvantages, in that you need to constantly adjust how you are sitting so you can face one end of the panel or the other, depending on who is speaking. The middle position probably gets a bit more of the spotlight as well.

The other strong position is the seat next to the moderator. This position has a kind of 'friend-of-the-moderator' or 'trusted advisor' connotation, in that often the moderator will turn to this person at the beginning or at key moments to advance discussion or pick up a point or enliven things if they go a bit quiet.

The chair furthest from the moderator can seem a bit isolated and marginalised. However, people seating furthest from the moderator often have the easiest time keeping everyone else in their range of sight – they are only looking one way down the panel.

Where to Look

Where to look is often a question I get asked. The simplest answer is: at the person currently speaking. You must feel free to be as natural as possible, which includes looking at other panellists, the moderator and also out at the audience.

Optimal eye contact one-on-one is usually two to three seconds, but you can probably extend that a bit on a panel discussion because the effect is not as concentrated. When you're looking at a portion of the audience, everyone in that section will think you are looking at them. This allows you to look as if you are engaging without needing to look at any one person in particular.

Getting Your Share of Voice

Probably the most delicate aspect is ensuring you get time to speak without being perceived as pushy and cutting people off.

This is very akin to knowing when to make a comment in a dinner party conversation – you need to listen for the natural cadence in the speaker's sentence. Almost everyone has a tendency to slow down and lower their voice as their last sentence is coming to a close. They effectively signal that they are going to stop speaking and when you hear and see these physical clues, get ready to jump in. Do not hover like a vulture waiting to pounce, but you can signal to the moderator with either your eyes or a subtle hand gesture that you would like to speak next. Normally, moderators are only too eager to take you up on that to keep the conversation moving.

There is a finely calibrated 'window' that you need to wait out and it is probably about one or two seconds after the person finishes speaking. Less than that, and your intervention will look abrupt or rude by effectively clipping the end of the person's comment. Worse, this may be perceived as too eager to make a point, signalling a less than mature orientation. But wait too long, and the opportunity slips on by.

Whatever happens, do not let whole chunks of the conversation go by without participating. This is a sure-fire way to self-marginalise. You need to be seen to be playing an active part in the conversation. Likewise, do not dominate – it looks really bad to take every other speaking opportunity as the panel discussion unfolds.

The Payoff

Pound for pound, panel discussions deliver. They allow you to get strong exposure with minimal time investment. And the requirements are relatively straightforward.

BOX 7.2 PANEL TAKEAWAYS FOR LEADERS

Panel discussions should be a natural communications forum for most leaders. They give good exposure without taking up too much time, and are usually focused on topics that allow for and encourage leaders' views on important trends and challenges.

As events, they do not carry the same risk quotient as dealing with the media and they do not require the same time investment needed for delivering a keynote address.

Panels are a good format in which to show diversity credentials. Women and ethnic minorities simply do not get the representation that they should get and event organisers are constantly looking to put together diverse panels. Leaders should encourage these executives to take these opportunities.

Note

1 https://www.goalcast.com/2017/04/03/maya-angelou-quotes-to-inspire-your-life/

Chapter 8

Handling Group Dynamics

Overview

This chapter deals with the skills in play when taking groups of people from one initial state to another different end state. These are what I call process skills and ironically are seen most clearly in two activities leaders rarely do formally – moderating and facilitating – but are constantly doing informally in executive team meetings, during town halls, at board meetings, away days and strategic events.

Formal moderating and facilitating is usually outsourced to specialists or non-c-suite executives. But strong, effective moderating and facilitating probably involve more of the modern leadership skill set than any other type of communicating and form the core of what a leader relies on day-to-day to get things done.

A premium is placed on the small group dynamics, interpersonal psychology and process management skills that enable leaders to ensure a controlled but creative and productive flow from the beginning state to the end. Success only really happens if everyone in the group gains and feels that the process has worked.

The key specific skills are those of listening, questioning, brokering, balancing and managing time and personalities, and are seen in spades in meetings and strategic brainstorms where the prevailing dynamic revolves around leading a group of senior executives through a crowded agenda, usually against a tight deadline, to make decisions and achieve results.

Because moderating and facilitating involves a lot of collaborative leadership and empathetic communication, they are like proxy 'boot camps' for observing and incubating modern leadership skills. These are the collaborative, authentic *discernment* skills that are increasingly demanded of modern leaders and will be needed to navigate and explain the disruptive change expected over the next few years.

Moderating

Overview

A good moderator is something more than an umpire or referee – that is, they play a role beyond simply adjudicating and timekeeping. A good moderator is confident enough to take a back seat and *keep watch over process rather than content*. Confident enough to shepherd, not posture, for others to come to the fore and definitely comfortable in their own skin.

Events that are well moderated and run smoothly have a kind of natural flow to them. Things just seem to happen at the right time and in the right order. Nothing feels jarring or out of place. And no matter what happens, the overwhelming feeling is that the event is in good, sure hands and that it is being professionally moderated.

DOI: 10.4324/9781003198994-12

The skill sets of a moderator and facilitator mirror the kind of positioning a leader increasingly needs to be comfortable with, as leading and managing become more collegial and collaborative and less about command and control. Leaders will want to see moderating type skills in emerging executives just as employees increasingly want and expect this approach in their managers and leaders.

Good moderators tend to be relatively easy-going, but at the same time have high standards. They project a certain gravitas and are masters of *process, flow, agenda and pace* – all increasingly important attributes for leaders as they are preoccupied with driving strategy and change rather than being able to focus solely on exhibiting expertise and growing the business.

A good moderator is a purveyor of confidence – encouraging presenters to be the best they can be and giving organisers of the event confidence that it will be adjudged to have been a very good experience by attendees and worth every penny by sponsors.

A strong moderator can make up or stretch time and make it appear seamless, just like a good news presenter. He or she needs to be a diplomat, listening carefully to distraught speakers or stressed technical directors. They need to be adaptable, nimble, flexible and agile – for what can go wrong will inevitably go wrong.

Most of all, they must be unflappable. Never letting on that anything might be amiss and constantly vigilant about what is happening both editorially and technically at all times. *They are front-of-house, but their major performing role is to make everything look easy.*

All this sums up the kind of enabling-of-confidence that will be a critical component for emerging authentic leaders.

Setting the Right Tone and Positioning

The first job of a moderator is to set the overall tone of the event. Moderators play a key role in 'projecting' the 'values' of an event and its positioning as well as signalling desired behaviours for all participants.

The moderator can make up for a lack of positioning by the event organiser by properly 'locating' the event in the current zeitgeist – why the event is important and is being held now. Good moderators do this as a matter of course.

Signposting and Ensuring Clarity over Process

The second major job for the moderator is to ensure that everyone is clear about what is happening now and what is expected next. We have talked about the importance of signposting in virtual presenting – it is equally as important for an event. The confidence of stakeholders is directly related to their comfort about the overall professionalism, tone and positioning of the event, and this becomes even more important as the event unfolds.

Clear management of time and expectations is crucial. Being able to explain clearly and succinctly what has happened and what is now going to change and to make the necessary adjustments is one of the key functions performed by the moderator. The parallels to modern leadership are obvious.

Encouraging Desired Behaviours

Part of a moderator's job is to model unwritten and unspoken behavioural expectations. Here are the ones I use when I moderate. As a quick credo for caring and authentic leadership it's not bad.

BOX 8.1 MODERATOR-SPECIFIC BEHAVIOUR

- Calmness and gentleness in settling any conflict.
- Decisiveness when decisions are needed.
- Thinking on your feet.
- Resilience in moving on.
- Creativity and flexibility when looking for solutions or making changes.
- Ability to see the bigger picture and not worry about small mistakes.
- Adaptability to changing circumstances.
- Ability to suggest programme or agenda changes, particularly if the event is running late.

Managing Conflict

In moderating, there is plenty that can go wrong, although outright conflict is rare. *The fundamental skill of acknowledging the situation and 'giving face' to those who feel aggrieved without necessarily agreeing with them or taking sides is the key dynamic that will help defuse a situation and sort things out.* Listening and being willing to compromise goes a long way in sorting out difficulties that are almost always caused by time pressure, different expectations or a lack of clarity. Again parallels to leadership.

Time Management

The third key skill of a moderator is time management. Along with setting the right tone and ensuring clarity, keeping the event running to time is absolutely critical.

Time management has to work on two levels, if it is to work at all. First, keeping to time inside the individual programme segment is important. That means reminding speakers they need to keep to time and diplomatically moving a presenter off the stage who is out of time. My preferred modus operandi is to grant them five extra minutes and then to start walking up to the podium, where they get wound down in the gentlest way possible.

A word about cancelled question and answer sessions (Q&A) – losing too many of these sessions can really change the nature and tone of an event. Suddenly, it is a lot more directive and far less participatory. And less valuable. Again, pointers for leaders but also a metaphor for more inclusive and less directive leadership.

This brings us to the second level of time management at an event – overall timekeeping so that the entire session runs to time.

The ability to mix and match and be flexible with overruns in individual slots, knowing you can claw back the time in other slots is risky and perhaps the skill that requires the most experience as moderator. Some of the most likely places to regain time include:

- Panel discussions – ten minutes light and no one minds.
- Q&A after a panel – because they've already spoken, this can be cut short.
- Lunch breaks –audiences happily accept 45-minute breaks.
- Concluding remarks – speakers and attendees want the quick goodbye.

BOX 8.2 TIPS FOR KEEPING TO TIME

- Remind all speakers about time.
- Take less time for yourself.
- Start sessions on time.
- Tell people what time to come back, not the length of the break.
- Tell speakers you will approach the stage with five minutes to go.
- Use breaks to recalibrate timings.
- Advise speakers beforehand if you are cutting their time.
- Trim number of panellists and panel Q&A rather than time slots for individual speakers.
- Allot more time to more interesting speakers.
- Reduce the number of panels.

Telling the Moderator's Big Story – Reminding Us of the Shared Human Condition

The final aspect of moderating is important and directly analogous to strong and enlightened leadership. At the best events there can be a real power in the shared experience of coming together, especially if that experience is tied to important changes in the industry and if the moderator has succeeded in encouraging speakers to outperform. Here are two stories that might show you what I mean.

BOX 8.3 THE POWER OF SHARING

In December 2017, a large company hosted a major event hoping to foster collaboration between patient advocacy groups in North America and Europe. The specific goal was to encourage them to form a loose network to better share knowledge and experiences in trying to improve patients' lives.

There were some inspirational speakers and creative sessions where delegates learned from each other and committed to trying to share best practice more formally.

But the highlight was the guest presentation from Ole Kassow, founder of Cycling Without Age, a Copenhagen-based organisation that began in 2012 with the simple idea of wanting elderly people to once again feel the 'wind in their hair' and the sheer exhilaration of being taken for a ride in a rickshaw.

Ole was the keynote speaker on the power of sharing and his talk was moving. Cycling Without Age grew from one man and one rickshaw to 3,300 rickshaws in 2,200 locations in 50 countries. They have 33,000 cyclists who together have served up more 1.5 million rides.

Ole talked about the power of vision, of keeping things simple and of giving back to those who have given so much. A great end to a truly powerful shared experience that I was privileged to have moderated.

BOX 8.4 THE POWER OF COMMUNITY

No one knew it at the time, but the last event in Asia for the International Council of Shopping Centres (ICSC) happened in October 2019 in Singapore. Shortly after this, the American-based group which represents the interests of shopping centre developers and operators pulled back from Asia to concentrate on its home market. Shortly after that, Covid-19 put a quick end to face-to-face events anyway.

I had moderated a number of events for ICSC over the years across China and Southeast Asia and I was always struck at the power of community I saw amongst these fairly straightforward business people.

They believed in the enduring power of retail and the industry's ability to use the Internet to innovate and evolve. Far from being pessimistic about the state of the high street and outmoded malls, they came together to plot the future of shopping.

I was always impressed by the optimism on display and the fact that most people knew each other quite well and had a genuine fondness for each other, as they pursued their business visions in wildly different places.

It was this shared power of community that I saw in action that has remained my lasting memory of moderating at these events.

BOX 8.5 MODERATING TAKEAWAYS

The skills in play are very similar to the skills needed to be an enlightened, encouraging, facilitative leader. Setting direction and process, ensuring clarity, modelling desired tone and behaviour and leading by example are all classic hallmarks of leaders with above-average emotional intelligence.

Modern leadership includes having the strategic knowledge and ability to navigate complex change, but effective moderating indicates the kind of temperament and soft skill set that authentic leaders should aspire to and will need.

Being able to bring people with you, articulate a process and move a group of people from point A to point B are all pertinent skills shared by moderators and leaders.

Moderating and facilitating skills lie somewhere near the very core of what it means to be an authentic leader.

Facilitating

Facilitating – Keeping Watch over Process so that the Group can Develop Content and Direction

In its broadest sense, *facilitation is a collaborative partnership* where the facilitator is responsible for the process and the group for the content or the outcome. In this, the facilitator's job is very similar to a coach – not to dictate content, but to ensure that the process is positive, professional, inclusive and delivers a valuable outcome.

These are core skills for authentic modern leadership when much of the old command and control style of mobilising people is being replaced by collaboration.

Facilitation is used in a variety of business settings to enable people to:

- Make decisions
- Explore strategic choices
- Evaluate potential courses of action
- Brainstorm ideas
- Test propositions
- Develop consensus positions
- Resolve conflict

The key goal is for the group to arrive at a shared understanding of their goal, strategy or way forward. The sense of achievement is focused around *clarity of direction and purpose.*

A good facilitation should be a two-way, invigorating and respectful experience. It should leave both facilitator and participants proud of the work they have done together.

Facilitation is probably the area of communications where the greatest range of skills comes into play and the one most affected by inter-personal behaviours and the resultant psychological landscape that is created (Table 8.1).

Table 8.1 Facilitator's behavioural playbook

Do	Do Not
Be confident and self-assured	Talk more than listen
Be authentic, inclusive and empathetic	Decide for the group
Listen actively	Inject personal opinion
Ask clear questions	Cut off discussion
Project a sense of calm and control	Belittle contributions
Manage conflict effectively	Be too directive
Keep sessions to time	Judge or being perceived to judge
Encourage wide participation and shared discussion	Feel you have to answer all questions
Be attuned to the mood of the group	Teach more than encourage discussion
Understand when to move on	Use poor verbal tone or body language

Core Competencies Involved in Facilitating

Effective communication skills lie at the heart of great facilitation. These skills include being clear and concise, offering simple directions, asking relevant questions, recognising what's important and identifying patterns in people's comments. Above all, a facilitator has to excel at listening and gauging if people are absorbing information and progress is being made.

Broadly, competencies divide into four main groups of skills (Table 8.2).

Table 8.2 Four key facilitating competencies

Performance	Skills directly associated with your own performance as a facilitator – voice, body language, confidence and the persona you are projecting. *These are the skills that build trust and engagement and determine how you are perceived as a facilitator.*

Discourse	Skills of conversation, listening, questioning and connection. *These are the skills that enable you to listen to what is being said and foster a positive atmosphere of sharing, clarity and understanding.*
Cognition	Skills that allow you to discern what has been communicated quickly, accurately and with nuance and understanding. *These are the skills that enable you to deconstruct conversations, identify patterns to isolate key points and help ensure the outcomes are being realised.*
Small Group Dynamics	Skills that allow you to manage effectively small group relations, interactions and dynamics. *These are the skills that enable you to ensure that a productive working environment is maintained as well as progress towards desired outcomes.*

Performance Skills

One of the key performance skills that a facilitator must use constantly is 'scanning the room', taking the temperature of proceedings to gauge in real time how things are going. This is very similar to listening for the mood of the room that we discussed earlier in the chapter on engagement.

Because success revolves around ensuring a smooth ecosystem for whatever the group is trying to do, this *constant 'checking-in' about the mood of the room is important.* It happens privately, with the facilitator keeping a careful watch on telltale cues and developments. It also happens overtly, with the facilitator not being afraid to 'call-out' what he or she is sensing or feeling and seeking to test this with the wider group.

Overtly calling-out a lapse or sag in the atmosphere for less experienced facilitators can feel like a risky thing to do, because it will intensify the feeling of being in the spotlight, expose the facilitator and put front and centre what may be an awkward or emotional issue.

As long as you are reporting what you are observing, knowing why it has happened isn't necessary. *A facilitator is not responsible for divining why something has happened, but for recognising that something has changed and asking participants what they think has happened.*

A strong facilitator is in the business of observing and recognising change and then helping participants work through what to do – not to offer their own interpretation and then direct participants to change.

It takes courage to be the 'honest broker' calling out what has happened and mobilising participants to work out what to do. But this is how facilitators build trust in themselves and the process. It is also liberating, in that it frees you of the responsibility for understanding everything and allows you to concentrate on the process of how best to move forward.

There are some parallels to leadership here but also some big differences. Leaders need to be able to switch seamlessly between recognising change and asking for input, but then overtly moving to direct change.

Savvy leaders will often separate their facilitative function from their responsibility as leaders to set direction – deferring the need for the more directive elements of leadership until they have facilitated a consensus on a shared understanding of the need, direction and quantum of change.

Discourse Skills

Listening is the fundamental discourse skill needed to facilitate. Listening to what participants have to say, what they think is important and how much they have absorbed is absolutely critical.

We have already covered listening in the engagement part of the overall framework – the importance of active listening, listening for what is not being said and listening between the lines for different levels of meaning.

In the context of facilitating, active listening is extremely important and perhaps harder to do than in any other setting. Many facilitators are so concerned with time management and making sure the process stays on track that they only half-listen or get distracted easily.

Active listening means being in-the-moment and paying attention to what is actually being said. It means being attuned to the other person as a holistic being, watching their body language and signals, their tone of voice and their facial expressions. Active listening signals to the person speaking that they are valued and respected. *Only by listening unreservedly can we really understand what someone else is saying.*

So how can you listen more actively? There are two key ideas:

Give yourself permission to listen: It is critical that facilitators slow down, trust that the process is unfolding as it should and take the time to really listen. You may feel so concerned about managing the process that you don't feel you can allow yourself to listen to the participants. The exact opposite is actually the case – the more you listen, the easier it becomes to manage the process because people are more willing to follow your lead on process if they have been listened to.

Try not to judge: Try listening in a non-judgemental way, so that you can really hear what is being said.

Again both ideas are firmly rooted in the coaching ethos and in the idea of creating or 'holding the space' for the group to listen to what each other is saying – an absolutely central tenet in authentic leadership as well.

This willingness to suspend process in order to listen for discovered truth is a fundamental dynamic in facilitating. And there is a cyclical pattern to it; after the listening comes the questioning where you seek to:

- Probe for further detail
- Confirm understanding
- Expand the discussion
- Turn to a new topic
- Challenge assumptions
- Encourage deeper consideration
  - Then a new round of listening to the information that has been elicited from the questioning

This cycle of listening and clarifying and confirming questioning goes on until a framework of understanding and consensus has been created that allows the group to move to the next stage of discussions. It is important not to hurry this iterative, revelatory process along. *This listening/questioning cycle is the key microprocess at work within the overall facilitation process.*

There is a real lesson for leaders here. On the one hand, the rush to action can be a powerful sentiment, especially as the pace of change accelerates. On the other hand, insisting, in the face of growing pressure to take the time needed to understand and build consensus, is critical.

Cognition Skills

Two skills are fundamental to the ability to identify what is really important in what is being said.

The first cognition skill is the ability to process information and isolate critical points in order to determine what is truly important. This is a fundamental facilitation skill.

This involves listening to the flow of information coming from one or more people and then accurately discerning what is important. This is sometimes called 'thin-slicing'. Thin-slicing is a term used in psychology to describe the ability to find patterns in events based only on 'thin slices' or narrow windows of experience. 'Thin-slicing' refers to the act of making very quick inferences about the state, characteristics or details of an individual or situation with only minimal amounts of information.

Most seasoned facilitators split processing information into two steps. First, they record (on flipcharts and whiteboards) as accurately as possible what has been said. Or they repeat back information to participants, checking that what they have heard is what has been meant.

This check-against-delivery allows participants to see that you value their comments, which helps the facilitator consider the meaning of the information, look for patterns and isolate important points.

In the second step, facilitators look more closely at what is actually meant by the words. This is best done in collaboration with the participants, either by asking them to suggest what points are of most importance or by summarising what you think are the most important points and getting input and approval.

Either way, it is important to first capture the key information and then collaboratively to highlight what is most important (Table 8.3).

Dealing with Complexity

The second key skill of cognition – dealing with complexity – is needed frequently when facilitators are asked to help senior management teams navigate through a series of interlocking issues that each need evaluating and together can appear quite complicated and complex.

If an issue or concept is proving too complex, the best course of action is to *break it down into simpler chunks and tackle these in an order that makes sense.* Slowing down the pace of facilitation by recognising that an issue or series of issues is complex and inviting maximum participation are all good ideas in handling complexity (Table 8.4).

Disentangling what had appeared to be hopelessly complex is often a facilitator's greatest contribution to the process. *It is a useful metaphor: clearing debris or confusion and disentangling in order to crystallise what is important and germane. That is facilitation at its most valuable.* This will also be a key skill for authentic leaders in the coming decade.

Small Group Dynamic Skills

First and foremost, *facilitators need to be able to ensure they can create a productive and positive environment,* one in which the process is enjoyable, inclusive to all participants

Table 8.3 Tips for identifying key points

Tips for identifying key points	Ask participants to take notes on a flipchart or whiteboard – this frees you to focus on interacting and to consider the key points earlier
	Practice recognising key phrases, sound bites or emotive language – often the important points stand out for their power or the fact they are being repeated by multiple people
	Actively listen for meaning – this allows you to screen out unnecessary information and focus on what's important
	Ask for help – involving participants in identifying key points supports reflective learning and promotes a sense of collaboration

Table 8.4 Tips to break down complexity

Tips to break down complexity	Translate the issue into graphic or pictorial form – this can help understanding, especially for participants who are visual learners.
	Temporarily transform the learning environment – into a more reflective mode by having participants pair and share. Working in pairs, they can discuss the issue and report back to the wider group.
	Reframe the concept – take it out of the current setting and compare the concept to an everyday idea with similar characteristics. Reframing often helps participants think in a fresh way about a difficult concept.

Table 8.5 Typical rules of engagement

Typical rules of engagement	Respect all comments
	Respect all opinions and the dignity of individuals
	Allow and encourage participation from everyone
	Respect for the facilitator
	Respect for time constraints
	No physical aggression of any kind
	No raised or angry voices
	No foul, inappropriate or pejorative language
	No verbal threats, intimidating language or bullying
	Overall focus on completing the outcome journey

and aligned to delivering stated outcomes. Facilitators need to regularly check in with participants that this is being maintained as the session unfolds.

This requires some core 'process' skills, including intervening before conflict starts, interrupting in a positive and respectful manner, effectively moving the discussion on, summarising key points and checking that sufficient progress is being made and expectations for the process are being met.

Typical rules of engagement for maintaining a professional atmosphere tend to include the following (Table 8.5).

Often a facilitator will need to interrupt to get the process back on track, change the dynamic or nip dissention in the bud. You need to be wary of interrupting too quickly lest you are bringing your own judgements to bear.

If you need to interrupt, getting permission is the first step. Then recognise what has been most worthwhile in the discussion. And then change the dynamic by widening the discussion, bringing others in and/or moving on.

Moving the discussion on is a variation on interrupting politely. Here the key is to recognise the progress that has been made, but in the interests of time summarise key points and ask for permission to move on and refer outstanding issues to the 'parking lot'.

Most participants will perceive this reminder about time and reimposition of process as a positive development. One of the really valued attributes that is ascribed to a good facilitator and leader is fairness and that they have the group's best interests at heart. They want the facilitation to be a success and thus have as much invested in ensuring a good outcome as the participants. Often, participants are relieved that there is one person charged with the responsibility of ensuring time is used wisely and measurable progress is delivered. To use a sporting analogy, it's important to keep the scoreboard ticking over.

Summarising key information and distilling down to action points is something facilitators do frequently in managing group dynamics. Again, there's a three-step process for doing this effectively: listen for what is core, substantive and carries meaning. Then, summarise and ask for further input. And finally, get agreement that reflects the group understanding and move on.

Facilitation: A Profoundly Human Process

We started by observing that facilitation is probably the area of communication that puts the widest skill set into play. It includes all the engagement skills of presentations and pitches, the listening, questioning and summarising skills of coaching and the process and time management skills of moderating.

But to this is added managing small group dynamics and being judged on whether the final outcomes have been delivered. Often, there is a lot invested in the process being successful. Outcomes are business critical, involve senior executives and have important time and cost implications. As the saying goes, 'failure is not an option'.

Against this high stakes backdrop, the best facilitation sessions are profoundly human. They involve stretching comfort zones and delivering growth and learning experiences. They can help strengthen bonds, forge identities and clarify strategic direction.

For most of the facilitations I have led, there has been a palpable sense that we were engaged in important work. And for almost everyone, this feels life-affirming. The end of a successful facilitation can feel revelatory and cathartic, and often these sessions lay the groundwork for changes in culture between key individuals or within senior management teams. An example of a recent facilitation assignment I had will give you a flavour of what I mean.

BOX 8.6 REBUILDING TRUST IN A TIME OF CHANGE

We worked with a firm that was going through significant changes. They were dealing with a competitor undercutting them on price, managing a series of re-dundancies and trying to compete on quality rather than product and price. Their operating situation was made more difficult by the fact that the c-suite had become frustrated with their senior leadership team and there was a gap in trust between layers of management and between management and employees.

We started work with the c-suite on their communications skills and helping them engage with employees.

They agreed to a facilitation to improve the situation with the other executives. The facilitation was chunked into two sessions, with the first session focused on discovery and clarifying what had happened and why and what expectations were now in play. The unwritten goal was to begin laying the groundwork for restoring trust. The second session was a practical exploration of what needed to change, how they could begin to structure this process and a framework and timeline for delivery on this.

That first facilitation set in motion a change programme that saw both the c-suite and senior leaders unite to form an effective team and deliver more transparency during a difficult period of change for the firm.

All the key facilitation skills we have discussed were in play: listening, questioning, summarising and managing small group dynamics. Having professional facilitation helped bridge the initial distance by giving them a process to help guide their discussions.

BOX 8.7 FACILITATION TAKEAWAYS

Leaders will likely not do too much overt or formal facilitating. But they will use the facilitating skill set all the time.

The skills in play are closely aligned with the coaching and collaborative style appreciated in modern leaders. Listening for tone, managing the room, brokering consensual decisions from a wider group, aggregating comments up to meaning and effectively moving a group from point A to point B are all classic modern leadership skills, and easily observable in board meetings, strategic away days and longer change management programmes.

Team Meetings

A good team meeting should of course allow for discussion and debate. But they should principally be about decision-making. Short presentations made and evaluated with more complex agenda items delegated to working groups. So that when the issue comes back to the team meeting, it comes in summary form ready to be discussed and decided.

Team meetings are also regularly hijacked by provocateurs, showboats and blowhards. The leader in charge will be cognizant of the different players, but fully containing them can be a challenge. Sometimes, the leader is the biggest problem in this regard.

A strong leader should be adept at bringing the major skills of facilitation into the team meeting: scanning the room, moving the discussion along, summarising key information and managing small group dynamics. Apart from being efficient with debate and discussion, the key thing is to not have too many agenda items. I'm always amazed by the number of items executive team meetings regularly expect to cover.

Focusing on a handful of substantive agenda items is enough for any one meeting. If you go by the rule of thumb that a substantive issue may need 15–20 minutes to deal with, you only really have room for about three per hour.

Many team meetings last either 60 or 90 minutes and of course board meetings can last one or two days in length. But expecting to get through a number of substantive issues in a short amount of time is hugely unrealistic.

Likewise, I'm not sure about the efficacy of board meetings that go for two days. I got an interesting insight into board efficiencies and behaviour when I was Head of Corporate Communications for an asset management firm in the Noughties. This little story illustrates some noteworthy points.

BOX 8.8 CHAIRMAN OF THE BORED

I had been asked to present a half year strategic look-ahead to the board. My slot was on day two at the end of the day and part of the 'back office ghetto' section of the agenda – that is, HR, IT, Legal and Compliance and Communications. Day one was given over to the CEO and CFO, strategy, numbers, the revenue-producing portions of the business and market and operational risk.

The meeting ran for two full days. I was kept waiting in a hotel room until day four and then summoned to present. When I walked in, the room was in disarray, the men (no women on the board) looked exhausted, ties dishevelled and faces grim. My 40-minute slot was reduced to five minutes and all they wanted was to be told what reputational risks, if any, the firm was facing. To focus only on important issues where a decision was needed. What resulted was a short discussion that lasted five minutes.

I've never forgotten this for many reasons – the profligate time wastage, the exhaustion, the lack of diversity and the relegation of support functions, but most of all for the key dynamic of the senior executive team wanting to focus on risk, variance and the bottom line. When the chips were down, these leaders rightly wanted only to talk about the most important items and in double quick time.

Lessons abound there for meetings in general. One wonders when they would have finished if they had adopted this stance from minute one.

Getting to the Conversation

This experience reminds us of the importance of being able to cut to the chase, ditch the slides and engage in conversation about the things the c-suite really care about. This is why practising an 'elevator pitch', understanding the key questions in the Imaginary Dialogue and being able to focus on bottom-line information and meaning are crucial skills for senior executives to use in conversing with a CEO. Equally it is a skill that all leaders would do well to remember in board meetings themselves.

Most meetings would benefit hugely from dropping some of the preordained items, shortening the pro forma presenting and getting to the conversation as quickly as possible. This is what c-suite executives want and find valuable. It is also the reason meetings run too long. Because the conversation is precisely the part that is valued most, it cannot be cut out or lessened and has to be planned for and included. This, in addition to the presentation parts of the meeting, really lengthens timelines.

To give a meeting any chance of finishing on time, the only parts that can really be cut are the number of agenda items and the upfront presenting that accompanies each item.

The Power of the Prototype

Another important lesson came via a Head of Corporate Communications who was having difficulty presenting to her board. The story resonates with everyone I have shared it with and it illustrates the counter-intuitive power of the prototype.

BOX 8.9 THE POWER OF THE PROTOTYPE

The Head of Communications was working hard on crafting and fine-tuning her presentations to the Board, and this work never seemed to pay off. Even on a topic for which they had asked for further information – her efforts to research and come back with a well-balanced presentation that evaluated options and made a recommendation – did not go over well at all. Instead, they gave her a hard time, ripping into the presentation and making her feel as if she did not know the business or her communications craft and was not adding value.

Some of this might have been gender bias as her board was all-male, but she was genuinely mystified at the negative reaction, because her relations with each board member were reasonably good and previous injections of insight or communications advice had been received well.

After some coaching, she recognised that their reaction was almost in inverse proportion to the amount of effort she put into the presentation. She decided to go counter-intuitive and not do the work. Instead, she prepared a prototype presentation – laying out key points and options, but then deliberately getting to the conversation faster and taking on a more moderating rather than presenting role by asking questions. To her amazement, the difference was immediate. She was praised for preparing a stimulating presentation and leading the discussion, even though she had done far less work.

Keeping a presentation in prototype form does five positive things:

1   Helps you get to the conversation more quickly and then own or broker the discussion
2   Gives you some detachment from your ideas, so you are not so personally invested
3   Positions you as a conduit bringing ideas to the table
4   Repositions the presentation as a co-creation that they can help finalise
5   Diffuses the 'hunt for negatives' dynamic as together you assess risk, benefits and costs

For leaders, this volte face in dynamic allows you to move from assessing weakness and 'proving the presenter wrong' – unfortunately the dynamics of many presentations made at board level – to collaborating to 'solve the problem'. It also helpfully shifts the spotlight from the leaders and the presentation to the putative solution.

Navigating Personalities

Finally, leaders intent on running an efficient meeting will obviously be aware of the 'power dynamics' present and how best to navigate the personalities in the room.

The key goal is to make sure the discourse is strategic and productive and that 'troublemakers' have minimal opportunity to hijack proceedings. Limiting 'presentation time' is one good way to cut down on behaviour that is excessive, unfocused or unhelpful. It's lot less likely to happen if they aren't given much time in the spotlight.

Often, the easiest course of action is to not confront directly, but instead isolate, marginalise and sideline the behaviour by simply moving on. Focusing on the process not the person starves the incident of oxygen, but can be the fastest, most effective and most easily supported course of action.

Remember, it is the process that is the core driver and dynamic here. Navigating personalities is subordinate to the time-bound nature of moving from point A to point B and invoking the demands of the process (and group) is usually sufficient for leaders to keep difficult behaviour in check.

Chapter 9

Managing a Crisis

Overview

Most people intuitively understand what constitutes a crisis. Something that has the power to fundamentally change, disrupt or destroy certainty, reputation, wealth and life itself.

Crises can be natural or man-made and are usually thought of as being unexpected – random events that visit with visceral power and perhaps unknowable provenance.

But most 'crises' are actually planned events when leaders needing to implement a significant change plan for and engineer a trigger event that sets in motion a major event or crisis for the organisation. These planned crises differ from change management in their importance, longevity and scope. A planned crisis is an important but short-term rupture or reset – like the removal of a CEO, the announcement of a redundancy programme or a merger with another company.

Major change programmes usually unfold over months and years and involve changes to business models, competitive positioning and behaviours.

Crises can be the making or unmaking of a leader. During a crisis, leaders are subjected to the highest levels of scrutiny and tested often to the limit in very trying circumstances.

In a crisis, the two key imperatives for a leader are:

- To act with clarity, alacrity and decisiveness
- To mobilise and manage an executive team (executive committee [EXCOM]) to direct communications

For leaders, a crisis is predominantly an exercise of character and communications that focuses on delivering efficiency and effectiveness. A change programme is predominantly an exercise in values and vision that focuses on mobilisation, persuasion and leading.

Crises come in all shapes and sizes. The Table 9.1 captures some of the ones we have dealt with on behalf of clients over the past 15 years (Table 9.1).

Table 9.1 Different types of crises

Environmental breaches	Civil emergencies	Litigation	Financial restructuring
Activist campaigns	Terrorist threats	Regulatory	Management change
Public health	Workplace incidents	Competition and cartels	Data breaches
Product recalls	Clinical trial deaths	Operational	Fraud and criminal acts
Catastrophic events	Personal difficulties	Industrial disputes	Cyber security

DOI: 10.4324/9781003198994-13

Crisis versus Issue – What's the Difference

People often ask: what is the difference between an issue and a crisis? A cheeky answer might involve the old story of the frog slowly being burned alive in a saucepan. The issue is that he is in the saucepan – how did he get there and can he get out? The crisis arrives at the tipping point where he can either use his last bit of energy to jump free or boil to death.

Essentially a crisis is an issue in a hurry. There is a time element that is useful in separating an issue from a crisis. In handling an issue, time is a strategic consideration – you need to make progress and get on with it. In a crisis, time is of the essence – a strategic imperative – and delay means defeat.

A good way of explaining the timing element is with another popular 'warning' story of the farmer and his pond filling with lily pads. The farmer needs to keep the pond clear of lily pads to keep the pond's ecosystem thriving. The lily pads double in number every day. The farmer, being busy, says he'll wait until the lily pads have covered half his pond before he takes action; but that only gives him one day to save his pond. The issue is the fact his pond is being covered by lily pads. The crisis comes on the last day he can do anything about it.

Issues, by their very nature, are simmering, complex and move at variable speed as they play out. A crisis is much more time-bound and telescopes into a tight timeline that will run its course until resolution. It needs to be immediately dealt with.

Two Types of Crisis

The hallmark of the unexpected crisis is the suddenness with which they confront us. They demand our attention and require immediate response and mobilisation of effort to prevent serious consequences like loss of life, destruction of property and reputations, the eradication of a business or the fundamental undermining of the ability to compete and be self-sufficient.

The other kind of crisis is effectively the sharp end of an issue and represents the culmination of an issue evolving and accelerating until it reaches a crisis point. Often, these types of crises have been recognised and worked on all the way through the process, and the actual trigger event or 'crisis' is deliberately engineered by a senior management team or head office at a time and place of its choosing.

For both unforeseen crises and the planned variety, the point at which they are 'triggered' is the indisputable call to action. It is the 'trigger' event that causes the crisis handling process to start.

At this point, let's separate the two types of crises and look first at the unexpected crisis. We'll focus particularly on stage one where the differences with a planned crisis are the most profound.

The Anatomy of an Unexpected Crisis

Most unexpected crises unfold in three main stages.

The first stage is about responding and getting the situation under control. With an unexpected crisis, the primary dynamic in stage one is to understand or establish what has happened, acknowledge this with stakeholders and scope out or diagnose the crisis to determine the best response or course of action.

The second stage involves working the problem and stabilising the situation. This is where the 'heavy-lifting' is done and this stage is typified by action.

The third stage is often referred to as the return to normalcy or business as usual (BAU). This stage focuses on planning and communicating how and when the crisis will end and how that will be recognised and communicated.

The focus in the third stage shifts to a forward-looking orientation – making good for the future – where the underlying causes of the crisis are addressed and reparations made. Here, there is an important opportunity to overtly reset strategic direction, to commit to new values or to change the business model or key operating procedures (Figure 9.1).

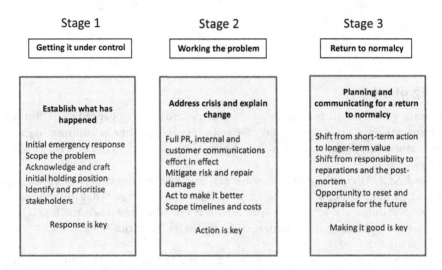

Stage 1	Stage 2	Stage 3
Getting it under control	**Working the problem**	**Return to normalcy**
Establish what has happened	**Address crisis and explain change**	**Planning and communicating for a return to normalcy**
Initial emergency response Scope the problem Acknowledge and craft initial holding position Identify and prioritise stakeholders	Full PR, internal and customer communications effort in effect Mitigate risk and repair damage Act to make it better Scope timelines and costs	Shift from short-term action to longer-term value Shift from responsibility to reparations and the post-mortem Opportunity to reset and reappraise for the future
Response is key	**Action is key**	**Making it good is key**

Figure 9.1 The three stages of an unexpected crisis.

Stage One – Understanding, Acknowledging and Communicating What Has Happened

Stage one focuses around the trigger event and overwhelmingly involves fast reaction to the crisis. Protocols are immediately invoked such as a business continuity plan (BCP) that may move equipment, employees and assets to an emergency and more secure site. The crisis team is mobilised. In most companies, this consists of the CEO, CFO and key heads of departments such as IT, Legal, Human Resources and Corporate Communications. Best practice suggests that this emergency EXCOM is kept to under eight people, as one of the primary dynamics in this first stage is the need for fast decision-making.

Job one in this first stage is to find out what exactly has happened, to analyse the available inputs accurately and to work at speed to decide an initial way forward.

Time spent upfront, working through basic questions, is never time wasted. Figure 9.2 shows some of the key questions that need to be answered as soon as possible.

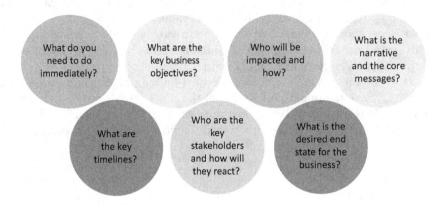

Figure 9.2 Time spent upfront is never wasted.

The Fog of War

The military term 'fog of war' is often used to describe the confused situation initially, where information is coming in from many sources, adrenaline is running high and the operating landscape is unclear. This initial confusion represents the first major challenge for leaders.

Can the EXCOM cut through the noise and analyse the situation fast enough to produce an initial diagnostic or 'reading' of what has happened and what immediately needs to happen to stabilise the situation? And how does this happen when the EXCOM is not privy to all the necessary information or is removed from the front lines of where the crisis is playing out.

The short answer to both questions is that reliable lines of communication must be established as soon as possible from the front lines to the EXCOM and particularly to the leader. The war analogy is useful. The EXCOM cannot direct operations if they don't get accurate information. In a crisis, it is the people at the coalface who are crucial in getting accurate information flowing.

The other key aspect at this point is not to wait until you have all the information you need. Colin Powell, the US general, used to say you need to take the decision once you have 40–70% of the available information – you will never have 100% because things always change.

In a crisis, you cannot afford to wait nearly that long. *You need to act as soon as possible and on the least amount of information you need to make a reasonable and accurate determination of what has happened.* You don't need to know what has caused the crisis or even what you will do about it in detail. But you cannot afford 'paralysis by analysis', which is one of the key failings we see in EXCOM teams when we game crisis scenarios with them. Too often, leaders, used to having all the information at their finger-tips, fail to adapt to the need to move at pace to get initial 'positioning' information out.

Developing and Communicating an Initial Holding Statement

The EXCOM usually work together to understand what has happened and prepare key messages based on what they know. This process continues throughout the crisis, but at the beginning you need to produce a holding statement designed to acknowledge what

Empathise and reassure	Be specific and decisive	Be open and transparent
Emotional statement Empathise with those affected Acknowledge what has happened without admitting liability Recognise impact on stakeholders Reassure stakeholders about the efficacy of your planned actions	**Outline your actions** What you are doing to fix the situation Actions need to be SMART (specific, measurable, action-focused, realistic and timely) The expected timeline and process for returning to normal	**Reaffirm commitment** What you believe is important How you will commit to safeguarding that. Show how you will strengthen processes and invite more dialogue on how they can be improved. Offer to make post-mortem findings public.

Figure 9.3 The basic messaging template.

has happened and reassure that the problem is being worked on. The goal is to buy time to better understand what has happened, what the risks, costs and impact may be and to whom and to formulate a plan for action.

The other key consideration at this point is to identify, prioritise and communicate with key stakeholders, using the holding statement initially and more detailed messaging later as the situation becomes clearer and progress is made.

The holding statement in written form is usually very short and designed to be delivered proactively or reactively, depending on the overall media strategy. In verbal form, the holding statement is delivered via the messaging template in (Figure 9.3).

Media Strategy

Broadly speaking, in an unexpected crisis, it is wise to go proactive and not wait for media and other stakeholders to hunt you down for a comment. You need to be seen to be reacting to a crisis, and going proactive puts you on the front foot from the beginning and sends a message that you care, are engaged and actively working the problem on behalf of stakeholders.

A good example of this is Richard Branson helicoptering to the site of a Virgin train derailment. He got there after first responders, but well before media and certainly before any officials. This kind of gesture creates the right 'optics' whether or not it is heartfelt and genuine. Rudy Giuliani got good marks for reacting quickly to 9/11, George Bush not so good for waiting 14 days to go to New Orleans after Hurricane Katrina.

The Anatomy of a Planned Crisis

A planned crisis also has a three-stage shape.

Planning/Stage One: The planning that happens is so closely linked with the delivery of the trigger event stage one that they really should be examined together. Here, activity

Stage 1	Stage 2	Stage 3
Rationale	**Embedding change**	**Return to normalcy**

Prepare a credible story of change	Move swiftly to implement change	Planning and communicating for a return to normalcy
Ensuring credible rationale and clear positioning and messaging Cascade info to employees Acknowledge and craft initial holding position Identify and prioritise stakeholders Preparation is key	Focus on winning hearts and minds of employees/customers Explain ramifications of change Signal change through new behaviours Communicate timelines and key milestones Decisiveness is key	Shift from short-term action to longer-term value Shift from responsibility to reparations and the post-mortem Opportunity to reset and reappraise for the future Making it good is key

Figure 9.4 The three stages of an expected crisis.

is first characterised by intense planning, including working out the rationale for the change, the new positioning for the organisation, the narrative to explain the change and the key messaging. Then the trigger event signals the start of stage one where the dynamic is all about ensuring a smooth delivery of key messaging to stakeholders and gaining initial understanding and support for the change that has been triggered.

Stage two focuses mainly on embedding the changes and moving to implement new positioning and procedures.

Like unexpected crises, stage three revolves around a return to normalcy, convincing stakeholders that the changes have been embedded and the transition has been smooth, and then monitoring employee and customer acceptance of the changes (Figure 9.4).

Planning/Stage One – Initial Communication Imperatives

In a planned crisis – before the trigger event – the rationale, positioning, narrative and key messaging are all worked out first. What is going to happen will have been studied in detail with different scenarios gamed. Once the business ramifications have been clarified the communications planning starts. Figure 9.5 outlines preparations during this stage.

Once the messaging 'bible' is complete, the pathway immediately before and after the trigger event, often described as D-Day, is clear (Figure 9.6).

In the planned crisis communications process, there is usually plenty of time in which to work out strategic positioning and messaging and identify and prioritise stakeholders. We have worked with clients where this has taken one to two months. But we have also worked where the whole process was telescoped into less than two weeks because an issue had suddenly morphed into a crisis with an imperative to act quickly.

Stage one ends in both types of crises when the trigger event has happened and initial efforts to communicate and work the crisis or explain the changes to be made are well underway. At this point – moving into stage two – activity in the two types of crises becomes more similar. We'll take a look at the commonality of what happens in stages two

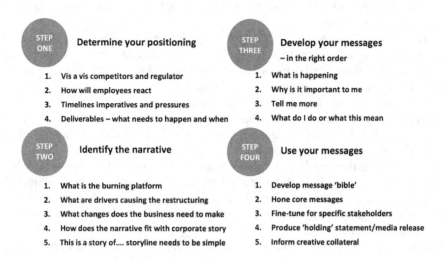

Figure 9.5 Preparations during stage one.

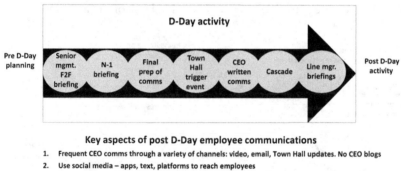

Key aspects of post D-Day employee communications

1. Frequent CEO comms through a variety of channels: video, email, Town Hall updates. No CEO blogs
2. Use social media – apps, text, platforms to reach employees
3. Monitor firm and private social media platforms for reaction
4. Identify and influence the 'influencers'
5. Be clear with and trust your employees but be controlled around releasing information
6. Expect what's said internally to go external within 10 minutes

Figure 9.6 Prepare all communications from the same messaging bible.

and three, but first a word on the criticality of understanding the stakeholder landscape in the first stage.

The Importance of Identifying and Prioritising Stakeholders

There is a best practice template that guides stakeholder communications in all crises: *you have to move from the inside out.* That is, your first and primary stakeholder must always be your employees. They should not hear from the media or clients about an important change that affects them.

Employees are the linchpins of effective corporate communications in general and crisis communications specifically. If employees understand what has happened and need to happen to return the business to a stable positioning, your chances of navigating smoothly through the crisis are immeasurably enhanced.

Employees are your best brand ambassadors and can 'sell' a necessary course of action to other stakeholder groups. If they're not on board or kept in the dark, they can fatally undermine progress, be prime fodder for enterprising media and act directly via social media to brief against the organisation.

The only caveat to this inside first approach is that if the regulator or government needs to know about the crisis, then this needs to happen first – quietly, in a behind-closed-doors verbal briefing – before employees are told. The last thing that any firm wants is for the regulator or government to hear about a material crisis on the grapevine or via an employee tweet or phone call.

Next in priority has to be customers and clients. A key goal in managing almost any kind of crisis is to be able to return to BAU status as soon as possible. Communicating early and often with customers and clients is imperative. The rule of thumb here is that size matters.

Communicate with your key large accounts first and always verbally, the second tier by email initially and then follow up with a call and third tier customers can be emailed or written to. Segmenting by size and importance is a quick way to begin identifying and prioritising customer stakeholders.

Figure 9.7 shows some of the key stakeholder considerations in a planned restructuring.

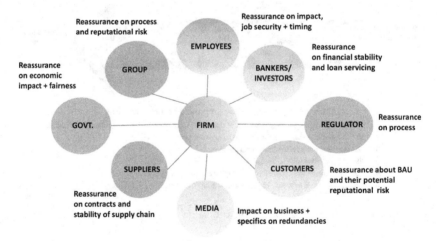

In a restructuring scenario – all these audiences are important – with employees, customers and the regulator being first tier

Figure 9.7 Stakeholder mapping – who needs what when.

Some stakeholder groups tend to get forgotten or underplayed and others may be overestimated. *When we work with clients in crisis scenarios and simulations, we find that employees are routinely underestimated and inadvertently moved down the priority list.*

Other groups that tend to be underestimated include suppliers and people with a direct financial stake in the firm such as financiers, investors and banks. Shareholders tend not to get forgotten. EXCOMS are good at rightly prioritising communications with the regulator, governments and head office or Group plc level.

The ability to correctly identify and prioritise who needs to know what and when is one of the most important responsibilities of the crisis leader.

Media as a Stakeholder

Almost everyone overestimates the importance of media as stakeholder. In a planned crisis, using a reactive stance can often be preferable if you don't want to be drawn into a protracted discussion in public with the media and prefer initially to prioritise proactive communications with other stakeholders.

Even in an unexpected 'live' crisis, once you get a holding position out, it is usually far better to work the problem and come back to the media with more concrete facts and progress than to spend a lot of time engaging initially with them. It is worth putting up with initial aggravation from the media in order to move to a more factual basis as quickly as you can.

For the most part, a measured stance with the media works well. Adopting a reactive-only strategy can at first appear very risky and courting of controversy. But if you put out a strong initial statement or comment and update on your terms, even in an evolving 'live' crisis situation, as long as you are seen to be trying to solve the problem, most traditional media will play ball and not invest too much time and money in trying to circumvent the process to get deeper or additional information.

In an unexpected crisis, you do have to regularly update the media, and this should be a specialist-delegated position or the CEO if reputation is at stake. For planned crises, the media strategy can be more nuanced, less 'cooperative' and less frequent.

Social media is a different ball game. Today, monitoring the full range of social media is part of being strategically prepared. Social media is a key stakeholder during both types of crisis and may be more time-consuming than and at least as difficult to manage as traditional media.

In an unexpected crisis, monitoring and responding in a timely fashion to social media is a key part of running an effective EXCOM operation – and it should not be the CEO who responds. In a planned crisis, again there is less immediate need to respond, although monitoring how the change is being received by various stakeholder groups and moving quickly if an issue arises within the crisis process that needs to be addressed is best practice.

Stage Two – Working the Problem/Embedding Change

Stage two in both types of crises kicks in when efforts redouble to work the problem or embed the change. Actions focus predominantly around putting in place new systems and processes that will help pave the way for stage three and an eventual return to normalcy.

The key deliverables needed in stage two are resilience and flexibility. This is the tough slog stage and physical endurance is often a key consideration.

In stage two, the focus is less on creating messaging and engaging stakeholders and more on monitoring progress and embedding change. On the internal front, it is important to ensure that employees are coping with the crisis or understanding the change that was set in motion.

The middle of a crisis can see employee energy, motivation and morale flag as the familiar patterns recede, the road to recovery still looks long and certainty has been replaced with uncertainty and challenge.

On the external front, the issue is much the same. Do stakeholders understand that you are making progress in handling the crisis, righting the situation and returning to a more stable operating stance? Or in the case of desired change, is this change being embedded and implemented in a way that benefits them?

In some ways, it is this middle stage that is the most challenging, because the adrenaline and focus of stage one has gone but the resolution of stage three has yet to come into view. Fatigue is a real factor and 'staying the course' not often a popular message.

Stage Three – Return to Normalcy

Stage three communications are a balancing act between two very different types of messaging. On the one hand, communications need to be very straightforward and rational. Focused on clear and concise messaging about **when** and **how** things will get back to normal. This is typified by directive messaging that clearly explains new processes, procedures, timelines and policies. Communications should aim to project confidence and competence and a firm sense, not only that the crisis is ending but that what is in place now is an improvement.

On the other hand, stage three communications must also not be tone deaf to what has just transpired. Messaging must acknowledge pain, disruption and loss and make room for the organisation's story of itself and how it has journeyed through the crisis. Communications must be forward-looking, signalling a willingness to reflect and offering a more emotive vision or promise to do better for employees, customers and the wider business ecosystem. This is where authentic leaders can make a big difference in being willing to tackle these imperatives head-on.

There are two common mistakes made in stage three by communications and business leaders. The first is to declare victory too early, to accelerate to a 'BAU' stance before it is warranted, sustainable or credible.

The other big mistake is to assume that it's 'BAU' emotionally for employees, customers and other stakeholders. The aftermath of a crisis needs to be very finely judged. Some people will want to move on fast and forget, while others will still be grieving, for tangible loss of life, material and wealth or for surety, identity and certainty.

Stage three requires real sensitivity to get this communications balance right and to clearly signpost activity, goals and objectives on both sides of the rational/emotional divide.

Key Overall Success Factors

There are a handful of clear critical success factors in handling a crisis. Most are operational in nature, but the most fundamental are a cluster of character traits – typical of the authentic leader – that absolutely have to be present or the effort to manage the crisis successfully will be undermined.

Leaders need to take responsibility and be accountable. This is different from admitting legal liability and a much bigger concept than parsing where legal fault sits. Authentic crisis leaders hold themselves and their organisations accountable. They take full responsibility for what has happened because it 'happened on their watch'.

Nothing undermines smooth operational efforts more than a leader uttering weasel words and shirking a sense of moral ownership. Honesty and transparency are absolute moral requirements. Again, this does not mean that CEOs must speak in a profligate fashion or offer too much information too soon. You must be prudent, measured and consider the timing of remarks. But it does mean committing to tell the truth and making information available as soon as is reasonably practicable.

For an event that has been planned, the same character issues are in play. You will be privy to information that you don't want to or cannot divulge immediately and there are often legal covenants governing what can be said to whom and when, especially if there are redundancies involved. Due process has to be followed.

But honesty and transparency about what is happening are core character traits that pay dividends in winning hearts and minds and ensuring that employees and customers feel reassured about the direction of travel. The vast majority of employees recognise they cannot be privy to the details, but a commitment to communicate with them frequently and honestly goes a long way in bolstering belief, loyalty and support.

This dynamic is exactly the same in the unexpected crisis, where customers, suppliers, shareholders and the general public will let you 'work the problem', if they are first satisfied they can trust you to tell the truth and do the right thing.

People tend to be reasonable and fair, even more so in a crisis. But this initial positioning on character has to first be in place, or that window of trust closes very quickly and seldom reopens as the crisis plays itself out. If these values are not present, what happens far more frequently is that senior leadership is removed or changes quickly after the crisis.

So what are the operational critical success factors? Ten stand out.

BOX 9.1 CRITICAL SUCCESS FACTORS – TAKEAWAYS ON MANAGING A CRISIS

1 Act as soon as you can
2 Be decisive
3 Have a clear overall process and chain of command
4 Use as few spokespeople as possible
5 Insist on a clear and believable narrative
6 Be proactive in communicating with stakeholders – this is what you will be most judged on
7 Communicate face-to-face or by telephone with government and regulators
8 Acknowledge the power of social media – stay on top of 'viral' comment
9 Be mindful of tone – humility and professionalism goes a long way
10 Stonewalling does not work – get out ahead of a problem, never cover it up

---

What Typically Goes Wrong

Crises are by their very nature amorphous, shifting, protean events. Circumstances are constantly changing and the best organisations stay agile, adaptive and flexible.

Too many firms stick with flawed plans for far too long because it's the only plan they have. They are too slow-moving, too indecisive and too hampered by institutional constraint to perceive what is working and why and make requisite changes.

What goes wrong most frequently is:

- Having an unclear or disjointed plan
- Allowing problems to escalate quickly, rendering initial efforts ineffective or inadequate
- Employees or customers actively briefing against you
- Multiple spokespeople delivering mixed messaging

In addition, we see three overriding areas of risk that need specific monitoring attention. These are:

1   **Disruption to distribution or supply chains** resulting in a broken business pipeline and/or loss of revenue that must be repaired or your competitive positioning is threatened.
2   **Regulatory and legal pressure** that must be addressed in a timely and specific manner and at senior level or your 'licence to operate' is threatened.
3   **Reputational damage** from one or more employees, customers and media where your 'trusted credentials' are threatened.

Any one of these threats is strong enough to pose a mortal challenge to the organisation.

Addressing possible discontinuity of distribution or supply chains should be the prime focus of all BCPs and crisis protocols and should be the most important focus of initial messaging after the empathy and safety message. Implementing a system that allows you to constantly monitor this primary function of the business is critical.

Keeping regulators on board and getting on top of all legal requirements is a fiduciary requirement and should be an immediate priority for the CEO and Chief Legal Counsel. Being seen to be working closely with the regulator or government in a crisis helps with messaging and positioning; but these relationships need constant attention and must not be taken for granted.

Finally, monitoring the health of internal and external reputation and tracking changes in how key stakeholders perceive your handling of the crisis is critical.

The risks may be slightly more muted and less visceral in dealing with a planned crisis, but they are all present in one form or another.

Preparing and Practising for a Crisis – Simulations and Scenarios

The very nature of a crisis means that it cannot be simulated or gamed in a completely accurate manner. But practice helps enormously. Many firms regularly work to simulate realistic scenarios or likely eventualities with the goals of testing existing protocols and teams, identifying weaknesses in their response and allowing EXCOMs to practice. They are intense experiences that have real value in helping companies be ready. Simulating crises is by its very nature a time-bound and limited exercise providing a kind of snapshot of what it might feel like to have to manage the initial hour or two of a rapidly unfolding crisis.

There is no equivalent exercise for managing change. Nothing can prepare you for the vagaries, reversals of fortune and the emotional and behavioural issues that always accompany any organisational effort to change. But understanding the key aspects of what needs to happen and what to be aware of will help. This is what we'll turn to now.

Chapter 10

Navigating Change

Understanding the Change Process in Business

Successfully navigating change is the number one issue CEOs are facing. In coaching sessions with leaders, there is broad agreement that coping with constant change is top of the priority list, followed by identifying where growth will come from, identifying, recruiting and retaining the talent that the business will need in five years and dealing with what they call 'the regulatory burden' – the huge expansion of regulation in many industries in the aftermath of the global financial crisis.

Change is moving so fast and in such a fundamentally disruptive way that the idea of three- to five-year strategic plans – that used to be commonplace – now seems unrealistic and quaint. There is a need to move from proactive, strategic planning to a 'fast reactive' stance, where scenario plans and ramped-up agility and flexibility allow for quick adaptation to fast-changing circumstances rather than trying to game the system and predict ahead of time how things will change. This is a huge departure from how almost all businesses were run even a decade ago.

The pace and quantum of change is eliciting fundamental questions about the impact on business models and core assumptions. Questions are about owning or offshoring production, proprietary IP versus open architecture, the relative security of supply chains, outright ownership or licensing, franchising and partnership to grow and how to build first-mover advantage in a fluid environment.

Change is daunting for business. On an existential level, there is real fear about making an extinction-level decision and getting it wrong fundamentally. Statistics show that of the 12 original members of the Dow Jones Industrial Average created in 1896, only General Electric still remains in its current form,[1] and from 1999 to 2015, 51 of the FTSE 100 have left the blue chip index, victims of mergers, breakups or collapses.[2]

Just think for a moment about Kodak-Eastman, one of the largest firms in the world when I was growing up and now utterly defunct having failed to adapt to the era of digital cameras and smart phones.

Extinction level change can be externally delivered, usually in the form of disruptive innovation and technical improvements that quickly render products and services redundant. But it can also be self-inflicted through rampant merger and acquisition (M&A) activity. M&A can of course be a fast and cost-effective way of scaling a business, broadening portfolio lines or entering new markets and neutralising competitors. But it can be lethal in destroying value if the strategic vision is unclear, valuations and pricing off or if the cultures of the two firms are fundamentally irreconcilable. Peter Drucker is said to have famously opined that 'culture eats strategy for breakfast' in warning about the need to get culture right before setting strategy.

DOI: 10.4324/9781003198994-14

As well as externally driven change via market forces or disruptive innovation and the self-inflicted change of ill-judged acquisitions, there is also the corroding effect of constant organisational change. These are the 'business unit realignments', the 'pivots to an outward-facing orientation', the attempts 'to deliver a unified "One Firm" to the customer' that regularly get trotted out by leaders and senior management teams, usually after a change at or near the top.

The equivalent in the television industry was the 100% predictable set makeover always demanded by a new boss so he or she could instantly signal their arrival and influence – before they were all too quickly yesterday's news.

When I worked in banking in the early 2000s, one of the most influential research papers I ever saw was one that showed that *almost all well-meaning internal business re-organisation programmes destroy rather than enhance value*. It showed that the rewards from the 'reorg' were almost always overshadowed by a resultant decline in productivity, morale and institutional memory. By the time this had been brought close to original levels again, it was time for another change. Some long-term colleagues had been through a major 'reorg' every few years.

I hope this opening scene-setter does not sound too negative or cynical. Many change programmes are hugely necessary and valuable. And the idea of constant improvement with its genesis in the Japanese idea of 'kaizen' is hard to argue with. But far too many change programmes are ill-conceived, poorly communicated and undertaken for vanity rather than business reasons.

Change is difficult and understanding the key phases and important communication imperatives is a critically important part of delivering a successful change programme. Doing change in a genuine, authentic manner that clearly recognises the rational and emotional needs and likely responses of employees and customers and makes an effort to let them be the 'heroes of their own story' is the only way of making sure that you are not destroying value.

In the end, for all the return on investment and share price projections, the consultant models and the financial targets and spreadsheets – change is a people business. Getting it right from a communications point of view is a matter of listening, leading and learning. All of which is a long way removed from the average 'get-change-done' playbook.

Crisis versus Change Management Programmes

The biggest difference between crisis management and change management are the overall goals, the key dynamic involved and the most important stakeholder.

In a crisis, the overall goal is returning at speed to a business-as-usual stance and familiar operating landscape. Good crisis management should capitalise on the opportunity to create a new and improved working state after the crisis is resolved. But this is not the main goal.

In a change programme, the goal is completely different – to deliberately change the business-as-usual operating mode and move to a fundamentally new way of operating.

The dynamics involved in each are also diametrically opposed. *In crisis management, the core dynamic is the need to demonstrate competence* – to get on top of a crisis and handle it effectively and efficiently.

The core dynamic in a change programme is persuasion and behavioural change. Change agents within the organisation are trying to win the hearts and minds of employees, seeking an initial shift in employee perception that then needs to be converted into tangible action and real behavioural change.

The key stakeholders in a crisis are the customers, shareholders or both – the generators of revenue and the providers of investment. At its most extreme, a crisis is an existential affair – it is about survival – and cuts straight to the heart of an organisation's ability to continue to exist. *And interestingly, for all the emotion surrounding crises, the process is predominantly rational.*

In a change programme, the key stakeholder is the employee, the means of production. Here, it is not immediately an existential issue about survival, but an actualisation issue about optimising the ability to compete. *And for all the rational procedures that typically dominate a change programme, it is predominantly an emotional process.*

These differences mean that change programmes are infinitely more difficult to execute to a successful conclusion than managing a crisis. Because there is a major behavioural component involved, they are more complex and often play out in a series of waves of change, where early adopters may be months ahead of other employees and everyone is at a different stage emotionally in their acceptance and support for change.

Change is a far more nuanced landscape in which to direct communications or to lead an organisation. As difficult as leading through a crisis can be, what needs to be done is relatively clear-cut. Leading through change is more amorphous, with fewer natural milestones and signposts, and is always subject to major reversals or slippage where the overall change process slows, plateaus, stalls or even reverses itself for a while before moving on again.

Think about the difference between Churchill's task in 1940 and Margaret Thatcher's task in 1979. Churchill faced an *existential crisis* that no matter how dire and difficult, the leadership imperative and message was clear. In 1979, after decades of decline and institutional defeatism, Thatcher faced a far more complex *actualisation challenge* – mobilising the British people to be persuaded that change was needed and to buy-into the behavioural changes implicit and explicit in having more individual responsibility and less reliance on the State.

These differences in goals, dynamics, stakeholders and complexity help explain why the track record of most change programmes is poor. Very often, they get part way towards their end goals only to dissipate in lethargy, difficulty, fatigue or yet more change ladled on top of the original programme.

Securing the internal buy-in and support from employees, moving clearly through the different stages of accepting change and delivering a real difference in actions and behaviours is a tall order and takes time. It also helps if leaders have a good understanding of what they are up against and what will be required of them.

Change Theory Models

Since navigating change is the most fundamental aspect of business, there is no shortage of change models out there that posit a theoretical framework through which to conduct and move through the different stages of change. The one we find most useful is Dr. John Kotter's change model,[3] because it has been developed and refined as the distillation of real conversations with leaders spanning four decades.

Kotter's model is also strong because it intuitively feels right, puts the heavy-lifting where it belongs at the beginning and avoids all of the esoteric mumbo jumbo of some of more complicated models (Figure 10.1).

Kotter identifies eight stages – the first four of which describe actions that happen before D-Day – before the change is communicated to all employees.

Stage one: create a sense of urgency – Laying the groundwork. CEO and executive management team begin to build the case for change amongst senior management.

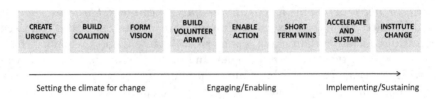

1. Create a sense of urgency
2. Build a guiding coalition
3. Form a strategic vision and initiatives
4. Enlist a volunteer army
5. Enable action by removing barriers
6. Generate short-term wins
7. Sustain acceleration
8. Institute change

| CREATE URGENCY | BUILD COALITION | FORM VISION | BUILD VOLUNTEER ARMY | ENABLE ACTION | SHORT TERM WINS | ACCELERATE AND SUSTAIN | INSTITUTE CHANGE |

Setting the climate for change   Engaging/Enabling   Implementing/Sustaining

Figure 10.1 Kotter change framework.

Stage two: build a guiding change coalition – Out of these conversations comes a clearer appreciation of who is going to lead the process.

Stage three: form a strategic vision and initiatives – One of the most critical aspects of the change process. Clarity about direction and goal is one of the most critical success factors.

Stage four: enlist a volunteer army – Mobilising change agents and influencers in the run up to D-Day, the actual 'trigger' communications and the cascade afterwards. It is imperative to keep up this level of attentive, clear and focused communication through the process.

Stage five: enable action by removing barriers – Dealing with obstacles and leveraging past successes to create a climate of success.

Stage six: generate short-term wins – Building momentum, energising supporters and enlightening the naysayers. Delivering the low hanging fruit and celebrating early wins helps to acknowledge that change is possible.

Kotter's fifth and six stages are really about igniting change – quickly creating a sense of momentum and a sense that something different is happening and will continue to happen.

Stage seven: sustain acceleration – Monitor progress, be mindful of fatigue and publicise wins to keep progress on track.

Stage eight: institute change – Make sure change is tied to the culture of the firm, overtly aligned to values and expected new behaviours and that this is celebrated and recognised.

Stages seven and eight are about perseverance and embedding lasting behavioural change which are both fundamental aspects of the change process. Change takes time and is supremely difficult to stick with and make stick. It is in these later stages that the change process can often become derailed or unstuck.

Kotter's model is based on what should happen. In reality, many change programmes do not follow a model and are not pre-planned months before beginning. Instead, often it is the numbers that drive the need for change and the behavioural aspects are often left to HR to worry about on the fly, once the process has started and change is unfolding.

The other ignition route that is common is that CEOs will often engage support when there is an immediate need like a D-Day speech to write, dire financial results to handle or a regulatory order to comply with – and they need far more immediate results. Sometimes it comes in the form of an unexpected change in leadership, a need to make fast cost savings or to handle a PR disaster.

All of the above really fall into the realm of crises rather than change programmes, and it would be fair of change experts to say the two things are not the same at all. But our experience has been that *a lot of change processes start first with an assignment to handle a crisis*. And that once the crisis has been handled and the organisation agrees to implement a change process, there is little appetite to start from scratch implementing a change model that may call for elaborate setup work.

Instead, leaders choose to convert the success of handling the immediate crisis into a real-time improvement or 'special measures' plan, where the strategy and objectives are often concluded over a few conversations and then executed tactically, flexibly and relatively quickly.

Having an understanding of the basic building blocks of change and how change should happen is important. But often the reality is a lot messier and less pristine.

It is particularly interesting that the least planned part of the process is the human and behavioural aspect. Given that when we say 'change' we are really talking about 'changing people', this is poignant and a little bit worrying.

Driving Behavioural Change

Far more important than the theoretical models that inform change management should be the ideas that help management and communication teams encourage behavioural change.

Given the fact that the key stakeholders in change programmes are employees and the core dynamics are persuasion about the need for change and embedding new behaviours, it makes sense that understanding the behavioural underpinnings to how people react to change is hugely important. In our experience, these considerations do not happen nearly enough in most change programmes.

Most people do not like change, and given a choice will opt for the status quo. Many experts have compared going through a change process as akin to the grieving or bereavement process. Elisabeth Kubler-Ross was a Swiss-born American psychiatrist who pioneered our understanding of these stages.[4] A graphic illustrating her ideas is shown in Figure 10.2.

There is the initial shock of someone dying which is quickly followed by our feeling that 'it can't be true' – we're in denial. Often, this denial stage deepens and can turn negative as we become frustrated with our new circumstances. We may find it harder to cope, be disillusioned with what can appear a lengthy journey ahead of us to recovery and anger can set in.

This moves into depression when the enormity and finality of loss is felt and we bottom-out in our emotions. Hope for a new reality is faint, everything feels like it is a struggle and we are low in energy, motivation and mood.

Things begin to change as we take the first tentative steps to experiment with our new status, not coming to terms with it but learning to live with it, accommodate it and see if we can carve out some new way of being. This initial engagement with our new status deepens as we grow in confidence, and at some point an often tacit decision is made to accept the change and get on with things. We feel more positive. The last stage is typified when the changes have largely been internalised and integrated and a 'renewed' person is ready to truly move forward.

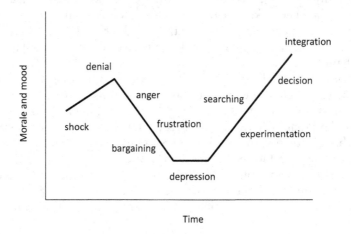

Figure 10.2 Kubler-Ross change curve.

This process, to which anyone who has been bereaved can attest, can take a number of months or even years to fully work itself out. It is not uncommon after the death of a spouse for people to report that it took them the better part of three years to move through all the stages.

This comparison of bereavement with our reaction to change is instructive and powerful and the first warning to executives not to rush things. Instead to expect that fully coming to grips with change may take months or longer and that the process cannot be rushed or speeded up.

The other huge insight that behavioural models bring to change management is that everyone moves through the process at different speeds. We go through the change process by going through the stages in the same order but at very different speeds.

Some people need far longer to negotiate a particular stage than others and how long people have known about the change plays a role as well. It is common that senior management, having been privy earlier to the need for change, will be further advanced in their stages of acceptance – and this can create a major commitment gap or multiple curves with employees lagging behind. Leaders need to be cognizant of the differing pace of acceptance or commitment and understand they have a huge head start (Figure 10.3).

Employees and even middle managers – the ones who really drive change – need time to get accustomed to the changes. If this happens smoothly, you get the positive outcomes of: awareness, understanding, acceptance and so on. If not, a negative reaction at the same stage (unaware, confusion, negative perception) is likely.

As well as people moving at different speeds through the change process, there are real differences in how people are predisposed to view change in general. People's innate reaction is located across the entire spectrum, from fully positive and eager through neutral and tentative to feeling negative and outright resistant to change.

Figure 10.4 is based on Professor Everett Roger's model of early adoption[5] and charts people's reactions to new technology and how quickly they move to adopt and embrace

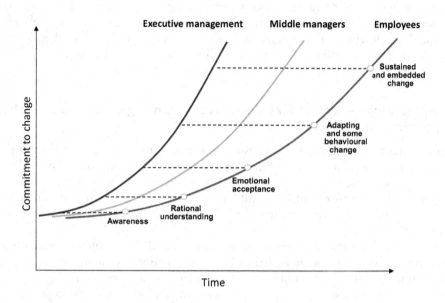

Figure 10.3 Differing commitment curves.

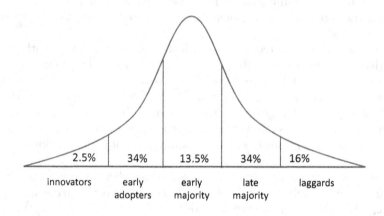

Figure 10.4 Adoption and innovation curve.

it. The idea that someone's perception about change has an innate positioning is another key insight into our understanding of possible reactions to change and therefore change management programmes.

Finally, it is important to note that progress along the change curve is not necessarily linear, that is, you cannot expect a continual and inexorable moving forward. In reality, the change process is a series of small victories and progressions that cumulatively outweigh the set-backs and reversals.

Patience and resilience is needed to cope with the numerous set-backs that will happen at the individual, team, department and even organisational level, when two steps forward may be followed by three steps back. Employees may feel a kind of roller coaster effect where highs are followed by renewed dips, and it seems for every step forward, there is the real or perceived danger of one or two steps backwards.

Primal Pathway – What Grief Recovery, Change Curves and the Storytelling Arc have in Common

It is interesting to compare the Kubler-Ross grief curve, the organisational commitment curve and the early adoption of technology curve with the traditional storytelling arc. Each has classic phases of struggle, retrenchment, trying out or seeking a new reality, fighting through doubt or conflict, climbing and progressing, getting within sight of a resolution or objective, often slipping back near the end and then a cathartic arrival or achievement.

In their book *Illuminate*,[6] authors Nancy Duarte and Patti Sanchez explicitly make the connection between change and the classic storytelling arc or trajectory. The book is a communicator's guide to change and the importance of recognising the stages of the change journey and the different emotional needs of employees at each stage.

Duarte and Sanchez advocate using a wide range of different communications and talk about the need to create powerful symbols and celebrations of change.

It is intriguing how the grief, change and storytelling trajectories coincide. It is almost as if this arc of setbacks and stages, peaks and valleys describes a primal pathway that is deeply wired inside us – and that we intuitively recognise and are drawn to this path because it illustrates the three fundamental and compelling journeys of our lives:

- **The grief journey** – Our recovery from losing those dear to us with its attendant lesson that we navigate through life as solitary beings and no matter how close the connection, we ultimately cannot take others with us.
- **The change journey** – Life is change and is marked by the stages of growth and decay. Everything is always changing. Nothing ever stays the same.
- **The story of our lives** – As we move through the other two journeys, we are creating in real time the story of our lives with its similar arc of highs and lows.

What does all this mean for the change process? I think there is something about the act of change that we intuitively recognise. And although we may tire of constantly having to face this arc, it is the essential human condition.

I think this is a powerful notion for leaders to remind people about at the outset when change is required. We have all successfully navigated hundreds of changes large and small in our lives. We know how to do this. It is in our DNA. However, there is another interesting and philosophical point to be made here.

All the change trajectories have a similar shape, in that they describe a journey that is overwhelmingly time-bound and linear – moving in one direction, that is, forward. The expectation is that there will be a recognisable, definable outcome with real achievements, changes made, actions taken and lessons learned and shared before embarking on the next change journey.

The causal assumption is that the prevailing direction of travel is forward and positive. Each of these models is built on a belief that change is progressive, rational and able to be fulfilled. The provenance for this kind of thinking is rooted in the Western enlightenment belief in man's perfectability and the absolute trust in rationality.

And so we have moved from the Enlightenment in the late 1700s through the Victorian era of relentless 'progress' to the early 1900s and the standardisation of mass production, on to mid-century management mantras of 'what can be measured can be managed' and our present-day faith in algorithms that offer 'certain' projections of what can be expected.

Today, this entire thesis is increasingly under attack with behavioural economics, black swan events, increasing complexity, interconnectivity and major challenges, all assembling to posit the idea that *a positive direction of travel should not be taken for granted.*

Rational drivers of change are certainly not the only drivers and sometimes not even the key drivers. Irrationality plays a bigger role in how we react than we might believe, and *we should not assume that these change processes can always be easily understood and navigated as we move towards their expected resolution.*

The strong assumption at the heart of many change management programmes – that they can be directed, controlled and driven to deliver positive outcomes – is essentially flawed and naïve or at least worthy of a far more critical eye. Effecting real change is a lot messier, more equivocal, more difficult and takes more time than expected.

The Change Communications Process

Articulating a clear change process, with transparency about objectives, timelines, milestones and deliverables, can immeasurably help to keep the process on track, understandable and moving forward.

Change communications have much in common with planned crises. The overall narrative and key messaging is decided well before D-Day, messaging is completed and there is a trigger event where the rationale for change is announced and key expected changes and actions are explained to employees.

But a change management programme is far larger and more fundamental in scope than handling a crisis. There are three key considerations right at the beginning that differentiate change management communications from those of a crisis.

Three Key Considerations

Selling the Case for Change – The 'Burning Platform'

In a change programme, job one is to clearly communicate the 'burning platform' – the reason why a change programme needs to be undertaken and why at the magnitude that is indicated. In one case, we worked with a firm that wanted to move from a product to customer focus, to fundamentally drive deeper value for the company. But the immediate 'burning platform' was the need to reduce the number of fines they were accruing for aggressive product selling.

This is a good example that shows the difference between a planned change event and a change management programme. If the issue was only the increasing number of fines and the potential financial and reputational fallout, then that would be serious. But the remedy would almost certainly not have been as fundamental as changing an entire business model.

But the firm made the call that the fines issue was a symptom of what was wrong – not the problem itself. And that what was needed was a complete re-imagination of the business.

Pivoting from product to customer, from price to quality and from commoditisation to tailored service was about 'actualising' the company – making it more differentiated and competitive across the sector landscape and more valuable to customers. The burning platform was the need to change. *The fine issue was a lightning rod for discontent and a symbol and symptom of what was wrong – but not the issue itself.*

Articulating this 'business case for change' is what the burning platform is all about. Too often, in communicating the burning platform, leaders are not clear enough and do not keep the story simple enough for employees to immediately understand. This should be the goal. The reason for change has to be easily articulated by all employees.

Getting the 'Vision Thing' Correct

The second communications consideration is the vision – the ultimate strategic objective for the change programme. George Bush Senior famously had difficulty with what he called 'the vision thing', feeling uncomfortable articulating the grand idea and preferring to explain **what** would happen and **how** rather than the bigger notion of **why** it was important.

Vision traditionally is meant to be a distillation of why a company exists. A classic vision aims to be both aspirational and inspirational and it should be future-orientated – something the firm is aiming for but not yet attained. A nice framing of the relationship between purpose, mission and vision is:

• Built for purpose
• Driven by mission
• In pursuit of vision

In a change management context, if the burning platform is **why** you are making the change, the vision is **what** you hope to achieve. Being able to clearly articulate this new end-state is as critical as being able to articulate the burning platform. One without the other does not work, and you have to be crystal clear about each before embarking on the change journey or you will lose employees immediately and be in a poor position to win hearts and minds further down the track.

Again, the same principles apply as with the burning platform – simple and easily remembered and articulated. The vision needs to offer a clear goal and it should be convincing and credible.

Making the Overall Process Clear

The third communication's consideration is to make the process as clear as possible. People are far more likely to support change if they know what is expected of them, roughly how long it will take, what good looks like and key milestones along the way.

This is not so different from the 'cognitive map' we discussed earlier. Audiences need to know how your presentation will unfold – what you are trying to do and what you are going to focus on and cover. They do not react well at all to being kept in the dark.

There is a lazy arrogance at work in how many executives plan to communicate about change. Many prefer the idea of drip-feeding employee information at key stages and when the time is right for the executives not the employees. This is a major mistake.

Most of the conditions for success in a change programme are set right at the beginning of the process and revolve around how executives treat employees. It is critical to set off from a position of openness and transparency and by building not abusing trust. The basic character and values of leaders are on display like never before at the beginning of a change programme and employees are experts at calibrating authenticity and assessing whether a leader is telling the truth or dissembling.

We spend a great deal of time at the beginning of a change programme making this point to leaders – that so much is riding on securing employees' support and that they need to commit right from the start to being as open, trustworthy and honest as they can. Employees will understand there are some details that cannot be made public at certain times and that executives will always be privy to the fine detail, but the broad direction of travel, the key goals and timelines and what will be expected of employees all has to be spelled out.

These three considerations – being able to articulate the burning platform, offer a clear vision and clearly identify the road ahead – are all necessary at the beginning of a change programme in a way that is just not as applicable in a crisis.

Celebrating Milestones – Tracking Progress and Avoiding Mission Creep and Fatigue

Once the change process is underway, it is vitally important to track progress and to celebrate key milestones met and passed. Change programmes are like a quest or long journey and it is easy for people to get discouraged and fatigued. It's also easy to take on additional goals or initiatives and celebrating key milestones is also a way of making sure the programme stays on track and resists mission creep.

Often, a first major milestone is reached when whatever redundancies involved are completed. This is an important time when those employees who are staying can feel somewhat bruised and vulnerable, but relieved. They are effectively in the lifeboat and part of the company's future.

A recommendation we often make is to try and get to this marker as soon as possible because then the focus of communication becomes unified around a shared future goal – the vision as articulated at the beginning of the process.

While redundancies are happening, the focus of the entire change programme is divided between the present-focused process of letting people go and the future-looking process of building that new desired end-state. This is a real communications challenge because you are effectively running two parallel and completely different narratives – a positive one for those who will stay with the firm and a negative one (albeit hopefully humane and smooth) for those being let go.

Experience shows that it is very difficult to fully get traction on the future until everyone is in the lifeboat and can move on with security and confidence – and those who are going to go have gone.

The moment that this process completes is worthy of being acknowledged in the most appropriate way, but it does mark a huge turning point for the change process as a whole.

It is important to celebrate achievement milestones – those targets set initially that indicate progress is being made. The product-to-customer focus company mentioned above found several natural points to celebrate such as the opening of a new model shop, new call centre scripts, the launch of the new website and advertising and the implementation of a new backbone technology system.

Leadership during a Change Programme

Leadership is the most important component of a successful change programme. Successful change leaders vary significantly in terms of charisma, disposition, humility and business expertise. What they tend to have in common is a set of very similar character traits and values.

In our experience, successful change leaders are:

- **Resilient and tenacious** – they do not easily weary, flag or get discouraged
- **Big picture thinkers** – directing, motivating, delegating and trusting are far more important than micromanaging
- **Clear communicators** – concise and simple
- **Authentic and caring** – able to show genuine empathy while remaining resolute
- **Self-aware** – understanding of their own strengths and weaknesses

Key Success Factors

All change programmes are unique and uniquely challenging. Being able to clearly explain the burning platform, the end-state vision and the pathway, while being aware of employees' emotional needs, are key success factors.

Building a strong change team, creating a network of change agents and early adopters is also critical to success. Assembling and encouraging a growing network of people who 'get it' helps to create momentum and a 'herd instinct' among the wider employee population that a tipping point has been reached and this is the way forward.

Perseverance and resilience are critical success factors. Change is mentally and physically tough and the pathway long and arduous. Keeping a sense of proportion and a sense of humour in addition to paying attention to well-being are all important.

Finally, for change to really be successful and mean something, it must be tangible. There have to be tangible changes to concrete things like policies, compensation programmes, product offerings and services as well as intangible but clear behavioural and value changes.

This embedding of a new and different 'way of doing things' is the real prize of change and the most difficult aspect to achieve.

BOX 10.1 BUILDING A CUSTOMER INTIMATE CAPABILITY

A few years ago, we were asked by a consultancy to work on a different kind of change programme. It involved their analyst team of about 12 people. The MD didn't want to make any structural changes to the business, no change of business model and there was no crisis event that triggered the process. He also needed no messaging and no D-Day planning, but most interestingly of all was that he was starting with behaviour change, the very thing Kotter warns to leave for the end.

The consultancy's clients tended to be medium-sized firms that were family owned and run by patriarchs in their 60s and 70s. Very proud and resolutely 'old school', they were being turned off by the detached, analytical professionalism of the 30-something analysts. The older executives felt they were being shown up and talked down to – never a good way for a consultancy to make clients feel. More than that, they felt that the control and responsibility of turning around their failing firms was being taken away from them in favour of analyst models, algorithms and spreadsheets (a preview look at the future?).

The brief was to help build a 'customer-intimate' capability. Analysts who would have stronger empathy would be able to forge real connections with clients and be able to read motivation and mood with far more deftness and nuance.

Over the course of 18 months, we implemented a behavioural change 'boot camp'. Facial recognition exercises, emotional intelligence assessments and metrics, role plays where actors were brought in to play the older bosses and a wide selection of bite-sized training modules focused on slowly changing habits and behaviours for the better.

The change programme worked well and the analysts felt more confident with their senior clients and better equipped to understand their situation. Their clients came back with very positive feedback.

The burning platform, vision and pathway were in play, but this change programme focused on behavioural restructuring.

Notes

1 https://www.investopedia.com
2 Article in *The Guardian* on February 25, 2015, cited from https://www.theguardian.com
3 https://www.kotterinc.com/8-steps-process-for-leading-change
4 Kubler-Ross, Elisabeth (1969), *On Death and Dying*, New York, USA, Macmillan Publishing.
5 Everett Rogers, *Diffusion of Innovations*, 1962, Simon and Schuster.
6 Duarte, Nancy and Sanchez, Patti (2016), *Illuminate: Ignite Change Through Speeches, Stories, Ceremonies and Symbols*, New York, Penguin Random House.

Chapter 11

Dealing with the Media

Overview

A media interview is undoubtedly one of the most intense and concentrated communication experiences. For most people, it is something to be endured and survived, not looked forward to.

Adrenaline runs high, performance is on demand and the spotlight is something most people do not crave.

As well, comments are made for the public record, usually in a one-on-one format that requires a considerable amount of trust on the part of the interviewee. They are giving comment in the hope that the information will be transmitted accurately and faithfully by the journalist into a story.

No one expects a direct transcription of comments, but there is not nearly the control over the messaging that exists in other formats such as presentations or panel discussions. Interviewees are effectively trusting in the process of going through the 'filter' that is the media to get air time for their content and views.

This lack of control is the chief reason that leaders usually do not like dealing with the media, and tend to dislike it the more they advance in their career. There is another reason as well.

The media requirement to synthesise, summarise and simplify knowledge down to packaged and marketable sound bites is anathema to many leaders, senior executives, scientists, academics and business people who trade in nuance, balanced probabilities, context and uncertainty. It's simply too black and white to be credible.

Having to play this game to gain entrance to public discourse and debate via the media is deeply off-putting to many leaders. And yet, knowing that this is the landscape you need to deal with gives you tremendous insight. If you know what they want and what it looks like, you can beat them at their own game by giving them what they need, but on your terms.

Effectively handling the media is about taking back control and about understanding how to connect with and manage media, so that you are effectively in the driver's seat, not them.

The process of taking back control is not antagonistic at all. It's wonderfully counter-intuitive because for the vast majority of interviews and journalists, the more you can efficiently package information, deliver meaning and 'take back control', the more the media like it. They find it valuable, time-efficient and effective. Let me explain.

As mentioned in the chapter on content, when I was a television journalist, my worst nightmare was an erudite guest who told me ten amazing things in an interview, but failed to prioritise or signal what information was most meaningful. I would get back to the studio with one hour to write my story and edit it together, not having a clue where to start.

DOI: 10.4324/9781003198994-15

The great secret in dealing with most media is that *they do not perceive you as being patronising if you tell them that this piece of information is important or meaningful.* Instead, it turns out media are like us after all – they crave meaning. For both parties, what good looks like is information that is clear, concise and meaningful. If you are overtly directive about this, so much the better.

For the media, it makes crafting the eventual story so much easier and the story infinitely better.

And you as a leader have liberated yourself from feeling that the interview is a high-risk, low-value and low-control channel of communication. Instead, it can and should be about articulating meaning.

When it works best, this process becomes a shared partnership.

Eighty-five per cent of all interviews are not controversial at all. They are transactional. The story is unknown and it is up to both parties to co-create the story. The journalist has come looking for something newsworthy. The leader's job is to offer insightful, well-packaged remarks that summarise key information. Hopefully the journalist plays his or her part by asking penetrating and perceptive questions that encourage storytelling and meaning transfer. But make no mistake, *it is actually the interviewees who are in the pole position and have the opportunity to drive and direct the encounter, because they are the ones in charge of the content and delivering the meaning.*

In my experience, far too few leaders understand this core dynamic and do not take this opportunity. For them, the media experience seems unremitting, like facing a Gatling gun-like interrogation.

Three Types of Interviews

Table 11.1 shows that there are three types of media interviews, and it is the transactional interview which has this co-creation of meaning as the prime dynamic.

In transactional interviews, focusing on meaning is the key. By structuring comments so that meaning is delivered in the summary statement at the end of answers, the leader can subtly 'control' the flow of the interview. A seasoned journalist will always want to be in charge of the questions, but they will almost always follow-up on an important point made at the end of an answer, by asking a supplementary question, probing for more information or clarifying a point. In this way, the executive – by focusing on delivering meaning – has a good chance of influencing the follow-up questions he or she gets asked.

Table 11.1 Three types of interviews

Transactional 85% (trade media)	Challenging 10% (national media)	Verificational 5% (financial media/analysts)
Key goal – transfer meaning	Key goal – protect reputation	Key goal – convey confidence
Knowledge – significant gap	Knowledge – less gap	Knowledge – little gap
Key dynamic – 'packaging' story	Key dynamic – handling emotion	Key dynamic – sticking to narrative
Key skill – summarising knowledge	Key skill – staying on message	Key skill – projecting reassurance
Performance – energetic	Performance – controlled	Performance – confidence
Tone – respectful	Tone – aggressive	Tone – forensic
Reporters – appreciate guidance	Reporters – try to goad for reaction	Reporters – 'guidance' on numbers
Answers – 50–60 seconds	Answers – 10–25 seconds	Answers – 30–45 seconds

A good transactional interview should resemble a lively conversation, with each playing off the other.

The challenging interview is the kind you see in films and on television. The journalist is aggressive and confrontational. The story is in dispute and the journalist is figuratively hitting the executive. The executive's job in this case is to protect reputation and hit back. Meaning goes out the window. What is important is recognising risk, correcting the record and defending reputation. Good is short, sharp answers where the leader deals with the allegation head on, bridges to a positive comment and does not to go down the rabbit hole of negativity set by the journalist.

The verificational interview is a specialist interview usually given only by CEOs and CFOs. It is a financial interview and the story – focused on the numbers – is already known. The figures get announced in quarterly, half-year or full-year results.

Here, the dynamic is more respectful. Reporters and analysts know a lot, are used to following the firm and have almost as much skill in interpreting the numbers as the executives. They have the story, but what they are looking for is 'guidance' that the market can believe and take confidence in the narrative behind the numbers.

We are going to focus first on the transactional media interview and how to give yourself the best possible shot at controlling the process of delivering meaning, the core dynamic in play.

How to Feel in 'Control'

Before we look at how to exploit this 'meaning' dynamic, we need to take a step back and acknowledge that for most people, giving a media interview is about the most fraught communications experience they can imagine doing. For many, it is a source of considerable anxiety, akin to public speaking.

The first element in equipping yourself to deliver an effective media interview is that you must feel 'in control'. You cannot perform effectively if your anxiety level is too high. Some performance anxiety is unavoidable, normal and even necessary as your adrenaline is signalling for you to get ready to 'perform', but you must feel you are in control.

The two best sources of feeling in control are your own knowledge and preparation. As a leader, you are being interviewed because you know the subject matter.

The gap between your knowledge and that of the journalist in a transactional interview is significant and this should produce some level of residual comfort. It should give you a 'vote of confidence' that all will be well and that you can handle anything thrown at you.

A far more likely issue is that you will end up having to simplify and summarise your knowledge so that you are able to 'transmit' effectively. *This is the real knowledge issue – not being challenged on the quantum of what you know, but being challenged on your structuring, packaging and presenting of your knowledge. For most leaders, this is the core challenge they face and what can make transactional interviews far more difficult than other interviews.*

After your own knowledge, the best source of confidence is good preparation. The minimal preparation time for a substantive interview is 45–60 minutes. You need to:

- Know why you are doing the interview – your bottom line objective
- Prepare content for the questions
- Assemble proof points, statistics or case studies
- Craft a few key messages that sum up your position
- Have a one-sentence summary that clearly articulates your main point
- Anticipate the difficult questions
- Rehearse

Rules of Engagement

For transactional interviews, the rules of engagement tend to be similar for all organisations and go a long way to ensuring a fair and level playing field between you and the journalist. Following these rules of engagement will take a lot of potential pressure off and allow you to focus on preparing your content. Here are the most common rules:

1 **Always go through corporate communications** – do not freelance and do not contact media directly.
2 **Corporate communications agrees a 'contract' for each interview*** (see qualifying note below) – this sets the 'ground rules' for the interview such as focus, 'no-go' areas, length of interview, questions seen beforehand, right to review draft story, right to review/change quotes. This contract gives structure and protection to your planned interview.
3 **Corporate communications to sit in on all interviews** – if a delicate question comes up or one that is clearly off limits, it is preferable that they intervene to say you are not authorised to comment rather than you – let them act as the 'bad cop'.
4 **Do not give off the record comments** – there is no upside for you and 'off the record' means they can use the information, but without identifying you. This places you entirely in their hands and leaves you trusting them to keep their word – not a great position to be in with a journalist. Sometimes journalists will suggest your comments could be 'not for attribution' which is a subset of 'off the record' and means they will quote you but not name you. Either way, it is very easy to identify someone by either the quote or the positioning offered by the journalist which often sounds like 'it is understood that XYZ company believes (quote)' or 'a senior spokesperson for XYZ said (quote)'.
5 **Do not comment on Group topics** – such as strategy, share price and financials.
6 **Do not comment on clients, competitors or individual employees**.
7 **Do not offer personal views** – you are too senior to have that luxury. If you do, all your comments will be attributed to you as the leader of your organisation.

*Qualifying note: The 'contract' with the media is mainly something that gets used with trade and national media – it tends to weaken to the point of non-existence the more you engage in a live or live-to-tape format or with a very senior correspondent or editor, who will baulk at having too many rules imposed on them.

Understanding Risk

The notion of better understanding the media you are dealing with is also an important aspect in giving you more confidence. Figure 11.1 shows the basic media risk spectrum in play. As you move to the left on the spectrum you take on more risk. The typical 'trade media' interview is totally different than a television, radio, social media or wire services interview (Figure 11.1).

Managing Anxiety

A final word on feeling 'in control'. No matter how well you prepare, you still may feel anxious.

A key source of worry is 'anticipatory anxiety'. Instead of focusing on what they are saying and staying 'in the moment', many people start thinking about their whole answer, or entire interview or presentation. Before they know, it their thinking has morphed into

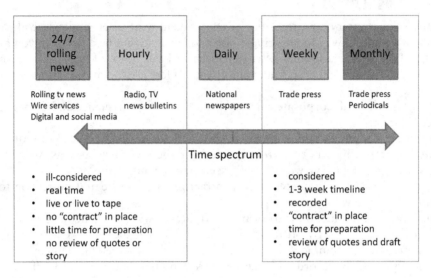

Figure 11.1 Understanding the risk landscape.

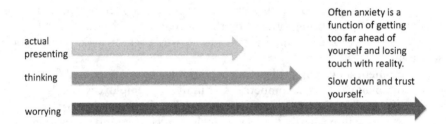

Figure 11.2 Managing anxiety while presenting.

worrying and they become detached from what they are talking about. At this point, the link with speaking is destroyed and they lose track of what they are saying and falter or stop entirely (Figure 11.2).

The antidote to this anticipatory anxiety is to slow down, focus on the point you are making and perhaps the gateway to your next point and trust that as you arrive at the other points in your answer or presentation you will deliver them equally well.

The twin ideas of slowing down and trusting yourself are probably the two best pieces of performance advice. Do not get too far ahead of yourself. Don't think about the whole enchilada. Pay attention to the points you are making now and trust that when you arrive at the next point, you will be fine. Don't forget: what you leave on the cutting room floor, they never knew existed.

This disaggregating of anxiety into manageable chunks is a recognised strategy for dealing with performance anxiety. But it is particularly applicable to media interviews that must be delivered in a calm and clear order if they are to convey meaning.

Transmitting Meaning

We talked earlier about using the Imaginary Dialogue to cognitively structure your information so that what you deliver aligns with the order in which people expect to receive information – that is, it makes sense to them. We saw how the structure also acts as a GPS system directing your answer and telling you when you've reached your destination.

Here are the two key templates again (Figures 11.3 and 11.4):

The information (in order) people expect to receive when we communicate

Question	Type of information	Best delivered with
What is it ?	Title Main Point Sound-bite Setting out your stall	Emotion
Why me?	Relevance Context Background	Emotion
Tell me more	Details	Reason
What do I do now?	Call to action Value and Benefits Meaning	Emotion

Figure 11.3 The imaginary dialogue.

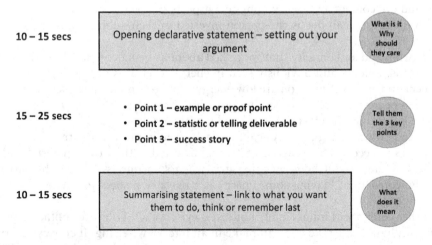

Figure 11.4 Template for delivering a message.

First and Second Box Communication

In a transactional interview, the two boxes are critical – they are where meaning lives and from where the media will quote you. Journalists will sum up the relatively dense information you include in the middle of your answer and look for quotes in the more emotive and big picture two boxes.

The first box often includes the de facto answer to the question that the journalist has asked. It can also include context, relevance and your point of view; so there are rich pickings here for a journalist looking for quotes.

Most interviewees do well at providing first box information. It's the second box that is the issue. Many leaders do not sum up the meaning of their information – feeling it is either not needed or patronising.

But utilising the second box is precisely the dynamic that allows us to control the process of developing and delivering meaning which is the core dynamic at play. By populating the second box with 'meaningful' comment, we give the journalist real incentive to take us up on the point we are making and probe further.

It is this aggregation of information up to meaning – the province of the second box – that is ultimately of most use to the journalist and where the best quotes are to be found. As we discussed previously, leaders give up a lot if they do not engage with and deliver meaning.

The second box doesn't feature much in either the challenging or the verificational interview. In the former, there is no requirement to transmit meaning – you are hitting back and protecting reputation. And in the financial interview, meaning is found in the numbers – the whole interview revolves around 'what does it mean for the company' – but that meaning is found first and foremost in the numbers, not the narrative. Too much focusing on second box meaning can be counterproductive and seem like a 'spin'.

You cannot use the second box technique all the time. It will sound contrived and formulaic. It is more a reminder to talk about meaning.

Body Language for Media Interviews

Energy and eye contact are the two physical aspects that stand out most in media interviews. By energy, I mean the 'is-the-person-invested-in-their-subject-and-enthused-to-be-here' test.

The passion and authenticity that we talked about as being core to effective communication is most quickly and obviously seen in energy level. It is pretty difficult to convey investment and enthusiasm if you are low energy, tepid or timid. That doesn't mean to say you need to be extroverted – a quiet, but powerful, reflective personality is very engaging and can generate significant intellectual and moral energy.

By far and away, the biggest physical feedback given in most media training sessions is that the person needs to be more energetic and invested in their own material and story. We talked already about how engaging it is when someone is telling a big story with power and conviction. Having some energy is a mark of respect for the media and it is always noticed.

The other component immediately noticed is eye contact. Poor eye contact is probably the biggest physical mistake you can make in an interview setting. It conveys everything you don't want to convey and is easily misread and escalated by the journalist. What to you may be indicative of nerves can come across as lack of interest or even disdain and can fatally undermine an otherwise content-rich interview.

Actual physical body language tends not to be so important in an interview setting. There is a constraint put on how much positive body language you can project anyway, and excessive movement of body or hands is not a good idea. The key points remain: keep hands away from your face and be positive, inclusive and welcoming in your general demeanour.

Challenging Media Interviews – Protecting Reputation

Although participants worry about their ability to come through this kind of interview unscathed, they tend to perform better on the challenging interview than they do with the transactional interview.

In a challenging interview, the prevailing dynamic is simple. It is like an argument where you need to react in real time, with a credible comeback line and not get unnerved physically. People don't like facing emotion and aggression, but virtually everyone is well equipped to handle this if they keep their answers short and factual. In a challenging interview, the requirement to summarise, synthesise and simplify information to deliver meaning has vanished.

Figure 11.5 shows the significant difference between the two types of interviews.

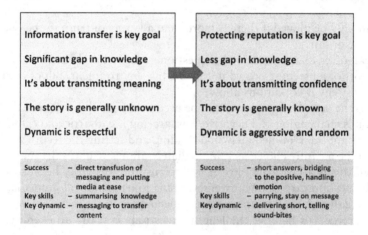

Figure 11.5 From transactional to challenging interviews.

I am always impressed by how well people rise to the challenge of defending reputation and setting the record straight. It almost seems as if there is something liberating about not having to worry about articulating meaning and instead just going directly at someone with one aim in mind: putting them back in their box.

How to Answer a Challenging Question

And so, what does good look like in a challenging interview? It's very simple and unequivocal: short answers of 10–25 seconds, a declarative and factual answering of the question or allegation and then bridging to the positive, so you do not end up debating the negative assertion with the journalist.

Strategy	When To Use	Advantages	Examples
Agree	If assertion is true or fair	Draws sting and charms/disarms	I think that is mainly true but more important is .....
Disagree	If assertion is so heinous it needs to be corrected	Corrects the record	I completely disagree because...but this is the really important thing.
Ignore	If you can answer by moving to your own info	Moves you to positive quickly but you may be asked again	What is important is this...

Bridging –build a bridge from the negative to the positive. Bridging helps you stay in control by keeping you focused on your main points

Figure 11.6 Handing a negative question.

Figure 11.6 outlines the three initial choices you have upon hearing the question and reminds about the potency of the bridging technique.

The three choices are interesting and go a long way to determining how successful your answer is going to be. You can agree, disagree or ignore, which is a politician's favourite tactic.

Agree – can only be played if there is more than a kernel of truth in the question or the assertion is true or fair.

Agreeing can often charm or defang a questioner, throwing them off balance and winning the support of a listening crowd if it is in a live environment. But of course, you can only use this strategy if conditions allow.

Disagree – is the default strategy and can be used in almost all cases since the very nature of the question is challenging and negative. Disagreeing is cathartic and categoric and gets you off on the right track immediately in defending and setting the record straight.

Ignore – can be a canny choice as it immediately allows you to start making a positive statement. But this is a favourite ploy of politicians and it is risky because you have not answered the question directly. Many enterprising journalists will immediately take you up on that and call you back to answer the dodged question.

The entire exercise of fielding challenging questions is really an exercise about three things:

1   Recognising and mitigating risk
2   Using lines-to-take naturally
3   Staying in control

Recognising and Mitigating Risk

One of the biggest differences between a transactional and a challenging interview is that in the latter, you do not get sight of the questions first. You can anticipate and prepare for a difficult question, but this is not the same as hearing it live for the first time, in situ and with the spin, angle or perspective that the reporter is putting on it.

A big part of coping well with challenging interviews is your ability to recognise risk. Like insects with antennae that are highly tuned, your ability to see the danger in a question, to surmise where it might lead to and to calibrate your organisation's level of exposure to the risk implicit in the question, all has to be done in real time and without you looking as if you are doing this.

So much is about staying calm and projecting confidence. 'Reading the risk' in a question has to be done coolly and without visible effort, yet quickly. It is like most things with the media – the more you do it, the better you get at it. This is one skill where you can practice before hand and should.

Using Lines-to-Take Naturally

Your ability to stick to your organisation's lines-to-take for tackling a certain issue is a key skill. You need to be able to sound natural without deviating from the meaning of the lines. Building in a certain amount of flexibility and tailoring to the official lines-to-take is a good idea, otherwise leaders will not use them effectively and will sound wooden and inauthentic in media situations.

Staying in Control

Finally, challenging interviews are always an exercise in staying in control. Not letting yourself get riled or emotional. The best way of staying in control is to treat it as an exercise or game with specific rules:

* Keep it short
* Do not complain
* Do not take it personally
* Do not blame
* Stay factual
* Be positive

Another good tip is not to allow yourself to be browbeaten. Once you have answered a question twice, it is well within your rights to suggest that you have answered that question and it's time to move on. *Do not agree to field the same question more than twice.*

These kinds of interviews are always a power struggle. But remember, you know more than they do, short answers are good and you are liberated from needing to care about meaning. Make your retaliation firm and decisive and just keep doing it until the interview ends.

Verificational Media Interviews – Projecting Confidence and Reassurance

In most ways, verificational interviews are the easiest to prepare for and deliver. There is a lot riding on them, but the key difficulties of the other two interviews – the need to craft and convey meaning and the need to stay in control, respectively – are not present.

The key dynamic here is the need to reassure and project confidence. As long as the overarching narrative is credible and can be 'proven' with plenty of statistics and 'guidance' and the key numbers are satisfactorily presented and located in that narrative, then the interview tends to go smoothly.

First of all, the dynamic is much different. The gap in knowledge with financial journalists and analysts is minimal, and often they are better versed in what the overall market and other competitors are doing than the people doing the interview.

This reduction in the knowledge gap means executives do not have to worry about dumbing down information or about simplifying, synthesising and summarising. Some of this may still be done in the interest of conveying the overall narrative, but that packaging of the information to a simpler format is not needed. Everyone understands the jargon, the shorthand and the meaning behind certain phrases and lines.

This liberates the conversation to move at pace to get to the heart of the matter, which is whether or not the numbers support the story the leader is trying to peddle.

Crafting the Overall Story

When I worked at four banks in the Noughties, this process of settling on the overall narrative would begin perhaps three weeks before the results were due to be announced. The shape of the numbers would indicate certain stories, all of which came encased in the familiar corporate speak:

- 'Resilience in the face of significant headwinds' – for a slightly disappointing financial story.
- 'Further rationalisation of revenue sources and a refocusing on core portfolio businesses' – for a retrenching of activity and numbers.
- 'Transformational growth and accelerating investment to embed competitive advantage' – for taking a boom and converting it into a lasting advantage.

The investor relations team and senior corporate communications people should work hard to shape the story and identify the specific numbers to hang the story on.

If the story was negative, what the topic analysts and journalists wanted to know about was the strategy to turn the numbers and story around – the key actions and timelines to be taken to improve the situation. If positive, it was about how the state of play could be sustained, defended and converted into lasting competitive advantage.

Today's verificational interviews are much more complex than they used to be. They now focus on an institution's sustainability record and agenda, its stance on climate change and social justice and equality issues like 'Black Lives Matter', diversity and inclusion positioning and a host of other societal and regulatory issues that never used to be on the agenda.

But the key dynamic is relatively simple and is always phrased as a question: 'can you provide guidance to the market that your confidence (or other prevailing sentiment) is supportable and not misplaced'. In other words, reassure us as journalists and analysts that your views are reasonable, credible and based on real numbers.

For the interviewee, this requires having a good grasp of the overall story, a facility in navigating the core numbers and the ability to project confidence.

Social Media – When Two Tribes go to War

Social media is an enigma. On the one hand, for anyone under 40 it is completely normal. Far more relevant, widespread and powerful than traditional media, far more connective and resonant with the whole sharing and collaborative ethos that lies at the heart of the Millennial and Gen Z modus operandi. And according to this view, far more deserving of the term 'media' than the traditional channels of television, radio, magazines and newspapers.

But if you're much over 40 or a leader, company owner or member of a senior executive management team, social media tends to be anathema. A potentially out-of-control demi-monde of visceral and often feral emotion, populated by ignorant trolls out to cause mischief. A 'viral' landscape that is hard to control and where discourse and debate is often simplified beyond black and white to something tribal.

Of course, the truth lies somewhere in the middle of these two crude caricatures. *For the youngest two generations, social media is now just media, completely mainstream and a preferred channel for receiving and distributing all kinds of information.* Business has been relatively slow to adapt to the uptake in social media, although it is now a fairly standard tool used for recruitment, marketing and employee engagement.

Growth Areas for Social Media – Engagement, Amplification and Analysis

Proactive communicating via social media with employees, potential employees and customers has become a cornerstone activity and although time-consuming, when it works well it is very effective.

Social media is being used effectively to complement, and in some cases drive public relation programmes, activist campaigns, client relationship outreach, product marketing, talent spotting and recruitment. It has a reach that is unparalleled at building awareness and profile, where amplification of a cause or issue is of most concern rather than inculcating knowledge or embedding meaning.

Social media activity is also at the core of a lot of algorithmic-driven analysis on influencer and topic mapping aimed at uncovering patterns of communication and discourse between people and institutions. 'Scraping' publically available social media information from Twitter, Facebook, Instagram as well as accessing digital information conveyed by smartphones is increasingly moving to the centre of strategic communications efforts, where the generation of insight like real-time political analysis, customer footfall in retail environments, customer preferences and the key influencer effect on product demand is becoming one of the central requirements for communications planning.

In these three areas – engagement, amplification and analysis – the influence of social media is inescapable and growing.

The Limits of Using Social Media

But particularly business-to-business (B2B) firms still draw the line at using social media as a replacement or even a supplementary channel for more traditional media. Financial, pharmaceutical, energy, technology or infrastructure firms, used to operating in heavily regulated environments – where the rules of engagement are many and specific and the potential penalties for breaching them significant – are not great users of social media.

These types of firms tend to baulk at proactively using social media to further any communications objectives other than internal engagement and external analysis. Amplification via proactive engagement, which is increasingly normal in business-to-consumer (B2C) firms, is still a bridge too far for these firms. They worry about the time and cost involved in committing to constant dialogue and about the potential for reputational damage if an issue is misrepresented and 'goes viral'.

Many leaders readily acknowledge that social media is growing in importance and they know they should be doing more to proactively engage with all their stakeholders. And there are signs of change. Already major banks are encouraging their leaders to use social media channels far more. But most leaders put this change at least a few years away and worry about the implications of opening up in an area that can be very difficult and challenging to control. They are happy to defer this issue to the next generation of millennial CEOs and leaders.

The basic issue in question is the medium itself. Social media simply does not handle complexity well. It doesn't allow for nuance, grey, context, reflection or creative equivocation.

Twitter, for example, demands messages that can be conveyed in 280 characters or less and that have primary and primal appeal to our emotions. It is like the imperative to simplify, summarise and synthesise that lies at the heart of crafting efficient media messaging and which leaders instinctively dislike because they fear it means 'dumbing down' information.

Most CEOs do not want to explain strategy, policies or objectives in the truncated form demanded by social media. And so, for better or worse, many organisations and virtually all in heavily regulated sectors are currently only in 'monitoring mode'.

Many B2B firms prefer to follow the curve rather than lead. They are happy letting B2C organisations take the lead in working out how best to use social media in dialogue with customers and media and how to adapt to changing social convention rather than trailblaze.

This positioning sits well with risk averse B2B CEOs, who worry about the potential ramifications of adding real and potential operational and reputational risk to all their other operational considerations. *But increasingly, this stance will come under pressure as all businesses face calls from younger stakeholders to 'modernise', get involved and show commitment in the social values debates we have discussed.*

Organisations will need to find ways to mitigate the specific risks of using social media in order to take up this challenge. Those who do this well will be tapping into a relatively new and powerful source of competitive advantage.

Looking to the Future

Social media is embedding as the primary media conduit and it is highly likely, as millennial leaders assume control of companies, to become far more widely used as a proactive channel of media communication.

Traditional print media may move to occupy a far more niche and bespoke positioning of comment, analysis and insight, leaving the day-to-day delivery of commoditised news and messaging to television, social media and websites.

Given the higher relative importance of direct and 'real time' customer engagement to B2C firms, it is these firms that will lead the way in using social media. Change will not be as fast or as ubiquitous with B2B companies. But the overall direction of travel is quite clear.

Part 4

Activating Authentic Communications

Chapter 12

Coaching, Leadership and Communications

A Coaching Approach Is the Key Ingredient in an Authentic Leader's Communication

In Chapter 2 we explored what authentic leadership looks like, why it is based on foundational values like integrity, kindness and trust, and why over the coming decade it will be required more than ever before.

If real authenticity is the primary imperative and ingredient for future leadership, adopting the key components of the coaching approach will be the best way for leaders to communicate in an authentic and effective manner.

The themes in this chapter tie directly to the central thesis of the book – that authentic and effective communications will be needed more than ever before as a counterbalance to the accelerating digitisation and automation of the business world. And that the rich panoply of coaching skills and the positioning of the coach as kind, generous of spirit, optimistic, worthy of trust and keen to transfer competence and guide rather than dictate is very similar to the positioning of the authentic leader.

My belief is that coaching and the coaching approach to communicating is the best model we have for what authentic and effective communications looks like, especially for leaders. Forward-looking, non-judgemental, recognising the primacy of the individual as the prime generator of insight and meaning, committed to securing positive outcomes and genuinely invested and interested in other people.

We mentioned earlier that facilitating is the type of communication that demonstrates the widest range of leadership communication skills and the best facilitators act almost like coaches. The same central dynamic is on display – helping people move from starting state A to end-state B. And the emotional 'wrapper' of wisdom, respect, listening, focusing on meaning and perseverance mirrors the key skills of coaching.

Simply put, this approach to communications is the best way in which to understand, articulate and mobilise to meet the great changes and disruption to come.

The coaching approach rather than the old style of directive communicating will be the best way of bringing people together and instilling some measure of control, agency and understanding over the trends that will increasingly impact our world. When allied to an authentic leader's character, this will be a powerful and effective combination.

Coaching is the ultimate calm mode of communicating. The warm, inviting coaching approach will be a powerful counterbalance to both the detached, cool and rational flavour of the technological imperative and the red-hot emotion and feeling associated with roiling social values.

For those listening and reporting to leaders, it will be the difference between feeling marginalised, isolated and at the behest of forces that are moving with unnerving speed and disruption, and feeling they are still a part of this process and can influence the conversation.

DOI: 10.4324/9781003198994-17

Coaching – An Overview

Coaching has taken off over the last 20 years, going from a narrow provenance rooted in sports performance to a fast-growing sector offering business and personal support across a wide range of areas. Coaching is the newest of the helping methodologies, and compared with therapy, counselling and mentoring has the shortest track record.

John Whitmore wrote *Coaching for Performance*[1] in 1992, and before this date coaching was inextricably linked to the sports world and was active, hands-on, and directive in seeking performance improvement.

When it first started to gain credence, coaching was often confused with therapy, counselling and mentoring, all of which occupy adjacent but critically different territory. Unlike therapy, coaching is concerned more with the present and future rather than examining the past. It is founded on humanistic principles rather than medical or psychiatric analysis, and recognises the individual's own knowledge, awareness and agency as being the primary catalysts for change rather than the interplay between the therapist's expertise, possible medication and the individual patient's understanding of the sources of their trauma.

Counselling differs, in that it is overtly directive – that is, the counsellor listens to the client and then offers advice on what they should do. Wise counsel plays an active part in the business world and many leaders observe that confiding in other people can be difficult. Having a sounding board and someone to bounce ideas off or get a different perspective from is important and worthwhile. Wise counsel differs from counselling, in that the former is relationship-driven and collaborative and less overtly directive.

Mentoring is similar to counselling where the mentor passes on his or her experience and lessons learned. The mentor guides and implicit in the guidance is an evaluative function calibrating how the individual is doing in implementing the mentor's information.

Mentoring has become more commonplace in organisations, particularly in succession planning and promotion where stronger diversity and inclusion is the aim.

Coaching is fundamentally different because there is no overt passing-on of expertise, guidance or direction. And *the evaluative function is directed by the individual reflecting on progress made, guided by the coach, rather than the other way round.*

Coaching is meant to be non-directive, with *the core premise being that the individual or client has what they need inside them* and that coaching is a process that helps them recognise, clarify and better understand what this is and how to mobilise it. Coaching helps clients improve performance and deepen their self-awareness of the ability and knowledge that was there all along waiting to be activated by the individual themselves.

It is this liberating of self-knowledge and ability that sets coaching apart and gives the best coaching a transcendent and transformative character and quality.

Some aspects of this sense of liberation are shared with therapy, counselling and mentoring. But these three differ greatly from coaching because they do not begin from this fundamental belief in self-empowerment and discovery. Liberation may be a beneficial side effect of these pursuits, but the individual is not in the driver's seat. This, more than anything I think, explains the fast growth of coaching. It is focused on an individual doing something for themselves, not having something done to them – a very clear signpost for enlightened leaders.

The Desire for Change

About the only existing condition needed to embark on coaching is the desire to change.

The coach acts as a catalyst for change. But the desired change is something that the client wants to happen. Coaching has a forward direction of movement that is just not as strong in any of the other three disciplines. *Coaching towards no change is a non-sequitur. Coaching is always aligned to changing the status quo* – there is an implicit forward direction of movement in coaching from beginning state 'A' to end-state 'B' that gives it an action orientation that businesses and performance-focused individuals find appealing.

Leaders using a coaching approach to change may find their employees more receptive to the 'burning platform' and quicker to understand that the status quo is not an option.

Where change is not explicitly endorsed and desired, coaching sessions quickly slow down and get subsumed within a morass of descriptive detail about the prevailing situation. Very little progress is made because change is not the goal. Again, this is a major point for leaders to consider: make change an explicit, desired goal and resist the temptation to spend too much time debating the status quo.

I have found that coaching clients who want to change always have the ability to describe why they want to change, what a changed state might look like and what is driving the need for change.

Sometimes this initial statement of intent or commitment to change is rational and reasonable and can sound like any other business action in a way that belies it is individual behaviour and belief that is being talked about. But often, this initial articulation is emotional, heartfelt and cathartic. The final, clear and more precise articulation of change can often wait, but *it is critically important that the desire to change is present* and that some articulation of what needs to happen can be made before beginning.

This idea is absolutely critical for leaders as well. Articulating what change looks like should not be the biggest challenge for leaders, provided they have cultivated the receptivity to change in the first place. They should not wait until they can articulate it perfectly. Start the process, talk about why it's needed and the precise description will emerge over time.

These two ingredients – the desire to change and the ability to articulate why that is important – are the only imperatives that need to be in place for coaching to start, exactly the same two ingredients a leader must focus on in communicating about change.

Directive versus Non-Directive Coaching

Most coaching is non-directive, in that the coach has not been hired to tell the client what to do. But this does not mean the coach is an empty vessel or cannot have a view on what insight is important, what line of questioning may elicit deepened awareness or growth or what topic areas may benefit from further exploration and clarification. *Non-directive certainly does not mean non-invested.*

At all times, the coach has the client's best interests at heart and is their strongest champion, and this includes at times their fiercest critic and most honest interlocutor. A good coach will hold his or her client's feet to the fire and demand honest and accurate self-appraisal.

This quick snapshot of the internal 'engine' for a coach is again remarkably similar to that of an authentic leader: invested in their employees and customers, championing their needs, having their best interests at heart and being honest about progress made and the road ahead.

Clients do not want coaches to withhold understanding, insight or specialist knowledge that will help them. The great skill is in how this is done. Strong coaches get met with requests for their views all the time, and for the most part they rightly resist offering their own views as this is not coaching. What good coaches do instead is to turn the request into a coaching session: what does the client think they will hear from the coach, what is their sense of what is important, what would their advice be if someone came to them asking what to do.

Often, a coaching client may intuitively know what needs to happen, but asking the client to identify what is important is infinitely preferable than just divulging the answer. The rule of thumb is always to turn the locus of control and the responsibility for 'agency' back on the client themselves – 'what would you do', 'what do you think you should do', 'what is important here', 'how could you do this', 'what are obstacles to doing this' are all open-ended ways of transforming the responsibility for growth and insight back to the client themselves, which is what delivers real value and growth and is memorable and liberating for the client.

Authentic and effective leaders will tend to do exactly this as well. The more a leader can bring stakeholders, particularly employees, into the conversation about what needs to happen – explicitly giving them agency, power and a seat at the table – the more they build trust, engagement and commitment.

The strongest coaching – client relationships display a symbiotic quality where the interplay of questions, answers, reflection, awareness and learning becomes something quite efficient and powerful – and show an 'in-the-zone' relationship working at a highly tuned level to deliver growth and insight.

It is a little like the sympatico that sometimes spring up between two people who find they play off each other so well that what is being created is fresh and startling. This idea of co-creation in coaching is very powerful. This is what leaders should be aiming for particularly with their senior executive teams, to build a creative, high-performance leadership team.

A leader who is skilled at steering a group through an important and possibly contentious process towards shared understanding, consensus and a new state is using exactly the same skills as a coach or facilitator. Managing that process while delivering the change and growth desired is the hallmark of good coaching, facilitation and leadership.

How Coaching Works

Coaching Models

A number of coaching models have been developed to help explain and guide coaches and clients through the process. The most common models all deconstruct the coaching process into a series of stages through which to move the conversation. They differ in how much time and emphasis is spent in each stage.

The GROW model was developed by Graham Alexander and popularised by John Whitmore and is one of the best known and most used models. Each letter stands for a key phase in the process:

Goal – What does the client want to achieve?

Reality – What is the client's current situation: the key issues, constraints, barriers and driver's influencing the client's ability to attain their goal?

Options – What options are open to the client and of these which ones look most promising and feasible?

Will – When and how will the client act on the option(s) he or she has chosen, what do they need to do this and do they have the will to do it?

The GROW model helps explain the overall direction of travel of coaching. The coach and client tend to move in a linear fashion discussing and clarifying the change or **goal** the client is trying to achieve, through a situational analysis of the operating environment or current **reality** that is informing, constraining, shaping or holding back attainment of the change or goal. They then move through a discussion evaluating possible **options** for action to a more specific focus on what the client **will** do, and the specific action plan that the client will put in place and execute to deliver the goal.

The CIGAR model developed by Suzy Green and Anthony Grant in 2003[2] stands for:

Current reality – An initial discussion about the client's situation.
Ideal – What they would like to aim for: their ideal goal or ultimate change they want to make
Gaps – Gap analysis aimed at producing a clear idea of what is needed to get from current reality to the ideal end-state
Action – Action needed by the client to close the gap and deliver the ideal
Review – A review of which actions have worked and which haven't and a recalibration of subsequent efforts

The CIGAR model recognises the utility of beginning with the issue rather than the goal, and then reframes the coaching process as a gap analysis with a check against delivery as the last phase. Both GROW and CIGAR come from the traditional 'transactional' end of the coaching spectrum – built around the recognition that for most clients exploring their situation and goal informs and is inextricably linked to how they are going to change this reality.

The DiSCO model, popularised by Alan Seale, a core proponent of 'transformational' coaching in 2010,[3] is very different. DiSCO stands for:

Drama – What is happening and who is at fault?
Situation – How does the client fit in?
Choice – Who do they choose to be and what do they choose to do in this situation?
Opportunity – What is the opportunity to grow or change?

Transformational coaching has become more popular in the last few years and focuses around the idea of turbocharging coaching sessions to make possible transformative change. Here the idea is to get through the drama and situation as quickly as possible to focus instead on who the client 'chooses to be' or the opportunity 'waiting to happen'. In this view of coaching, the energy in a session should be focused on three fundamental questions:

1   What wants to happen here (or what is the opportunity here)?
2   Who is that asking me to be (or what is the shift that needs to happen)?
3   What is that asking me to do (or what is the breakthrough waiting to happen)?

Transformative coaches favour getting past the clutter of the current reality stage as quickly as possible and spending more time helping the client frame the choice in front of them. Transformative coaching can appear fairly New Age-like in its insistence on clients *feeling* what needs to happen – but when it works it is powerful.

In contrast, transactional coaching suggests the current reality stage is so crucial that it should never be rushed through, and provided the client is not indulging in a morass of detail or emotional angst – insight gathered at this stage is crucial in driving lasting change. This view says that all coaching is potentially transformative and that turbo-charging the process can work for some clients, but that a clear understanding of what is happening and why is a fundamental building block in helping clients deal with complexity and create lasting change.

My view is that positive change happens both ways: through a slower accumulation of insight and self-awareness and the more declarative acts of choosing and reframing change and growth as opportunity and that neither are mutually exclusive. The transformative approach is less common. Most clients expect the more traditional approach where talking about current reality is expected and valued.

BOX 12.1 IMPLICATIONS FOR LEADERS

The key challenge for many leaders is how to balance the need to understand and interrogate the current situation with the need to change and move forward to a new reality. Having a clear understanding of the current operating landscape must obviously be the basis for any change. But many leaders will feel the imperative to move at pace to fundamentally transform. And that means being able to destroy as well as build – as coaches say – *moving from* something old at the same time as you are *moving towards* something new. Balancing the need to understand with the imperative to act and choose.

This evaluative weighing up of the old, letting go and coming to terms with why the old needs to change is hugely challenging and for many people painful and a time-consuming process. Doing this at the same time as you are identifying the new – making choices and moving to capitalise on new opportunities – is profoundly dissonant and discordant for some.

But for others, it is the best way to make the changes needed. Some people feel acutely the ambiguity and incongruence between the old and the new and prefer a slower pace of change. Others feel they can only make progress if they make a fundamental rupture with the past and move swiftly lest they lose heart or nerve.

Helping a client calibrate and balance these two fundamental reactions is one of the most important actions a coach is called to do. Helping an organisation do the same thing will be one of the biggest challenges leaders will face over the next ten years. As the pace of change causes fundamental restructuring and change to business models, dealing with this 'balancing equation' in a nuanced, caring and authentic manner will be a key critical success factor for leaders.

The Core Skills of Coaching

The two core skills of coaching are without a doubt listening and questioning. As we saw earlier, the ability to really listen to people is immensely powerful and confers tremendous gifts on the client. We saw the visceral and transformative power being listened to had on that elderly woman in Quebec. She wept because someone listened to her properly for the first time in 20 years.

Listening makes people feel valued and validated. It confers attention on the speaker and if done in an active manner signals a basic reaffirmation of worth.

Questioning is the companion skill to listening that moves the conversation along, elicits meaning and insight and helps turn what could be just an emotive and cathartic discussion into an experience in learning, self-awareness and change.

We saw earlier the power of asking the right question at the right time and how this key skill, when used correctly, can change the direction of discourse and create conditions for insight. It's worth looking at these core coaching skills from the perspective of a leader.

Listening

Listening is such a basic cornerstone of coaching that after about three months of coaching, I decided to put away my pen, stop taking notes and simply listen to my clients and aim for a level of respect and attention that was not diminished by note-taking. The result was significant. I understood more clearly, quickly and deeply. The connection made was stronger and more emotive and I saw so much more revealing body language than when I was scurrying to take notes. All important issues were easily recalled up to two days later. Foregoing note-taking during the coaching session deepened my under-standing of what had happened rather than lessened it.

We have dealt with the basics of good listening earlier: the importance of choosing an active mode of listening, striving to be attentive and holding yourself open to hearing truly transformative insight.

And we have talked about a deeper kind of listening – listening for what is not being said, for what resides between the lines of what people say – the hidden emotion that daren't be voiced or articulated. The importance of not rushing and of simply 'holding the space' for people to sort out what they want to say, or to say nothing at all and just reflect and feel.

All this is bread and butter for coaches and is probably the most transformative gift they can give to clients. It is also a bedrock skill for authentic, effective leadership.

After the listening itself, the key moment comes when it is time to play back to the client what they have said. To synthesise and summarise, or better still, quote their words back to them and ask them what it means or indicates. This constant cyclical interplay between listening, playing back, searching for insight and meaning and asking questions to clarify, clinch a point, deepen awareness and consolidate learning is the heart of coaching.

The ability of leaders to do this with key members of their senior leadership team and in a less intimate manner – with larger groups of employees, customer or other stakeholders – will transform a leader's ability to engender understanding, a shared sense of purpose and the willingness to replace disbelief and anxiety in favour of trust. All core components in getting people to support the changes you need to make as leader.

Insight tends to come when the process slows down to accommodate deeper ways of knowing. When there is profound silence as clients grapple with what has just been said or intuited or felt and when time is made available to be reflective and meditative.

It is at these critical moments when one of the most important skills for a coach comes into play: *knowing when not to talk*. At these moments, listening morphs into communing. You are not so much listening as waiting – holding yourself in abeyance for truth to emerge.

For leaders, much of this will seem very strange, counter-intuitive or perhaps laughable. Or else this kind of listening will appear to be a luxury in which they cannot indulge. After all, leaders are paid to have an opinion and lead. But listening is never time wasted. And the kind of issues leaders will be dealing with over the next ten years will lend themselves to this more enquiring, protean approach of seeking input, distilling, re-shaping, building consensus and then moving forward together. At the heart of this mode of knowing is listening.

For leaders grappling with complex or morally ambiguous issues, complicated change programmes or difficult decisions, really listening to others' views and input is absolutely crucial in assembling both knowledge and nuance. Rushed change based on poor listening and misconstrued meaning is the antithesis of what leaders need.

Listening is like a muscle – the more you exercise it, the stronger it becomes. But you need to let it unfold. That dynamic is well known to coaches, less so to leaders.

Questioning

The most effective questions are the shortest and the simplest. As we saw earlier, the two most effective one-word questions are **what** and **how**, with **why** being the dangerous question because it is perceived as being personal and somewhat judgemental.

Many coaches deliberately do not ask long or convoluted questions and probably the most frequent question asked is 'what else'? Getting the client to unpack what they mean and deepen their own description and understanding of what is happening sometimes requires little more than encouraging them to keep going.

I am always struck by the simplicity of the questioning used by the most experienced coaches. They are not the ones in the spotlight. It is all about the client and so there is no need to be complicated, witty or intellectual. What is needed is the elegance of simplicity, knowing what to ask and when.

BOX 12.2 TEN POWERFUL COACHING QUESTIONS

1 How do you know this?
2 What else?
3 What is waiting to happen?
4 If you could change one thing what would that be?
5 What needs to change?
6 How will you do this?
7 What do you need to do?
8 What is important here?
9 What does what you have just said tell you?
10 What do you know to be true?

Coaching and Business

Common Themes and Patterns

In a business setting, coaching is used for a variety of reasons and these differ markedly depending on the seniority of the client.

At the junior level, the key topics that come up frequently include helping people to:

- 'Get to the next level' and prepare for a position with more responsibility
- Add gravitas, emotional awareness and projection of authority
- Be more confident
- Present in a more concise and impactful manner
- Address habits constraining performance

These sessions often adopt a hybrid mix of coaching, mentoring and training where sessions include transfer of competence, skills exercises and role plays but within a non-directive coaching framework. The programmes tend to be sponsor-driven and expect clear progress, results and improved outcomes, and will typically include four to six sessions over three months. They are run in a more formal, 'boot camp'-type manner.

At the middle to senior management level, the assignments tend to focus more on a specific objective, such as:

- Securing promotion to an executive-level position
- Better understanding the challenges and complexities of leading
- Preparing to move from a number two to a leadership position
- Addressing performance issues
- Helping navigate career choices
- Preparing for a major business-critical presentation

These clients are often at a critical career crossroads or have some performance issues that the firm wants clarity on. These coaching assignments often result in the client making significant decisions in the wake of a fairly rapid acceleration in their awareness of what is happening, how they fit in and what direction they want to move in.

At the senior leadership level, the topic areas are more complex as you would expect. Assignments tend to focus on:

- Navigating a toxic executive team atmosphere
- Building a high-performance team
- Leading through a corporate takeover and sale of the business
- Leading a change in business model
- Communicating a major change programme
- Rebuilding trust with the management team and employees
- Competing for the managing partner's position

Almost all these assignments come directly from the leaders themselves and many arise as spin-offs from consultant or change work that is happening in parallel.

These sessions can include scenarios and role plays where different courses of actions are discussed, gamed or simulated. The coach is more heavily involved in helping the leader evaluate different courses of action and may act in a supporting role confirming what is becoming apparent to the leader. This confirmatory role stretches the definition of non-directive coaching, but often leaders take great comfort in having a coach discuss an insight they have had and provide some external validation of their views.

The act of working collaboratively towards finding the optimal path forward, particularly through a complex situation, typifies coaching sessions for leaders and is often referred to as hybrid coaching. The coach is playing the role of provocateur, encouraging the leader to think differently and creatively about the situation. By summarising, clarifying, confirming and encouraging, the leader feels supported and safe in the knowledge that the coach is playing a kind of fail-safe role – a second line of defence looking out for the leader and helping to ensure they do not take the wrong decision.

Here the focus is very much on offering trusted advisor support – being a sounding board for frustrations, musings and thoughts they cannot easily make known with anyone else. Often, this type of coaching can change quite significantly over time from a more formal beginning in non-directive coaching to a trusted partnership model where the menu of what is required is constantly shifting and can include these elements:

- Pure listening/sounding board service
- Significant push back or devil's advocate – stress-testing ideas or courses of action
- Consultant views or a second opinion
- Non-directive coaching to more fully explore issues

Since this type of coaching often happens within the context of a real-time change programme, the coaching itself is less formal and time-bound.

The Coaching Approach to Managing

The idea of coaching as an approach to interacting with people (in addition to being a mode of leadership communication) is a concept that has gained credence over the past decade or so. Many organisations now encourage their managers to adopt a coaching approach – this is one of the key responses companies have made to the advent of millennials and Generation Z in the workplace and the reset in values detailed earlier.

Adopting a less hierarchical and more collaborative approach in managing employees actively recognises these changes and aligns far more closely to how younger employees want to be managed and to their expectations, core beliefs and values.

A coaching approach to managing takes as its starting point the core coaching idea that people innately have the wherewithal to improve inside them. And so management becomes an exercise in supporting their process of self-awareness, heightened learning and insight and encouraging the employee rather than demanding improved performance via top-down directives.

Of course, direction, guidance and leadership are still needed and there is nothing more frustrating that an overly collegial manager who is not clear enough on overall goals and direction.

The coaching manager cultivates a learning and trusting environment where the impetus to collaborate trumps the old command and control dynamic. In this kind of managing, all the core ingredients of coaching come into play – good listening, incisive questions, focus on process rather than content, rigorous holding of the employee to account but within an overall framework of commitment to their best interests.

This sounds a long way from traditional management and increasingly is the way forward for most organisations. This trend will only increase as millennials move into the boardroom and are responsible for workplace culture and values.

Coaching and the Disruptive Decade

Coaching will come into its own as a direct response to the increasing complexity and accelerated change we will see in business over the next decade.

Leaders will need to adopt a fair slice of coaching methodology in order to help employees understand for themselves the changes they are living through – it won't be enough to only offer a top-down, directive, from-on-high articulation of what is happening if the idea is to help employees fully understand change.

The more leaders and managers can work collaboratively with employees and encourage their own learning and awareness, the less chance of huge disconnect developing between those that are 'in the know' and in the vanguard of change and others who may be in much earlier stages of acceptance.

This willingness to share, collaborate and coach through change will separate those organisations that cope well with disruptive change and those who find themselves overwhelmed. One of the most important initiatives any firm can commit to is the willingness to adopt a coaching approach to managing and communicating – so employees are encouraged to work through their understanding of what is changing and are not left to rely solely on hearing from their leaders.

In a fundamental way, it comes down to matter of trust, the same core driver of the values reset and a critical component in engendering authenticity. Will leaders and organisations trust their employees enough to develop their own skills for making sense of change? The corporate dialogue will have to deepen given the quantum of change to come, but so will the commitment to supporting individual employee's change and learning.

The coaching approach driven by an authentic, values-driven character will increasingly come to be seen as the core communication skill of the effective leader. Without it, all the charisma, knowledge and articulation in the world won't be enough to effectively mobilise employees. Helping them mobilise themselves will produce an infinitely stronger resilience and ability to cope with change.

Strengthening people's own ability to cope with change will help them deal with another fundamental need. I believe the core driver for most people who receive coaching is their desire to have what they are doing and who they are confirmed and validated.

It has often powerfully struck me that what most people seem to be looking for is a kind of absolution for all that they have done or not done. People worry greatly about their capacity to do the right thing and judge themselves quite harshly for all sorts of things. In many coaching sessions, I have seen an almost palpable need for validation and a real hunger to be told – even in the face of their own shortcomings – that by virtue of being human, they have an inalienable worth and are deserving of inestimable love and acceptance. *The biggest light-bulb moments I have witnessed are when people make this connection deep down and realise that they don't need to struggle, yearn or strive for what they've had all along.*

This may sound overtly spiritual or like New Age gobbledegook, but in reflecting back after each coaching programme ends, I have often found myself thinking that what that was really about was helping the person to see that they are intrinsically fine, powerful even despite any real or imagined failings.

For the most part, they are doing their best – they know exactly what they should be doing and what they are really looking for is reassurance and validation that this is enough. The second opinion that says – you are not alone, you're not crazy, you're doing alright – trust yourself.

It is this fundamental need for reassurance and validation that will be sorely tested by the accelerated pace of the changes to come. People's ability to cope with change will mix with their need to be reassured about their own self-worth and both will come under increasing pressure because of the pace of change. *This coming together of the organisation imperative to support employees coping with change and the individual need to be reassured and validated will make authentic, genuine, caring and effective communications – delivered through a coaching approach – critically important.*

What employees need as employees and what they need as people will coalesce. Our collective ability to deliver this will determine how well we deal with the disruptive decade to come.

Notes

1 Whitmore, John (1992), *Coaching for Performance*, London and Boston, Nicholas Brealey Publishing.
2 Grant, Anthony (2011), Is it time to REGROW the GROW model? Issues related to teaching coaching session structures. *The Coaching Psychologist*, Vol. 7, No. 2, December.
3 Notes taken from Transformational Presence for Leaders and Coaches course, offered by Alan Seale, January 2018, UK.

Chapter 13

Observations and Summary

We began this story with the observation that people are innately good at communicating when they cast aside expectations and inhibitions and simply talk about themselves – the story of me. But this positioning rarely lasts and instead gets hopelessly swamped in the urge to show credentials and expertise, deliver detail and offer more information in the hope that we can paper over what we fear is the hollowness of our own thoughts.

There is a profound psychological rift that lies at the heart of most people's communicating. Deep down, at an almost unconscious level, they know fundamentally what they want to say, what they believe, how to say it and what they feel. But this inner knowing, confidence and surety has over the years been so camouflaged and obfuscated by the weight of convention, expectation, fear and lack of nurturing that many of us have lost touch with this fundamental aspect of our humanity.

Storytelling and communicating with emotion and meaning are the key skills that have been lost.

And our awareness that this has happened only glows dimly – a faint impulse within that reminds us that there is a different way – that there was a time when we did this differently, with more authenticity and without calibrating and analysing everything so much.

On an individual level, this rift can be seen when people experience that powerful yearning for liberation that we spoke of earlier. The need for liberation and the sense of power, lightness and freedom that it brings for many people manifests itself most at times of great stress, inflection or change. People agitate for change when at long last they have had enough and feel compelled to restore this link to their deeper, more authentic selves.

I believe more people are feeling this way now than ever before. That there is a great undifferentiated yearning 'out there' to do things differently. To communicate without fear or favour and without pretence.

This need for a restoration of a fundamental aspect of our individual human selves is mirrored by a similar need at the collective, societal level.

It is the central thesis of this book that this individual yearning for liberation, for more authentic, heartfelt and effective leadership and communication is needed now at a societal level more than ever before. That the sheer complexity of our modern world and the turbocharged pace of technological change is such that being able to show emotion, storytell, articulate meaning and enable awareness will be absolutely critical to ensuring some kind of counterbalancing force is at work as we together move through this vortex of change.

This is the prime driver behind the second great mega trend that we have discussed in this book – the powerful rise of social values accompanied by roiling emotion and a strong thirst for justice and equality. It's no coincidence that we are seeing this demand

DOI: 10.4324/9781003198994-18

for an increasing reset on values at exactly the same time as we are experiencing such rapid and fundamental technological change and disruption.

But this emotional, messy, organic and powerful urge for social change can easily be hijacked by populism from the right and crippling intellectual orthodoxy from the left. And it will have such a power and weight behind it – just like the inexorable technological change – that the individual voice in this sea of change stands in real danger of being marginalised.

As individuals and as leaders, we simply cannot stand on the sidelines detached, aloof and uninvolved, watching as these two trends remake our lives. We must find our voice, identify the important stories and restore our ability to really communicate and engage in our businesses, in our relationships and in our daily lives.

There will simply be so much change in the next decade that the choice will be very stark – increased marginalisation or increased engagement. Either we find our voices or others will increasingly speak for us. We need to gear up, get wise and get ready to have a view, take a stand, push back and demand a better level of discourse, both on the individual and societal levels.

One of the key issues in the UK as I finished writing the first draft of this book was the unedifying and farcical crisis over exam marking for A levels and GCSEs (mentioned in the introduction). The hubris, lazy arrogance and sheer incompetence of the principals involved in this saga were plain for all to see. And although this was the core story reported at the time, the bigger point was missed.

This story showed in microcosm what we are going to live through thousands of times over the next decade. At its heart, this was a story about the unalloyed faith in an algorithm applied by so-called experts at the collective level which came up against strongly felt notions of fairness at the individual level. The story nicely embodies our two mega trends – the increasing ubiquity of artificial intelligence, automation and algorithms ranged against our sharpened emotional perceptions of the importance of values, particularly fairness.

What made the exam story so powerful is that the use of the algorithm was not by itself a bad idea, but it was the way in which it was constructed and the overt preference for a collective rational tool over the need to consider the 'fairness' impact on individuals that was illuminating.

It turned out that the algorithm was fatally flawed, skewing results in favour of smaller, private schools and outperforming cohorts and biased against high-performing individuals from state schools with poor records. You couldn't have constructed something less fit for purpose if you tried.

But this rational, 'mechanistic' problem was dwarfed by the emotional, 'values' issue. It was the disenfranchisement of this particular year cohort, the so-called COVID kids that set teeth on edge.

These students did not have face-to-face schooling for months, had been denied the opportunity to sit exams and were told their teacher's predicted grades for them would be hopelessly biased and unfair and that they could not be allowed to compete unfairly against the year that came before and the one that would immediately follow in the great lottery of life. The fact that the rage in Scotland happened a week before the same unfolding of events in England and Wales, made the government's inability to properly prepare for or appreciate the emotional quotient at play pathetic and worrying.

This story shows in outline the twin forces at play that will dominate the next decade. Increasing use of automated intelligence to drive business and political decision-making versus the viral and at times feral emotion tied to core social values.

We need to – individually, collectively and certainly as leaders – embrace better, more effective, authentic and powerful communications and storytelling as a middle way between this rational technological impulse and the emotional values response.

Navigating our way through the immense changes to come will require courage, conviction and commitment.

It will start with a desire to simply communicate more honestly, to tell stories powerfully and effectively, so that we can lead others and ourselves through change. And it will be driven by a deeper realisation that something has been diminished, misplaced or temporarily lost – that we feel a yearning and growing need to recover, reset and restore.

This book is a manual for those seeking to deepen or recover these innate skills and a warning that they will be needed in the coming years like never before.

Part 5

Appendices

Appendix 1

Alternatives to Slides

Table 1.1

Presenting alternative	Strengths and weaknesses	Where best used
Demos – A demonstration of how a product, service or system works	**Strengths** – Tactile, good for kinaesthetic learners and for getting attention as something physical is happening, good for illustrating tangible benefits of a product or service **Weaknesses** – Takes spotlight off the presenter, can be perceived as technical and geeky, often they go on too long or are poorly explained and not clear	Middle of the presentation. Needs set-up and not appropriate to use for summarising
Props – A physical object that helps you illustrate the main point you are making	**Strengths** – Tactile and tangible, can help to simplify a more complicated concept, memorable because it is simple and visual, good to use in conjunction with a story **Weaknesses** – Can appear unprofessional depending on the audience, can run the risk of oversimplifying or of confusing if the relevance is not crystal clear	Beginning of a presentation or to introduce a new section. To be avoided in summarising
Big Pictures – Graphics, drawings or photographs that provide a visual representation of the main point of the presentation	**Strengths** – Appeals to visual learners, can help simplify complicated concepts, memorable because it is simple and visual, good to leave up during a presentation **Weaknesses** – Can run the risk of oversimplifying or of confusing if the relevance is not crystal clear	Beginning of a presentation or to introduce a new section. To be avoided in summarising
Video – Usually a short film with sound and pictures that creates an initial impression, explains a key process or point or summarises benefits	**Strengths** – Changes the tone of presentation, gives relief from the presenter, allows audience to reflect and enjoy pictures and sound, can drive emotion and engagement, can illustrate more clearly key processes or points **Weaknesses** – Can show up disparities between video and presenter if video is more engaging, do not leave it to the video to make the most important points, otherwise the presenter is sidelined	Anytime. Do not end with a video
Flipcharts and whiteboarding – Presenter drawing in real time on a flipchart or whiteboard	**Strengths** – Aids in audience recall, strengthens engagement and interest level, can help a dry subject come to life, allows the presenter to shift gears and be more creative **Weaknesses** – Can be a distraction and not as useful for delivering the most important messages because the focus is off the presenter and on what is being drawn	Anytime. Do not end by using a flipchart or whiteboard

(Continued)

Presenting alternative	Strengths and weaknesses	Where best used
Animated slides – Using services such as Prezi or Miro to create movement or animation in the slides in real time	**Strengths** – Can import into slides the same strengths as whiteboarding, can bring drier slides to life **Weaknesses** – Can appear affected and gimmicky, propensity to be overused and 'wow' factor wears off quickly	Middle of the presentation
Stories – Told directly to the audience	**Strengths** – Universally preferred as audiences' most favourite mode of presentation, helps clarify and make presentation more personal and impactful **Weaknesses** – Can be overdone and not as useful for explaining detail and data	Anytime, but particularly good at the beginning and the end

Understanding Stakeholder Needs in Each Stage of an Unplanned Crisis

Table 2.1 Overview

	Phase 1 Trigger *This can't be happening*	Phase 2 Diagnostic *What do we do*	Phase 3 Adjustment *Working the problem*	Phase 4 Recovery *End of the tunnel*	Phase 5 Return to BAU *A smooth landing*	Phase 6 Aftermath *What should change*
Description and drivers	Denial, disbelief and panic. Initial triage, hyperactivity and/or slow to mobilise	Work the problem: Fact gather, risk assess, evaluate and mitigate	Fine-tune actions. Optimise risk mitigation. Fast reactive stance is best. Prioritise effort	Outline road to recovery: What new BAU will look like and timings. Manage expectations	Explain return to BAU process. Explain how you will future-proof measures, so crisis won't repeat	Assess damage. Renew covenant with stakeholders. Strengthen what works and change what doesn't
Key challenges	Reassert/ impose order. Understand what is happening. Move quickly	Get the initial 'business-critical' calls correct. Safety and legal issues first	Deal with flagging energy/ morale. Don't go proactive too soon. Work the existing issues	Demonstrate competence. Have a clear roadmap to recovery	Reaffirm customer connection. Keep or win back trust and determine pledge for the future	Display humility. Embrace innovation. Acknowledge need for and lead change
Key deliverables	Reassurance Clear leadership	Clarity	Resilience Flexibility	Expectation management	Delivery	Improvement Innovation

Table 2.2 Stakeholders

	Phase 1 Trigger *This can't be happening*	Phase 2 Diagnostic *What do we do*	Phase 3 Adjustment *Working the problem*	Phase 4 Recovery *End of the tunnel*	Phase 5 Return to BAU *A smooth landing*	Phase 6 Aftermath *What should change*
Leadership	Be united, speak with one voice, calm and reassuring. Invoke BCP. Be directive/ delegative, factual/ empathetic	Top-down on big picture. Mobilise middle management. Enable experts and invite bottom-up views	Critical phase. Early adopters are tired, sceptics are just getting started	Be clear and on front foot about plans and timelines. Signal confidence in nearing BAU	Thank people for staying on course. Need to celebrate/ return value to stakeholders. Expect emotion	Time for reflection. Opportunity to rededicate and recalibrate business and initiate change

(Continued)

	Phase 1 Trigger This can't be happening	Phase 2 Diagnostic What do we do	Phase 3 Adjustment Working the problem	Phase 4 Recovery End of the tunnel	Phase 5 Return to BAU A smooth landing	Phase 6 Aftermath What should change
Middle management	Cascade to staff. Client outreach	Be clear on what staff need to do. Manage/ motivate	Flexibly deploy resources. Encourage initiative. Delegate	Road-test solutions. Pilot and war game what's new	Rehearse BAU. Triage quick fixes. Invite feedback	Support change. Brainstorm, surface new ideas
Employees	Staff are key brand ambassadors. Need information. Use social media. F2F from CEO and managers	Keep staff informed. Establish hotlines, ask for their input	Big variability in understanding and acceptance. 'Influencers' are key	Give staff sense of ownership over new processes, they will implement them	Staff feel relief, pride and exhaustion. Needs to be acknowledged. No big changes now	Opportunity to involve employees in new vision, key changes or deepening innovation
Customers	Inform them asap. Key accounts need a phone call, others can be by email/letter	Monitor/ engage with customer reaction and get on front foot asap	Communicate often. Customers tend to be patient if they know what to expect	No false promises or exaggerations. Under-promise and over-deliver	Thank/return value to your customers. Understand what changes they need	Huge opportunity to involve customers in key changes being discussed
Supply chain	Often overlooked initially. Inform them asap. Key accounts need a call, can delegate this	Keep them informed and ask for their help if the crisis/issue involves supply chain	Keep them informed and ask for their help if the crisis/ issue involves supply chain	Critical stage for suppliers, they need to know new plans can be delivered	Thank/return value to suppliers. Understand what changes they need	Opportunity to rethink supply chain arrangements
Regulators/ HQ	Regulators are relaxed provided they know what you are doing. Inform HQ immediately as rep risk and share price are concerns	Keep regulators informed and join industry-wide consultations brokered by regulator. Liaise with HQ often.	Keep regulators informed. HQ will want to know costs, impact on their other businesses and timelines	Keep regulators and HQ informed on timelines, and HQ on impact and coordinating with their businesses	Regulators/HQ have a vested interest in you succeeding and returning to BAU in the 'correct' fashion. Clarity is key	Regulators keen to do a post-mortem and beware their potential rush to regulate. Likely time for fundamental HQ review
Investors/ banks	Often overlooked. Financiers are well informed and make quick judgements on investments. Set up a senior channel to communicate with them	Consider involving them if business model, strategy or risk calls need to be made. You need to factor in financial implications	Key topic will be financial cost of effort to mitigate crisis	Key topic will be financial cost of effort to mitigate crisis	A lot is riding on how the market views the return to BAU. It's all about outperforming expectations. Stay close to financiers on results	May be opportunity to re-negotiate financing or put on a different basis/model

Coaching Tips and Techniques

BOX 3.1 FIFTEEN COACHING TIPS AND TECHNIQUES

Generating initial insight

1 **Personality metrics** – Lots of different models and metrics are available and all coaches have their favourites. Models like Belbin, DISC, Business Styles and MBTI all focus on helping the client identify which typologies they are more predisposed to, what implications that has for them, how their innate disposition affects the current issue at hand, what changes they could focus on making and what adaptations they may need to consider making in their relationships with others.

2 **Strengths inventory metrics** – There are a number of strengths metrics, including Hogan, FIRO-B, StrengthsFinder and Leadership Strengths Inventory. These metrics focus on helping a client identify areas of relative strengths and weakness and can be useful in generating insight into particular challenges or in developing a better self-understanding of the client's own personal 'operating landscape'.

3 **Limiting beliefs** – Limiting beliefs are often gross generalisations that have been adopted and internalised years ago, like 'I'm not good at public speaking' or 'I never succeed in these sort of situations', but now are acting as barriers to progress and improvement. Successfully tackling limiting beliefs can be hugely liberating and embolden a client towards making greater changes.

4 **Empty chair** – Asking the client to detach from their own reality and look at the situation from a dispassionate and disinterested point of view can be helpful in generating a different view point and seeing their own situation in a new light.

Eliciting a different perspective

5 **Trusted friend** – Often ascribing the act of agency to someone they know well rather than themselves, frees the client up and gives them a way of thinking about their own situation with a clearer, more detached manner and free of some of the attendant emotion.

6 **Time traveller** – The client is asked to imagine 6–12 months in the future looking back on the situation and reporting how it was resolved and what lessons were learned. Starting at the end and working backwards can often

liberate new ways of thinking and allow a client to predict in advance what will prove to be the important breakthrough ideas and actions that need to be taken.

7 **Helicopter view** – Asking the client to focus on the most important aspects about the situation they are dealing with can turbocharge progress by allowing the client to leave behind less important items.

Action-oriented techniques

8 **Role plays** – Invaluable in helping a client try out new behaviour and gain insight into specific circumstances and specific protagonists.

9 **Location coaching** – Often changing physical locations can help refresh coaching sessions and stimulate new insight for clients. Conducting a coaching session outside or while walking can really free up new ways of thinking or give a session a more informal and more creative vibe.

10 **Coaching from different physical perspectives** – Changing the vantage point without changing the location can often generate breakthroughs and creativity. Naming say a rug as the 'issue' and having the client look at the 'issue' from behind, in front, below and above can elicit different viewpoints.

Generating clarification and insight

11 **Drawing for insight** – Getting clients to draw what they are feeling or the operating situation they are describing can often be very liberating both emotionally for the client, but also as a way of gaining extra clarity by seeing the situation depicted in a drawing. Often, clients will make a breakthrough in understanding by seeing the 'ecosystem' of different issues or protagonists displayed on one piece of paper. This can also be a good technique in helping clients weigh up two or three different courses of action. It can also elicit results to have the coach draw what they see as the challenges being discussed. This allows clients to open up by interacting with the picture, pointing to key aspects or redrawing it to be more accurate

Confirming action

12 **A 1–10 scoring** – Asking a client to rate on a scale of 1–10 how likely certain they are to take action usually leads to an interesting conversation. A rating of 8 or above suggests that the action will be taken and the conversation can focus on how to do this. Anything 6 or lower suggests the action will not be undertaken and the conversation can focus on what is holding the client back or preventing them from taking action. The middling area of 6–8 suggests indecision or lingering uncertainty, and this of course can be addressed.

Transformative coaching techniques

The following three tools are all taken from transformative coaching and are used by Alan Seale, a master practitioner of transformative coaching.

13 **The deep simple** – This consists of five questions that can be moved through fairly quickly to help identify the choice the client needs to make and the opportunity that is there for them:

a What three things do you know to be true and which of these do you want to focus on?
b What do you observe?
c What do you need less of?
d What do you need more of?
e What is the opportunity here? What wants to happen here?

The deep simple in action is impressive because it turbocharges conversation and cuts through the clutter to what is truly important. My impression is that it works best with clients who are already predisposed to change and familiar with coaching techniques. It is less effective if the client is less sure about what is happening, could happen or 'wants to happen'.

14 **Three intelligences** – This is an interesting tool that deliberately asks a client to think about their situation from three different perspectives:

a What does their intelligence (brain or ego) tell them?
b What does their emotion (belly or body) tell them?
c What does their intuition (heart or soul) tell them?

Using the three intelligences can produce some very different perspectives and can help a client sort out what they are really feeling about an issue. Often, the classic conflict is between intelligence (brain) and intuition (heart), and getting a third perspective from the (less appreciated) 'gut' can be helpful, liberating and occasionally startling.

15 **Using archetypal shapes** – Offering clients the opportunity to use the four archetypal shapes of square, triangle, circle and wavy line to help discuss or share insight into their situation can often lead to interesting results. Traditionally, each archetypal shape represents one of the primal elements:

Square represents earth – solidity, foundations and clarity but also boundaries.

Triangle represents fire – powerful, hierarchy, progress and direction but also potentially constraints.

Circle represents air – holistic, endless and bountiful but can also appear directionless.

Wavy line represents water – fluidity, journey and possibilities but also can appear misleading or aimless.

Very often, this technique yields surprising insight, with the shapes triggering all sorts of observations about their situation. Many people are visual learners and find the shapes useful proxies to talk about different aspects that could be more complicated to explain without the shapes. The archetypal nature of the shapes is particularly useful in talking about things like direction, boundaries, opportunity, freedom and hierarchy.

Acknowledgements

I would like to acknowledge the support of all those who helped make this book possible.

To my clients, who gave me the idea of writing a book to try and capture much of what we talk about in coaching and training sessions or in strategy discussions.

To Andrea Carpenter for her guidance and sound editorial suggestions. To Mar Sulaika Ochs for her enthusiastic review of early drafts and to all those who provided invaluable insight.

To the editing team at the Routledge – Taylor & Francis Group, particularly Meredith Norwich for her early and unwavering support and guidance and Julia Pollacco for helping me navigate the submission process.

I would like to particularly thank Michael Evans and Matthew Moth for their support and interest in the project. Specifically, I would like to thank and acknowledge the kind support of my employer The Madano Partnership, for generously making key materials and information available for me to adapt and use.

I would like to thank my wife Mozhgan and children Lara and Liam for their patience and understanding throughout the writing of this book. Writing a book at any time is a massive undertaking, but doing this during three lockdowns over much of 2020 and early 2021 was challenging.

In one respect, it provided a tremendous opportunity for focus and agency which was very welcome – but it also took me out of circulation for significant chunks of time. This may have been a hidden blessing for them, but whatever they thought about what was going on, they were always supportive. And for this I'm thankful.

Finally, I would like to acknowledge the challenges all leaders face today. It is my hope that this book will be useful as you guide your organisations through the coming years.

Index

Note: **Bold** page numbers refer to tables; *italic* page numbers refer to figures.

Printed in the United States
by Baker & Taylor Publisher Services